Anti-Bias Education

for Young Children & Ourselves

SECOND EDITION

Louise Derman-Sparks & Julie Olsen Edwards

with Catherine M. Goins

National Association for the Education of Young Children
Washington, DC

National Association for the
Education of Young Children
1313 L Street NW, Suite 500
Washington, DC 20005-4101
202-232-8777 • 800-424-2460
NAEYC.org

NAEYC Books

Senior Director, Publishing
and Professional Learning
Susan Friedman

Director, Books
Dana Battaglia

Senior Editor
Holly Bohart

Editor
Rossella Procopio

Senior Creative Design Manager
Henrique J. Siblesz

Senior Creative Design Specialist
Charity Coleman

Publishing Business
Operations Manager
Francine Markowitz

Former Editor in Chief
Kathy Charner

Through its publications program,
the National Association
for the Education of Young
Children (NAEYC) provides a
forum for discussion of major
issues and ideas in the early
childhood field, with the hope
of provoking thought and
promoting professional growth.
The views expressed or implied
in this book are not necessarily
those of the Association.

Permissions

NAEYC accepts requests for limited use of our copyrighted
material. For permission to reprint, adapt, translate, or otherwise
reuse and repurpose content from this publication, review
our guidelines at NAEYC.org/resources/permissions.

Page 23 is adapted, with permission, from Louise Derman-Sparks
and Julie Olsen Edwards, "Living Our Commitments: A Pledge to
All Children and Families," *Exchange* (March/April 2017): 34.

The vignette on pages 40–41 is adapted, with permission, from Julie
Olsen Edwards, "How to Get Started with Anti-Bias Education in Your
Classroom and Program," *Exchange* (January/February 2017): 78–79.

The excerpt on page 94 is reprinted, with permission,
from Linda Irene Jiménez, "Finding a Voice," *In Our Own
Way: How Anti-Bias Work Shapes Our Lives* (St. Paul, MN:
Redleaf, 1999), 32–34. © 1999 by Linda Irene Jiménez.

The excerpt on page 164 is reprinted, with permission, from John
McCutcheon, "Happy Adoption Day." © 1993 by John McCutcheon.

The vignettes on pages 29, 57, 136, 144, 144–145, and 147 are
reprinted by permission of the publisher from Louise Derman-Sparks
and Patricia G. Ramsey, with Julie Olsen Edwards, *What If All the
Kids Are White? Anti-Bias Multicultural Education with Young
Children and Families,* 2nd ed. (New York: Teachers College
Press, 2011), 45, 92–93, 134–136, 162, 163, and 165–166. © 2011 by
Teachers College, Columbia University. All rights reserved.

Photo Credits

All photographs © Getty Images.

Library of Congress Control Number: 2019935621

ISBN: 978-1-938113-57-4

Item 1143

Contents

Foreword: Welcome to the Journey

by Carol Brunson Day

As I was preparing my thoughts about what I would say in this foreword, I had one big question: Are we making any progress? As a society? As an early childhood profession? Is anything really changing?

And what came to mind was the opening line in Charles Dickens's famous book *A Tale of Two Cities*: "It was the best of times, it was the worst of times . . ."

I want to believe that anti-bias work is making forward progress. After all, doesn't this new edition of *Anti-Bias Education for Young Children and Ourselves* mean that this work is still vital? Even more significantly, anti-bias work with young children has permeated the field. It's rare to find a publication—no matter the topic—that doesn't mention bias or focus on diversity in some way. And the NAEYC position statement "Advancing Equity in Early Childhood Education," released in September 2019, is very strong and so very significant.

Yet it also seems like the worst of times. Our country is deeply divided. Inflammatory words and actions daily add fuel to the fire of bigotry and bias. What does it mean when white supremacy groups are not universally condemned? What does it say when we delay putting Harriet Tubman's image on the 20-dollar bill? What does it tell our children when they see or hear others mock people who have a disability? One's politics notwithstanding, this is a time of strife in public discourse around race, culture, gender, religion, and sexual orientation and discrimination around these and other identities. The discord surrounds us all—and without a doubt, it penetrates the lives of young children.

Children are listening. Children are watching. Children are learning from what is going on around them. And so my concern about progress notwithstanding, I remain thankful for this book, this anti-bias tool, as a resource to help children grow up strong.

In this spirit of thankfulness, what I said in the foreword to the previous edition of this book bears repeating: "What if someone told you that you could contribute in a small but significant way to making the world a better place? Would you want to do it? Of course you would. Then read on, because that is what this book offers—a chance to make the world fairer and more humane for everybody. And it offers the chance to achieve that grand goal from a place where you have already chosen to be—in your daily work with children and families."

In 1989, *Anti-Bias Curriculum: Tools for Empowering Young Children* hit the early childhood education field like a bombshell; both it and its 2010 successor, *Anti-Bias Education for Young Children and Ourselves,* have remained vital and provocative in the decades since. I expect this new edition to likewise generate both contentious debate and penetrating growth. That's because it is so compelling and inviting, filled with stories about real experiences of real teachers with real children and real families, simply and honestly told. And it asks the reader to interact with the text and reflect on deeply held beliefs and practices.

So be prepared to work hard, for the authors are demanding. They repeatedly ask you to try and try again. They challenge you to go deeply into issues such as class bias, and they want you to push past your comfort and ease. But rest assured, they are also gentle and supportive, offering reassurance along the way. Especially at the most precarious points, they provide scenario after scenario, walking *with* you step by step to capture and explain the subtleties of this anti-bias work through concrete examples. Becoming a strong anti-bias educator is a journey, and no matter how much you might already know about the topic, there's always more to master, more challenges ahead.

Our responsibility as early childhood educators to anti-bias education becomes more compelling in a period when racism and other isms are more overt in rhetoric and policies and are seriously harming children. In many ways, this work requires faith that we can make a difference, because it may be hard to see progress. But I offer a quote on perspective from Michelle Obama's book *Becoming,* made after a conversation she had with Nelson Mandela: "Real change happens slowly, not just over months and years, but over decades and lifetimes."

Stay strong and welcome to the journey.

Introduction:
A Few Words
About this Book

All children have the right to equitable learning opportunities that help them achieve their full potential as engaged learners and valued members of society. Thus, all early childhood educators have a professional obligation to advance equity. They can do this best when they are effectively supported by the early learning settings in which they work and when they and their wider communities embrace diversity and full inclusion as strengths, uphold fundamental principles of fairness and justice, and work to eliminate structural inequities that limit equitable learning opportunities.

—NAEYC, "Advancing Equity in Early Childhood Education" (position statement)

Since the publication of *Anti-Bias Curriculum: Tools for Empowering Young Children* (Derman-Sparks & the A.B.C. Task Force 1989) and the subsequent first edition of *Anti-Bias Education for Young Children and Ourselves* (Derman-Sparks & Edwards 2010), early childhood teachers across the United States and internationally have embraced anti-bias education (ABE) as a central part of their work. This third book about anti-bias—the second edition of *Anti-Bias Education for Young Children and Ourselves*—builds on the first two books. Its underlying intentions remain the same: to support children's full development in our world of great human diversity and to give them the tools to stand up to prejudice, stereotyping, bias, and eventually to institutional isms. To achieve this for children means that as educators it is not sufficient to be nonbiased (nor is

it likely), and it is not sufficient to be an observer. Rather, educators are called upon to integrate the core goals of ABE in developmentally appropriate ways throughout children's education.

What Is in this Book

This book has two major parts. Together they provide the information and strategies needed to integrate ABE into your work.

The first five chapters provide a foundation for understanding ABE. Chapter 1 describes the social and political landscape of the United States that makes ABE essential to high-quality early childhood education and explains the four core anti-bias goals. Chapter 2 discusses how young children and adults are shaped by the social and political landscape described in Chapter 1. This developmental information informs the work educators do with children and with themselves. Chapters 3, 4, and 5 present the basic tools of an anti-bias learning environment: materials and curriculum that make visible and honor diversity; clarifying and brave conversations with children; and collaborative relationships with staff and families.

Chapters 6–12 discuss social identities that fundamentally shape young children's development and learning—cultural identities, racialized identities, gendered identities, economic class, abilities, and family structure. Each of these chapters offers a big picture to help you understand how societal ideas, attitudes, and biases affect young children's development and provides a discussion of children's thinking and feelings as they try to make sense of their experiences. The four anti-bias education goals are then applied to each of the social identities, accompanied by guidelines, strategies, and specific ideas to foster children's healthy growth in a world where bias and discrimination are all too pervasive.

Being an anti-bias educator requires long-term commitment and persistence. In the final section, we offer some key strategies for "keeping on keeping on." We hope these strategies answer an oft-asked question, "What keeps you going?" and help you begin or continue your own ABE journey.

To illuminate and bring alive the ideas and strategies in this book, the chapters are filled with true stories about children, families, and educators. The stories, some of which we have combined or compressed, are ones we have observed ourselves or collected from others in our decades of working with children and teachers. Each chapter also invites you to "Stop & Think" with a series of questions about your own life experiences.

Self-discovery and heightened self-knowledge are essential to being an anti-bias educator. We encourage you to engage in self-reflection as you read each chapter and to share your insights with others and listen closely to their perspectives.

The Language of Equity and Diversity

Critical thinking and communicating about the forces that shape children's identities and attitudes require having appropriate language. As for all authors, the terms we choose to use reflect our perspective, experience, and understanding of our book's subject. As ideas change, people create new terms to describe them or use old terms in new ways. Additionally, people use a variety of names to describe themselves, even some that differ from those used by people in their same social identity groups. (See "What's in a Name?" in Chapter 2.)

In the anecdotes and discussions throughout the book, we name children's social identities when it is relevant to the topic being considered. We mostly refer to *children* or to *the child* rather than use the gendered terms *girl* or *boy* and *she* or *he*, except where it makes an anecdote clearer. We avoid pronouns where possible, and where necessary we alternate the use of *he* and *she* in the various examples and stories.

• • •

As you read, ponder, and implement the ideas in this book, we hope that you will add your experiences and knowledge to the ongoing work of creating early childhood programs that make it possible for all children to develop to their fullest potential.

Online at **NAEYC.org/books/anti-bias** you will find links to other resources to deepen your learning and provide new ideas and possibilities for your work with children.

It Takes a Village

Our most heartfelt thanks go to the many experienced social justice educators and activists who helped us make sure that this book says what it needs to say. They gave generously of their busy time to read through chapters at various points in the book's development. Their feedback, reflecting each person's own work with children and in social justice struggles, added important insights that we value greatly. In alphabetical order, deep thanks to Regina Chavez, Dana Cox, Robette Dias, Doralynn Folse, Jean Gallagher-Heil, Debbie LeeKeenan, Christina Lopez-Morgan, Mary Pat Martin, Deborah Menkart, Colette Murray, John Nimmo, Encian Pastel, Bill Sparks, Sean Sparks, Anne Stewart, Nadiyah Faquir Taylor, and Maureen Yates. In addition, we thank colleagues who wrote specific vignettes or contributed to specific chapters: Margie Brinkley, Nancy Brown, Carol Cole, Tarah Fleming, Doralynn Folse, Aimee Gelnaw, Luis Hernandez, Debbie LeeKeenan, Bryan Nelson, Laurie Olsen, Encian Pastel, Louise Rosenkrantz, and Nadiyah Faquir Taylor. We are also grateful to the many educators, named and unnamed, who shared the personal stories you read throughout the book.

We owe a debt of gratitude to NAEYC for the organization's steadfast commitment to publishing a book about ABE since the first edition came out in 1989. NAEYC has held strong in the face of criticism and unfounded attacks. To our current editors—Kathy Charner and Holly Bohart—we give many thanks for their never-failing warmth, support, and discerning editing.

Finally, we send our love to the many people in our beloved communities who have been a part of our ABE journeys. They were there for us in times of discouragement, frustration, confusion, or exhaustion—and in times when we got it right and when it was time to celebrate.

I, Louise, hug my many colleagues from Pacific Oaks, Crossroads, DECET (the European diversity/equity trainers network), and the numerous early childhood teachers of children and adults with whom I've have spoken in the past 35 years. And, as always, I am able to do what I do because of Bill, Douglass, and Sean.

I, Julie, always hold in my mind and heart my early childhood colleagues from across the country, from Cabrillo College, and from my union, the California Federation of Teachers; the commitment of my beloved Rob, Rebekah, and Toby; and my amazing sisters, Kathie and Laurie, who always have my back.

And I, Catherine, am grateful to my wife, Linda; my parents, Jessie and Bud; Brian; my colleagues at PCOE; the Sierra College faculty and students; and the circle of women who surround me with love, wisdom, and support—Louise and Julie, my extraordinary mentors, and Randi, Linda L., and Joy. All of you are the wind beneath my wings.

Dedication

To the new generation of anti-bias educators who will expand, deepen, and carry on this work. And to our parents Tillie & Jack Olsen and Ann & Al Robbins. They lived and taught that respect, belief in justice, and the power of ordinary people, organized to act together, can change the world. Their work goes on.

CHAPTER 1

Anti-Bias Education and Why It Matters

We find these joys to be self-evident: That all children are created whole, endowed with innate intelligence, with dignity and wonder, worthy of respect. The embodiment of life, liberty and happiness, children are original blessings, here to learn their own song. Every [child] is entitled to love, to dream and belong to a loving "village." And to pursue a life of purpose.

—Raffi Foundation for Child Honouring,
"A Covenant for Honouring Children"

Equal rights, fair play, justice, are all like the air; we all have it, or none of us has it.

—Maya Angelou, Academy of Achievement interview

What Is Anti-Bias Education?

Anti-bias education (ABE) is an optimistic commitment to supporting children who live in a highly diverse and yet still inequitable world. Rather than a formula for a particular curriculum, it is an underpinning perspective and framework that permeates everything in early childhood education—including your interactions with children, families, and colleagues. ABE is based on the understanding that children are individuals with their own personalities and temperaments and with social group identities based on the families who birth and raise them and the way society views who they are.

These identities are both externally applied by the world around them and internally constructed within the child.

ABE has four goals for children that have developed from the need to identify and prevent, as much as possible, the harmful emotional and psychological impacts on children from societal prejudice and bias. The goals are designed to strengthen children's sense of self and family (identity, Goal 1); to support their joy in human diversity (diversity, Goal 2); to enable them to gain the cognitive and social and emotional tools to recognize hurtful behavior (justice, Goal 3); and to develop the confidence and skills to work with others to build inclusive, fairer ways of being in a community (activism, Goal 4). The four core goals of ABE are described in detail on pages 15–19.

The Four Core Goals of Anti-Bias Education

Goal 1, Identity

- Teachers will nurture each child's construction of knowledgeable and confident personal and social identities.

- Children will demonstrate self-awareness, confidence, family pride, and positive social identities.

Goal 2, Diversity

- Teachers will promote each child's comfortable, empathic interaction with people from diverse backgrounds.

- Children will express comfort and joy with human diversity, use accurate language for human differences, and form deep, caring connections across all dimensions of human diversity.

Goal 3, Justice

- Teachers will foster each child's capacity to critically identify bias and will nurture each child's empathy for the hurt bias causes.

- Children will increasingly recognize unfairness (injustice), have language to describe unfairness, and understand that unfairness hurts.

Goal 4, Activism

- Teachers will cultivate each child's ability and confidence to stand up for oneself and for others in the face of bias.

- Children will demonstrate a sense of empowerment and the skills to act, with others or alone, against prejudice and/or discriminatory actions.

At the heart of anti-bias work is a vision of a world in which all children are able to blossom and each child's abilities and gifts are able to flourish:

- All children and families have a sense of belonging and experience affirmation of their personal and social identities and their cultural ways of being.

- All children have access to and participate in the education they need to become successful, contributing members of society.

- All children are engaged in joyful learning that supports their cognitive, physical, creative, and social development.

- Children and adults know how to respectfully and easily live, learn, and work together in diverse and inclusive environments. All families have the resources they need to fully nurture their children.

- All children and families live in safe, peaceful, healthy, comfortable housing and neighborhoods.

This vision of ABE also reflects the basic human rights described in the United Nations Convention on the Rights of the Child (UN OHCHR 1989):

- The right to *survival*

- The right to *develop to the fullest*

- The right to *protection* from harmful influences, abuse, and/or exploitation

- The right to *participate fully* in family, cultural, and social life

In order for children to receive these rights, their society, their families, and those responsible for their care and education must work together to provide what each child needs to flourish. A worldwide community of anti-bias educators shares this vision. They adapt its goals and principles to their particular settings as they work with children and their families to bring these rights into being.

Stop & Think: Imagine

Because of social inequities, too many children still do not have access to basic human rights. Imagine a world of justice, equal opportunity, and safety for all.

- What would that world look like for each of the children you work with?

- What would the world look like for the program you work in?

- What would you add to the vision of anti-bias education on this page?

Why Do We Need Anti-Bias Education?

Effective early childhood educators are committed to the principle that all children deserve to develop to their fullest potential. At the same time, the world is not yet a place where all children are equally responded to and have equal opportunity to become all they can be. Listen to the voices heard in early childhood programs:

A 10-month-old infant cries instead of eating when placed at a table with other classmates in his child care program. When the teacher talks with the infant's mother about it, she learns that the family still feeds the infant because in their culture, children do not begin eating by themselves until they are a little older. The teacher says rather indignantly, "Well, we do not have the staff to do that. You have to teach your child to feed himself."

• • •

A preschool teacher announces that the children will make cards for Father's Day. "I don't want to!" defiantly states a 4-year-old from a family with a single mom. The teacher shrugs and says, "We're making cards today. So, you make a card too."

• • •

A 4-year-old child newly arrived from Armenia starts his first day at a neighborhood preschool with an English-only policy. When he returns home, he tells his mother, "My teacher couldn't hear anything I said!" The next

day his mom asks the preschool director about this, and she suggests, "Perhaps your son wasn't paying attention."

• • •

"This is supposed to be a happy painting. Why are you using all that black paint?" observes a teacher to a young child at an easel.

• • •

"You're a baby, you can't play with us," a group of preschoolers tell a classmate who uses a wheelchair and who wants to join their play. "It's fun being the baby," the teacher says cheerfully, hoping to encourage the children play together.

Damage is done when children do not see their families reflected and respected in their early childhood programs and when they experience confusing expectations and messages about how to act that contradict those they get at home. Children are injured when they receive messages about themselves that say they are not fully capable, intelligent, or worthwhile.

Teachers become anti-bias educators when they recognize that it hurts children's development when adults do not actively support children's family identities or when adults remain silent when children tease or reject others because of who they are. Children need to feel good about themselves without developing a false sense of superiority based on who they are. Messages and actions that both directly and indirectly reinforce harmful ideas and stereotypes about people undermine children's sense of worth, especially when they come from someone as significant to them as a teacher. Lupe Cortes, a Head Start teacher, recalls,

I still remember that many adults put me down when I was a child, like saying, "Oh, she is just a little Mexican girl." These comments really affected how I felt about myself, and I vowed I wouldn't do the same to someone else. As a teacher, I wanted to break that cycle.

When teachers and families integrate the four ABE goals into teaching and childrearing and engage children in positive, informative conversations about human diversity, children develop the conviction that who they are is valued and important. When adults help children notice and address unfairness, even very young children are able to be strong and clear in standing up for themselves and others. Listen to the voices of children who have experienced ABE in their schools:

> Several 3-year-olds (Asian, White, and Latinx) are at the art table playing with small mirrors while they paint on paper ovals. As they look at their eyes, Jesse starts crooning to himself, "Oh, pretty eyes, pretty eyes. Lots of different eyes, pretty eyes, pretty eyes. Brown and blue, pointy, round. Pretty eyes, pretty eyes."

> • • •

> Some children are imitating the Native American characters they saw in a Peter Pan movie, running around the yard making whooping noises and pretending they have tomahawks. One of the children, Skyler, puts up her hand to stop them and says firmly, "That's not what Indians sound like. They have words. Real words. And you'll hurt teacher Claudia's feelings—'cause she's Cherokee."

> • • •

> In a pre-K class where the teacher engages children in examining stereotypes and omissions in their classroom books, 5-year-old Walker writes in awkward printing, "This book is irregular. It doesn't have any women in it."

A Professional Responsibility to Advance Equity

In 2019 NAEYC released a groundbreaking position statement on advancing equity, which affirms that "all early childhood educators have a professional obligation to advance equity . . . and work to eliminate structural inequities that limit equitable learning opportunities" (NAEYC 2019, 1).

In addition, this position statement declares that "advancing equity requires a dedication to self-reflection, a willingness to respectfully listen to others' perspectives without interruption or defensiveness, and a commitment to continuous learning to improve practice" (5). It calls on everyone involved in any aspect of early childhood education to take on the following actions, which are also foundational to using an ABE approach.

- Build awareness and understanding of your culture, personal beliefs, values, and biases.

- Recognize the power and benefits of diversity and inclusivity.

- Take responsibility for biased actions, even if unintended, and actively work to repair the harm.

- Acknowledge and seek to understand structural inequities and their impact over time.

- View your commitment to cultural responsiveness as an ongoing process.

- Recognize that the professional knowledge base is changing. . . . Be willing to challenge the use of outdated or narrowly defined approaches—for example, in curriculum, assessment policies and practices, or early learning standards. (6)

The Profession's Code of Ethics

As do all professional organizations, NAEYC has a Code of Ethical Conduct that describes the central ideals and principles of the early childhood education field. Many of these also support the vision and goals of ABE. Here are some specific examples (NAEYC 2016):

P-1.2—We shall care for and educate children in positive emotional and social environments that are cognitively stimulating and that support each *child's culture, language, ethnicity, and family structure* [emphasis added].

P-1.3—We shall not participate in practices that discriminate against children by denying benefits, giving special advantages, or excluding them from programs or activities on the basis of their sex, race, national origin, immigration status, preferred home language, religious beliefs, medical condition, disability, or the marital status/family structure, sexual orientation, or religious beliefs or other affiliations of their families.

I-4.3—[We shall] work through education, research, and advocacy toward an environmentally safe world in which all children receive health care, food, and shelter; are nurtured; and live free from violence in their home and their communities.

I-4.4—[We shall] work through education, research, and advocacy toward a society in which all young children have access to high-quality early care and education programs.

I-4.7—[We shall] support policies and laws that promote the well-being of children and families, and work to change those that impair their well-being. To participate in developing policies and laws that are needed, and to cooperate with families and other individuals and groups in these efforts. (9, 19)

Stop & Think: NAEYC's Code of Ethical Conduct and You

- Which specific parts of the Code listed above speak to you most right now? Why? (See NAEYC.org/resources/position-statements/ethical-conduct.)

- Which parts, if any, are you not comfortable with? Why?

- Which parts of the Code do you see practiced in the program where you work, send your child, or hope to work in someday?

Inequity Is Built into the System

Early childhood teachers welcome children and show respect for their families so children feel powerful, competent, and a sense of belonging. However, beyond individual teachers' hopes, beliefs, and actions is a society that has built advantage and disadvantage into its institutions and systems. These dynamics of advantage and disadvantage are deeply rooted in history. They continue to shape the degree of access children have to education, health care, and security—the services necessary for children's healthy development. These dynamics also greatly affect the early childhood education system, despite whatever values individual teachers may have.

As the NAEYC position statement on advancing equity (2019) explains,

> Advancing equity in early childhood education requires understanding . . . the ways in which historical and current inequities have shaped the profession, as they have shaped our nation. The biases we refer to here are based in race, class, culture, gender, sexual orientation, ability and disability, language, national origin, indigenous heritage, religion, and other identities. They are rooted in our nation's social, political, economic, and educational structures. Precisely because these biases are both individual and institutional, addressing structural inequities requires attention to both *interpersonal* dynamics—the day-to-day relationships and interactions at the core of early childhood education practice—and *systemic* influences— the uneven distribution of power and privilege ingrained in public and private systems nationwide, including in early childhood education. (4)

Teachers need to know how structural biases operate and affect their teaching and how these biases impact the development of children's identities and attitudes. This means understanding societal isms and explicit and implicit bias.

What Are Isms?

Ableism, classism, nativism, racism, and sexism are examples of an *ism,* a set of social beliefs, policies, and actions designed to keep power and privilege in the hands of one group at the expense of another. Isms are reflected in a society's institutions, such as education, health, housing, employment, and media. Institutional isms are often created through the laws or regulations of federal, state, and city governments and are expressed in organizational policies, regulations, cultural assumptions, and the thinking and actions of the people who carry out the policies (Rothstein 2017).

The structural advantages and disadvantages assigned to people based on isms depend on people's membership, or *perceived* membership, in specific social identity groups, such as citizenship, race, ethnicity, economic class, physical ability, gender, or sexual orientation. The biases that accompany the isms shape children's construction of their social identities and their attitudes toward others.

Direct and Indirect Effects of Isms

Many people equate the isms to blatant, easily identifiable ideas and actions—and sometimes isms do function directly and obviously. Historically, forbidding women to vote or own property was an example of direct sexism. So, too, were laws that created racial segregation in education (racism) or legally denied public education to children with disabilities (ableism). Laws prohibiting marriage to a same-sex partner, or prohibiting a same-sex partner from getting custody of a couple's children if the biological parent dies, are also direct consequences of a structural ism (heterosexism). The number of direct laws or regulations creating advantage for some groups and disadvantage to others has decreased over US history, usually as a result of years of many people working to end these direct forms of isms. The Civil Rights Act of 1968, the Education for All Handicapped Children Act of 1975, and the 2015 ruling of the US Supreme Court guaranteeing same-sex couples the freedom to marry are examples of structural changes that have resulted in greater equality.

However, while some forms of systemic inequality are eliminated or weakened, aspects of them may arise again (Kendi 2016). An example is the weakening of the Voting Rights Act of 1965 by congressional and Supreme Court actions in the 2000s. This has led to several states passing legislation restricting the right to vote, particularly hurting people of color, people with low income, students, and senior citizens. Another example, occurring during the writing of this book (2017–2019), is the action taken by the federal government and some state legislatures to pass new immigration regulations directed at restricting people—particularly those from majority Muslim countries and from Mexico, the Caribbean, and Central and South America—from coming to the United States. Yet another disturbing indicator is the data about hate groups and hate crimes. In the United States, the number of hate groups rose to a record

high in 2018 (Beirich 2019b), and crimes against people of color, Jewish people, and LGBTQ people were the second highest in more than a decade (Levin & Nakashima 2019).

Economic statistics also illustrate the continuing impact of racism and classism. The percentage of African American (34 percent) and American Indian (34 percent) children living in poverty in the United States is almost three times the percentage of White children (12 percent). The percentage of Latino children (28 percent) living in poverty is twice that of White, non-Hispanic children (Annie E. Casey Foundation 2018; terms of race and origin used here are those used in the Casey report). There is also a growing body of research about the psychological and emotional effects of racism and other isms, including poverty, trauma, and stress (NAEYC 2019). For example, many Latinx children, whether they have been directly involved or not, experience trauma and psychological distress as a result of parental detention and deportations (Rojas-Flores et al. 2017).

Isms Impact the Early Childhood Profession Too

The early childhood profession exists as part of the larger society and is not immune to the biases that are built into its complex world. The field's professional commitment to children and to families has laid a foundation for equitable treatment of all, yet the field often fails to address implicit biases and barriers that are explored in the chapters ahead. Consider the following:

- One long-standing early childhood education principle requires that curriculum meet each child's individual needs. However, individualizing frequently relies on a single cultural perspective of development and does not include understanding the cultural and social influences on children's learning. This approach results in misunderstanding either the strengths or the learning needs of children who are not seen as members of the dominant culture (see page 13). In addition, many teachers still do not receive preservice and in-service training on using children's cultural strengths as part of individualizing learning. Another factor is that for the most part, standardized curriculum and assessment tools frequently reflect an implicit dominant cultural perspective

(NAEYC 2019). While some do address ways to individualize learning, they do not explicitly include discussions about social identity issues and considering children's cultural strengths.

- Another research-backed principle states that it is developmentally best for young children to continue to develop their home languages while also learning English (Castro 2014). However, teacher training and resources for working with dual language learners are not always available, and many early childhood teachers struggle to effectively support dual language learners. Moreover, the idea of dual language learning continues to be a contested social issue and is not accepted in many school districts around the country.

- The field of early childhood education still reflects the stratification of the larger society and "the historic marginalization of women's social and economic roles—which has a particularly strong impact on women of color. Comprising primarily women, the early childhood workforce is typically characterized by low wages. It is also stratified, with fewer women of color and immigrant women having access to higher education opportunities that lead to the educational qualifications required for higher-paying roles. Systemic barriers limit upward mobility, even when degrees and qualifications are obtained" (NAEYC 2019, 14).

Biases Are Part of the System of Isms

Biases are beliefs that affect how individuals think, feel, and act toward others. They lead to acts of individual prejudice and discrimination. Starting in childhood, everyone absorbs and internalizes biases from larger societal attitudes (Bian, Leslie, & Cimpian 2017; Brown et al. 2017). As adults, early childhood teachers bring biased ideas, whether consciously or unintentionally, into their work (Yates & Marcelo 2014). This is why it is essential for teachers to understand how biases work—and uncover and get rid of their own.

For example, some teachers may assume that families are not interested in their children's education because they miss family conferences, meetings, or other events, without considering that families may be unable to attend due to such factors as the cost of babysitting, lack of available transportation, or inflexible work hours, or that discussions with their child's teacher are not in the family's language. Or, some teachers might unquestioningly accept the disproportionate number of White early childhood educators who work as master teachers, program directors, university professors, and administrators, excusing this situation with the rationale that people of color lack sufficient qualifications or degrees or interest. They do not take into account societal factors such as the economic conditions that permit people to be full-time students or consider the far-reaching, negative results of attending underresourced and overcrowded schools prior to college.

Biases Are Explicit *and* Implicit

Sometimes a person's bias is obvious, or *explicit*. Explicit biases are undisguised statements. They are attitudes and beliefs about a group of people that are applied to all individuals in the group. Examples of explicit biases in US society include the sexual harassment of women by powerful men; violence against mosques, churches, and synagogues by angry, prejudiced people; and white nationalist demonstrators chanting anti-Semitic slogans used by the Nazis. Most early childhood teachers are sensitive to explicit bias and, for the most part, work hard to avoid and address such behavior. Still, the field is plagued by some explicit biases, such as the belief that children in some racial groups are genetically more intelligent than those in other racial groups, that boys are inherently more destructive than girls, and that adopted children carry lifelong emotional damage.

In other cases, a person's actions reflect bias that is not so obvious—even to the person acting on it. This is *implicit* bias. Implicit biases are "attitudes or stereotypes that affect our understanding, actions, and decisions in an unconscious manner" (Kirwan Institute 2015). Individuals may not be aware that they have these biases or that they act or fail to act because of them. For example, in our experience, White teachers who say that they are color blind (i.e., are not aware of racial or ethnic differences because "children are children") tend to have classrooms in which White, urban, middle-class children are represented in the learning environment and curriculum while children of other backgrounds are not. Regardless of the teacher's conscious intentions, this kind of classroom sends all children the message that the "universal" child is White, middle class, urban, able-bodied, and from a two-parent family, and therefore the one who matters. Children who do not fit in those categories are "less than," "different," "exotic," not "regular." These teachers may not express *explicit* biases that being White or middle class is better, but their implicit bias of what the universal child looks like turns into bias in practice and reinforces the societal inequities and injuries the child meets outside the classroom. This implicit bias is also evident in many college child development textbooks that have chapters of research about White, middle-class children and short segments at the end of the chapter, or in a separate chapter, about "diverse" children.

> Teachers of young children—like all people—are not immune to such bias. Even among teachers who do not believe they hold any explicit biases, implicit biases are associated with differential judgments about and treatment of children by race, gender, ability, body type, physical appearance, and social, economic, and language status—all of which limit children's opportunities to reach their potential. Implicit biases also result in differential judgments of children's play, aggressiveness, compliance, initiative, and abilities. (NAEYC 2019, 15)

Implicit Biases Impact Teachers' Behavior and Children's Well-Being

Consider how girls often receive feedback about the way they look and the way they are dressed rather than about their abilities, while boys are praised for their efforts and accomplishments. Bit by bit, many girls become convinced that their value rests mainly on their appearance, a belief that becomes increasingly toxic for teens and young adults and tends to shadow the adult lives of many women (OWH 2019).

Another deeply hurtful—and well-researched— example of implicit biases influencing teacher behavior is documentation that African American boys are disproportionately suspended from preschool programs for behavioral issues. Oscar Barbarin was one of the first to look at this disturbing

reality (Barbarin & Crawford 2006). Several years later, the US Department of Education's Office for Civil Rights reported that African American children "represent 18 percent of preschool enrollment, but 48 percent of preschool children receiving more than one out-of-school suspension" (2014, 1). And although the teachers and directors who suspend these boys may not be acting with the conscious intent of being racist, their unexamined implicit bias results in racism.

Here is an example of a preservice teacher in one of Julie's college classes facing an important learning moment concerning how implicit bias resulted in an incorrect and unfair interpretation of children's behavior:

> A preservice teacher was recorded leading circle time. The activity had fallen apart, with children getting up, running away, and refusing to participate. That evening the college class discussed what had happened. The preservice teacher complained about the disruptive behavior of two African American boys who had "ruined" the circle. Then the instructor played the video recording. Everyone was shocked to see that the real disruption had come from two White boys, that one of the African American boys had joined in later, and that the second boy had been almost entirely a bystander. "But I remembered it as Alec and William!" the preservice teacher said in tears. "How could I have been so wrong?"

The following example shows Linda, a community college teacher, uncovering her own implicit biases and then changing the behavior that reflected that bias.

> When I first started teaching adults, I was shocked and distressed by the poor level of writing skill by my college students. Some

part of me felt like the students just didn't care enough to proofread their papers or were unwilling to put in the time to learn appropriate grammar and spelling. As I got to know the students, I came to realize that few had been expected or supported to write well in high school. Many were dual language learners, fluent in conversational English, but with little experience in academic English. At my community college, almost all my students worked full time in addition to carrying 12 units. Some cared for families at home. My willingness to blame them for their lack of preparation was an outcome of buying into the classist idea that everyone had the same opportunities to learn and the same exposure to skill building in school. I still needed to help them learn to write an academic paper, but coming to terms with the classism in my thinking allowed me to stop seeing them as lazy and uninterested, "less-than." And once that happened, I began to see their intelligence, their eagerness to learn, and their incredible commitment to becoming educated despite the barriers they experienced.

Even organizations can discover implicit bias in their publications and address it. The evolution of the concept of developmentally appropriate practice (DAP), for example, illustrates a significant implicit bias evident in the first NAEYC publication on DAP, *Developmentally Appropriate Practice* (Bredekamp 1986), and then the important uncovering and revising of the bias in subsequent editions (Bredekamp 1987; Bredekamp & Copple 1997; Copple & Bredekamp 2009). The original definition of DAP reflected a perspective that all children's development is essentially the same, which—given the commonly acknowledged research of the time—meant that White children's patterns of development were considered the norm for all children. In 1996, "NAEYC revisited its position statement on developmentally appropriate practice in response to new knowledge, the changing context, and critiques from within and beyond the profession" (Copple & Bredekamp 2009, viii). One of the major issues was "expanding the basic definition of developmentally appropriate practice to include consideration of social and cultural context" (viii). With another revision of the NAEYC position statement on DAP in progress at the time of this writing, NAEYC is continuing to address this bias.

Walter Gilliam, a leading researcher on the subject of implicit bias and early childhood education, explains with his colleagues that "Fortunately, recent research suggests that implicit biases may be reduced through interventions designed to either address biases directly or increase teachers' empathy for children. Useful guiding principles by which early educators may explore and discover their own implicit biases and strive to deliver more equitable services may also prove helpful" (Gilliam et al. 2016, 15). Strategies include acknowledging differences while also identifying shared qualities and goals (e.g., "We are all the same. We are all different" is one of the key concepts of anti-bias work), increasing teachers' interactions and familiarity with people whose social identities are not the same as their own, and learning to speak out when encountering examples of explicit bias (Cooper 2016). Some early childhood education programs at higher education institutions are now including these skills in their courses.

Stop & Think: Everyone Learns Explicit and Implicit Biases

- Choose a specific social identity that you are *not* a part of; it could be related to race, culture, language, economic class, sexual orientation, gender, religion, ethnicity, or physical ability. Make a list of all the biases or stereotypes you have ever heard about this group of people. Don't censor yourself. Write them down regardless of whether you believe them. (You cannot change your thinking or gain new knowledge unless you first uncover and face the messages that have surrounded you throughout your life.)

- Choose two or three items from your list and think about how, where, and from whom you learned these biased messages. Share your thinking with a colleague.

- How much real contact did you or do you have with people who are members of the identity group you are thinking about?

- How do your own social identities influence the implicit biases you learned?

Microaggressions

A microaggression is another form of biased comment or action that inflicts injury or insult and damages people's sense of themselves. The casual comments, jokes, and statements that constitute microaggressions may seem small and unimportant to the microaggressor. Even though unintended, they act as sandpaper grinding down the recipient's sense of self and confidence. For example, "You speak English very well for someone named Mendoza." Racial microaggressions are "brief and commonplace daily verbal, behavioral, or environmental indignities, whether intentional or unintentional, that communicate hostile, derogatory, or negative racial slights and insults toward people of color. Perpetrators of microaggressions are often unaware that they engage in such communications when they interact with racial/ethnic minorities" (Sue et al. 2007, 271).

Dr. Chester Pierce (1980), a pioneer in the study of the social and psychological impacts of racism on identity development, compares the many racial microaggressions children experience over time to physically poisonous microcontaminants, suggesting that microaggressions build up and undermine children's evolving sense of who they are and their place in the world. For example, consider the impact on young children of hearing their names mispronounced every day or even being given another name because their teachers find it difficult to pronounce their real names and do not make the effort to learn the correct pronunciation. White children may also learn racism through regular doses of microaggressions witnessed in their families. For example, some of our White students remember times when their families closed their car windows and locked the doors as they drove through a neighborhood where a majority of residents were people of color.

Sue (2010) expanded on this work to include identifying microaggressions that target other social identities, such as gender, sexual orientation, and ability. For example, consider the message to children with disabilities when someone says, "Oh, let me help you," or "I'll do that for you," before giving children a chance to do it themselves. Over time, such a message teaches children with disabilities to think of themselves as frail, not capable, and dependent on

others. "I need some strong boys to help me move this table" sends the message that girls are not strong and that physical strength is valued in boys.

Learning to uncover and name microaggressions serves two purposes. First, it supports people who are the targets of microaggressions to better address what is going on. People may feel insulted or put down but not be sure exactly why or how they should respond, which makes it more difficult to resist the microaggression and stand up for themselves. Second, it helps people gain awareness of the microaggressions they are inflicting on others and the effects of these acts and statements, which is a first step toward changing their behaviors (DeAngelis 2009).

Dominant Culture and Cultural Diversity

The term *dominant culture* does not necessarily mean the culture of the majority. Rather, it is the culture of the people who hold social, political, and economic power in a society. The United States has had both a dominant culture and ethnic and cultural diversity from its earliest days as a nation. These two realities have played out in different ways throughout history and have created tension over how its residents can be one and many at the same time.

The implicit rules of a dominant culture set a norm and become the lens through which all other ways of living are judged. These judgments become the basis for information, stereotyping, and biases, which in turn justify the societal power of the dominant group.

The typical images of dominant culture in the United States include native English speaker; Christian; well dressed; slim (for women); well-furnished and equipped single-family home (always very neat); heterosexual married couple with one or two biological children, each of whom has a separate bedroom; well-resourced schools; professional or business management employment; reliable health care and internet service; and one or more new cars. The consistency of these images conveys the message that this is *the* ordinary and desirable way to live. The more a person's life looks like that described in dominant culture, the worthier that person is as a human being in the eyes of that culture.

The term *mainstream* rather than *dominant culture* is sometimes used to describe this cultural image. *Mainstream,* however, not only signals that it is the correct way to live but also implies that most people (the "main" stream) in the society actually live like this, which is not the reality. The mainstream image becomes the standard by which people, families, or groups are judged, and the degree to which they differ from it becomes the basis for prejudice against them. *Dominant culture* is more accurate and descriptive.

Stop & Think: How Did Your Family Fit the Image?

- In what ways did the family of your childhood match or not match the prevailing images of the dominant culture where you lived? How did that feel to you?

- In what ways does your current family match or not match the prevailing images of the dominant culture? How does that feel to you?

- How do the families you serve fit into or not fit into the dominant culture image?

The Long Shadow of History

The United States includes Native Americans, immigrants and their descendants, and the descendants of those who came not by choice but by force and chain. Throughout history, each ethnic group brought its own languages and cultural ways of life. These were often considered "inferior" and "non-civilized" by the existing dominant culture and language groups (Roediger 2005). Considerable

pressure was put on immigrant groups to "melt" into the dominant culture. Prejudices prevented some groups from doing so. Yet many immigrants forged blended cultures that kept alive beliefs, practices, and languages of their original cultures and incorporated some dominant cultural elements. The reality was more "salad bowl" than melting pot.

Once public schools were established in the 19th century, they intentionally played a key role in the process of assimilating children into the dominant culture. The assumption was that children must give up their home cultures and languages in order to learn how to be part of the dominant culture. One particularly brutal example of this assimilation policy is the boarding schools created for Native American children. First established in the 1800s, the schools lasted all the way through the 1970s (Churchill 2004). Children as young as 5 years old were forcibly taken from their homes and kept in these boarding schools for several years. The children were severely punished for speaking their home languages and practicing their cultural traditions. In 1978, Congress worked closely with American Indian and Alaska Native (AI/AN) elected officials, child welfare experts, and families to pass the Indian Child Welfare Act. In particular, the act's intent was to stop the unnecessary separation of large numbers of children who had been removed from their homes, parents, extended families, and communities by state child welfare and private adoption agencies (National Indian Child Welfare Association 2015).

The call for a cultural diversity approach—in all aspects of education—was a component of the 1960s Civil Rights movement. Advocates argued for an educational approach that honored the importance of home culture to ensure that all children were fully supported in their learning while also teaching children how to live as part of one overall society. Advocates highlighted the value of cultural diversity to the building of a strong and democratic nation.

In Early Childhood Programs, Families Matter

One of the core values of the early childhood field is that "children are best understood and supported in the context of family, culture, community, and society" (NAEYC 2016, 4). The extent to which children's home cultures and languages are made visible or invisible in a program's learning environment and curriculum is at the heart of whether the dominant culture perspective or cultural diversity perspective undergirds that program. The invisibility of some children and the visibility of other children in the classroom's environment and curriculum send this message: "Some people matter—some do not." This message sits at the heart of isms.

Stop & Think: Your Experiences with Schools and Your Family

- How visible were your family and families like yours in your schools when you were growing up? Did your school support your home language? Were the people you saw portrayed in books, classroom materials, and the curriculum of the same racial, ethnic, or religious group or economic class with which you identified?

- Were the holidays that mattered to your family acknowledged by your school? Celebrated in your school? If yes, were you aware that not all families celebrated those holidays? If no, how did that affect your feelings about yourself?

- Did the adults in your family feel comfortable coming to school and talking with your teachers? If not, why not? If so, what did the school do to make that happen?

The Four Core Goals of Anti-Bias Education

The vital and fundamental connections between cognitive development and social and emotional development is a foundational principle of early childhood education. Together, these connections are the "bricks and mortar" of human development (NIEER 2007, 5). ABE is part of the bricks and mortar necessary for children to healthfully and fully become all they can be. Four core goals provide a framework for its practice with children. Grounded in what is known about how children construct identity and attitudes (see Chapter 2), the goals help you create a safe, supportive learning community for every child.

The four core goals support the following: children's development of a confident sense of identity without needing to feel superior to others; an ease with human diversity; a sense of fairness and justice; and the ability to stand up for themselves or others (the skills of empowerment).

Goal 1, Identity

- Teachers will nurture each child's construction of knowledgeable and confident personal and social identities.

- Children will demonstrate self-awareness, confidence, family pride, and positive social identities.

This goal means supporting children to feel strong and proud of who they are without needing to feel superior to anyone else. It means children learn accurate, respectful language to describe who they and others are. Teachers support children to develop and be comfortable within their home culture and within the school culture. Goal 1 is the starting place for all children, in all settings.

Adding to early childhood education's long-term commitment to nurturing each child's individual, personal identity, ABE emphasizes the importance of nurturing children's social, or group, identities. Social identities relate to the significant group categorizations of the society in which children grow up and live and which they share with many others. Social identities include but are not limited to gender, racial, ethnic, cultural, religious, and economic class groups. (Social identity is described in detail in Chapter 2.) A strong sense of both individual and group identities is the foundation for the three other anti-bias core goals.

Goal 2, Diversity

- Teachers will promote each child's comfortable, empathic interaction with people from diverse backgrounds.

- Children will express comfort and joy with human diversity, use accurate language for human differences, and form deep, caring human connections across all dimensions of human diversity.

between exploring differences and similarities. All human beings share similar biological attributes, needs, and rights (e.g., the need for food, shelter, and love; the commonalities of language, families, and feelings) and people live and meet these shared needs and rights in many different ways. A basic premise in ABE is "We are all the same. We are all different. Isn't that wonderful!"

Goal 3, Justice

- Teachers will foster each child's capacity to critically identify bias and will nurture each child's empathy for the hurt bias causes.

- Children will increasingly recognize unfairness (injustice), have language to describe unfairness, and understand that unfairness hurts.

This goal is about building children's innate, budding capacities for empathy and fairness as well as their cognitive skills for thinking critically about what is happening around them. It is about building a sense of safety—the sense that everyone can and will be treated fairly.

Learning experiences include opportunities for children to understand and practice using skills for identifying unfair and untrue images (stereotypes), comments (teasing, name calling), and behaviors (isolation, discrimination) directed at themselves or at others. This includes issues of race, disability, economic class, ethnicity, language, gender, body shape, age, and so on. These are early lessons in critical thinking for children, giving them ways to identify what they see and hear and testing it against the notions of kindness and fairness.

These lessons build on young children's implicit interest in what is fair and not fair. As children come to identify unfair experiences and learn that unfair situations can be made more fair, they gain an increased sense of their own power in the world. Children cannot construct a strong self-concept, or develop respect for others, if they do not know how to identify and resist hurtful, stereotypical, and inaccurate messages or actions directed toward themselves or others. Developing the ability to think critically strengthens children's sense of self as well as their capacity to form caring relationships with others.

This goal means guiding children to be able to think about and have words for how people are the same and how they are different. It includes helping children feel and behave respectfully, warmly, and confidently with people who are different from themselves. It includes encouraging children to learn both about how they are different from other children and about how they are similar. These are never either/or realities because people are *simultaneously* the same in some ways and different from one another in some ways. This goal is the heart of learning how to treat all people fairly and in caring ways.

Some early childhood teachers and families are not sure they should encourage children to pay attention to and learn about differences among people. They may think it is best to teach only about how people are the same, worrying that talking about differences causes prejudice. While well intentioned, this concern arises from a mistaken notion about the sources of bias. Differences do not create bias. *Children learn prejudice from prejudice*—not from learning about human diversity. It is how people respond to differences that can teach bias and fear.

Another misconception about Goal 2 is that exploring differences among people ignores appreciating the similarities. Goal 2 calls for creating a balance

Goal 4, Activism

- Teachers will cultivate each child's ability and confidence to stand up for oneself and for others in the face of bias.

- Children will demonstrate a sense of empowerment and the skills to act, with others or alone, against prejudice and/or discriminatory actions.

Goal 4 is about giving children tools for learning how to stand up to hurtful and unfair biased behavior based on any aspect of social identity. Biased behavior may be directed at oneself or another. It may come from another child or an adult, children's books, or television and films. This goal strengthens children's ability to consider other perspectives, interact in positive ways with others, and engage in conflict resolution.

Actions of teasing, rejection, and exclusion because of some aspect of a child's social identities are forms of aggressive behavior. They are just as serious as physical aggression. The old saying "Sticks and stones may break my bones, but names will never hurt me" is false. Children's developing sense of self is hurt by name calling, teasing, and exclusion based on identity. And children who engage in such hurtful behaviors are learning it is acceptable to hurt others, the earliest form of bullying. An anti-bias approach calls on teachers to intervene gently but firmly to support the child who is the target of the biased behavior and help both children learn other ways of interacting.

Children's growth on Goal 4 strengthens their growth on the other three goals. If children are the target of prejudice or discrimination, they need tools to resist and to know that they have worth (Goal 1). When a child speaks up for another child, it reinforces—for the children involved and for any bystanders—the importance of understanding other people's unique feelings (Goal 2). When children are helped to act, it broadens their understanding of unfairness and fairness (Goal 3).

Implementing All Four Core Anti-Bias Education Goals

Each Gear Moves Another

At a conference on early childhood anti-bias work in Berlin, Germany, in 2010 (Kinderwelten), teachers from 31 child care programs displayed storyboards documenting the work. One center had a wonderful way to show the relationship among the four ABE goals. They made four wooden, interlocking gears, each representing one goal. Moving any one of the gears moved all the others.

Goal 1 → Goal 2 → Goal 3 → Goal 4

Even though the four ABE core goals interconnect and build on each other, some programs choose to work on only some of them. Some teachers bypass Goal 1 to focus on Goal 2, because they think it is more important for the children to learn about diversity than about their own social identities. This tends to happen in programs primarily serving children from the dominant culture, where their social identities are seen as the norm. While it is very important for children from the dominant culture to develop an understanding and appreciation of diversity (Goal 2), it is also necessary for them to develop a positive sense of their social identities *without* learning to feel superior to others (Goal 1).

In contrast, other teachers primarily focus on Goal 1, because the children they teach—for example, children of color or children with disabilities—are targets of systemic oppression and harmful biases. Goal 1 *is* key to children's development of resilience and resistance to the harmful undermining of their social identities. At the same time, children who experience systemic oppression and biases also need to develop an understanding and appreciation of all the many ways people live (e.g., family structure, ability, culture, economic class).

Another problematic choice is to focus on Goals 1 and 2 while disregarding Goals 3 and 4. This is a watered-down approach to ABE. Goals 3 and 4 provide children with the critical thinking and behavioral skills that build their sense of "we all belong here, and we are all safe here." Children need the dispositions and skills engendered by Goals 3 and 4 to live competently and in caring ways in a diverse and complex world.

Fostering children's sense of empowerment—that they will recognize when something is wrong and know how to improve it—strengthens their sense of empathy and builds a sense that they will be safe and cared for. The best antidote to children's hurt, sadness, or worry is to help them develop a conviction that they can do something to make the situation better and that there are adults who also care and who do things to change unfair situations to fair, to shift feelings of hurt to safe. Naming unfairness and not liking it (Goal 3) are the first steps to learning how to act *for* fairness. And unless children feel they and others are working to make their world fair (Goal 4), they cannot truly feel safe.

Talking with Children About Identity, Diversity, Justice, and Activism

Here are some simple concepts related to the four ABE goals to share with preschoolers and kindergartners.

- Everyone wants a world that is fair, where all people are treated with kindness and no one is hurtful or mean to others. You can help make that happen!

- Sometimes children quarrel or want the same toy or don't want to play with each other. That happens to everyone. Teachers and families help children learn how to work kindly and fairly with other people.

- Sometimes people are treated badly because of the color of their skin or where their family came from, or how they talk, or because they are experiencing homelessness or because they have a disability. That is never okay.

- Saying someone can't cry because he is a boy is not okay (and it's not true—boys *do* cry). Saying someone can't run fast because she is a girl is not okay (and it's not true—girls *do* run fast). Saying someone can't play with you because their skin is a different color is hurtful and mean, and it's not okay. Saying someone can't sit next to you because they say words differently than you do, or because they use a wheelchair, is not okay. These things are hurtful and mean, and you miss out on making a new friend.

- When someone treats another person badly because of who they are, it's called injustice. That means it's hurtful and not fair.

- If someone is mean or unfair to you or to someone else, you can do something. You can help turn unfair into fair. You can tell people to stop! You can explain that unfairness hurts. You can be a friend to someone whose feelings are hurt. You can ask a grownup to help you. There are lots of things you can do.

- Sometimes hurtful, unfair things happen in our world. But there are always people who will do something about it. Sometimes they talk to the person who is doing the unjust thing. Sometimes they write letters or sign petitions (that's a letter signed by lots and lots of people who send it to people who could help make something fair). Sometimes they march in the streets carrying signs saying what should happen to make the world fair. Sometimes they go to meetings and talk to lots of other people to get ideas to fix the thing that's unfair and change it to fair. Sometimes they vote for people who want to make laws more fair.

- What kinds of things can you do or what we can do together to help make things fair in our class?

The Four Anti-Bias Education Goals Are for Adults Too

One of the great gifts of teaching is the ongoing learning that it requires. Quality ABE relies on teachers who embrace the four core goals as tools for their own growth. Understanding who you are—and how you came to be the person you now are—gives you a deeper understanding of how children develop and what shaped them. This is a lifelong process. Teachers are on a continual journey of self-discovery as they work with children, families, and staff, who sometimes reflect their own experiences and sometimes challenge them.

ABE goals for teachers parallel the four core goals for working with children:

Adult Goal 1, Identity: Increase your awareness and understanding of your own individual and social identity in its many facets (race, ethnicity, gender, ability, sexual orientation, family structure, economic class) and your own cultural contexts, both in your childhood and currently.

Adult Goal 2, Diversity: Examine what you have learned about differences, connection, and what you enjoy or fear across all aspects of human diversity.

Adult Goal 3, Justice: Identify how you have been advantaged or disadvantaged by the isms (ableism, classism, heterosexism, racism, sexism) and the stereotypes or prejudices you have absorbed about yourself or others.

Adult Goal 4, Activism: Explore your ideas, feelings, and experiences of social justice activism. Open up dialogue with colleagues and families about all these goals. Develop the courage and commitment to model for young children that you stand for fairness and to be an activist voice for children.

Stop & Think: Your Own Expectations for ABE

- What do you hope ABE could do for the children you teach? For their families? If your hopes are realized, how will it benefit them?

- What anxieties and concerns might you have about doing ABE in your particular setting or community?

- Where could you find support for doing ABE within or outside your program?

- What seems most interesting and inviting about becoming an anti-bias teacher? Which anti-bias goal interests you most right now?

• • •

You Have Already Begun

Whether you are an experienced teacher or a beginning student, ABE offers the opportunity to expand your understanding of how the social forces of systemic oppression and biases shape children. Deepening your knowledge of the dynamics of bias, fear of differences, and institutional inequity in the society at large and in your own life provides insight into your role as an early childhood educator in countering prejudice and discrimination. So too does coming to fully understand the four core goals of ABE as they apply to children and educators. This is urgent work that calls on all the best hopes you have for children, for the world, and for yourself. It is work that matters. Keep reading and learning! There's more to come.

Young Children and Their Families in Crisis: Immigrants and Refugees

Above all, we shall not harm children. We shall not participate in practices that are emotionally damaging, physically harmful, disrespectful, degrading, dangerous, exploitative, or intimidating to children. *This principle has precedence over all others in this Code*.

—NAEYC, *Code of Ethical Conduct and Statement of Commitment*

Early childhood education programs are not immune to debates, policies, and actions regarding diversity and equality in the larger society. Regardless of your opinion on immigration policy, your job as an early childhood educator is to consider the needs of the children you work with. As we write this book, many children of refugee and immigrant families seeking to enter the United States are facing traumatic separation from one or more of their parents or family members as they seek asylum at the US–Mexico border and in raids by the federal government to remove undocumented individuals from their homes and communities (Jordan 2019). Even children who are citizens or are in the country on official visas live with the anxiety of being removed from their loved ones. They may hear stories or see terrible images of other children being taken away from their families at the borders of the country in which they are living.

How do early childhood educators hold true to the ethics of their profession and to the goals of ABE when societal policies and actions challenge them? Rhian Evans Allvin, CEO of NAEYC, makes it clear in this excerpt from a letter to NAEYC members on February 3, 2017:

> In this country, there are 5.8 million children under age 5 with at least one immigrant parent. They are in our classrooms and homes. Some of them already live in fear and anxiety that their parents will be taken away from them. As a result of [recent] policies . . . these

fears are made worse, and the most essential relationships between these children and the caring adults in their lives are put at risk. The impact, which could deepen children's stress, disrupt their brain development, and negatively impact their short- and long-term health outcomes, will make the jobs of early childhood educators and parents—who already bear enormous responsibility to promote the development and learning of each child—that much harder.

Know the Context

During your career as an early childhood educator, it is highly likely that you will work with children from families who are immigrants and refugees. Consider the following facts (NAEYC & CLASP 2018):

> 1 in 4 children under age 6 in the United States is a member of an immigrant family.
>
> 94 percent of these children are US citizens. This is a right granted by the 14th Amendment to the Bill of Rights, which states that "All persons born or naturalized in the United States, . . . are citizens of the United States and of the State wherein they reside. No State shall make or enforce any law which shall abridge the privileges or immunities of citizens of the United States. . . ."

5.9 million citizen children under the age of 18 are living with a parent or family member who is undocumented.

1.6 million children under age 5 have an undocumented parent(s).

Families immigrate to the United States for many different reasons. Some come from wealth and privilege in their home countries; some are escaping poverty and violence. Some are in the country on student or work visas, some are on a path to citizenship, and some come undocumented seeking refugee status. Regardless of their legal status, their children experience the impact of heightened prejudice and discrimination directed against their families.

> When the constant dread of arrest, detention, or deportation of parents culminates in actual family separation— whether short-lived or permanent—the results are particularly detrimental and far-reaching for child well-being. Children of detained and deported immigrants suffer the consequences of economic instability, emotional distress, changes in daily routines, . . . family separation, long-term financial instability, and finally, in some cases, family dissolution. (Rojas-Flores 2017, 12)

Children of immigrant families need intensified and sensitive support from teachers to help them deal with their anxieties and fears of possible or actual separation from or loss of family members and friends. Very real fears of being taken from one's family and detained for a long time or deported are also keeping many undocumented families from seeking help for their children, such as medical care, or even allowing them to go to school. Moreover, even children in families who are citizens of the United States—especially in Latinx and Muslim families—are experiencing the tension of not knowing if they can be safe in their communities.

What Early Childhood Programs Can Do

Early childhood programs are not only important bridges between children's families and the larger society, they can be emotional sanctuaries for families and children who are immigrants. NAEYC and the Center for Law and Social Policy (CLASP) outline the following responsibilities for early childhood educators working with children in immigrant families (NAEYC & CLASP 2018):

Let families know that your program and you will do all you can to keep them and their children safe. Explain the policies and procedures you have put in place to families and staff. Also explain to families how you address hurtful comments by other children, should these occur.

Have information about immigrants' rights and make these public and available to all families in their home languages. Make sure that all staff members know what these are as well.

Understand your right as an early childhood program to refuse entry to immigration agents without a warrant. (See "Keep Current with Federal, State, and Local Policies" on page 22.) Establish a safety plan in case of illegal attempts by immigration agents to enter your program without a warrant. This should include identifying which staff will be responsible for speaking with the agent, which staff members need to be notified about a potential danger to their children, and how you will handle such situations when other children see or hear the interchanges.

Create a clear confidentiality policy about the privacy of family information. NAEYC accreditation standards require that programs have clear written policies concerning confidentiality of families' information. Make sure that your confidentiality policy includes assurance that immigration data aren't recorded or released. Share confidentiality protections with *all* families and all staff.

Connect new families who are immigrants with families in your program who will act as allies to them.

Keep Current with Federal, State, and Local Policies

The US Department of Homeland Security has changing policies regarding *sensitive locations,* where immigration agents are restricted in carrying out arrests, apprehensions, or other enforcement actions. At the time of this writing, licensed center-based and home-based early childhood programs, schools, places of worship, K–12 schools, and colleges are sometimes designated as sensitive locations. To know what your responsibilities are, it is essential to know the policies in your own state and city. In addition to information provided by the National Education Association (NEA) and the American Federation of Teachers (AFT), look for current information about designated sensitive locations on the CLASP website (www.clasp.org).

Resources for Families and Staff

Almost all communities have advocacy and legal organizations, as well as faith-based groups, dedicated to providing support and legal help to refugee, immigrant, and/or undocumented families. Create a list of these organizations and groups and help families who need services connect to the appropriate resources. Other families may be willing to accompany undocumented families to safe community services, or staff members may do so.

People working in early childhood programs— perhaps you yourself—may also be personally living with the impact of bias and fear toward immigrants. At the same time, there may be staff members who have anti-immigrant feelings. Creating a work atmosphere of respect and safety among the staff is essential for educators to effectively work with the program's families and children.

We wrote the following commitment statement during a period of sweeping arrests by US Immigration and Customs Enforcement (ICE) and heightened police violence against African Americans. We see it as one way to affirm our professional principles to teach, nurture, and protect all children. We also see it as a way to let families and colleagues know where we stand and to connect with those who stand with us.

We are in this together— working for a world where every child is protected and honored, exactly as they are.

All Children Belong Here

OUR PROMISE TO YOU

- We will build an open, safe, and mutually respectful school community in which each child and each family is an important and equal member.

- We will never allow differences of any kind to be an excuse to make fun of, exclude, or hurt you.

- We will listen carefully and lovingly to what worries you and give you thoughtful, age-appropriate information and support.

- We will nurture you to feel strong and proud about yourself and your family.

- We will facilitate your skills to be friends with classmates who are alike and different from you.

- We will honor your family's importance to you by building respectful partnerships with them.

- We will provide support to you and your family when they feel stress, anxiety, or fear because of current events or acts of prejudice or hate.

- We will learn about and help your family use legal and community resources to keep you safe.

- We will work to uproot our own personal biases as adults and will speak out against prejudice and bias wherever we encounter it.

- We will mobilize our courage and become active with others to resist and change any policies and practices that threaten to hurt you or your family.

Reprinted, by permission, from L. Derman-Sparks & J.O. Edwards, "Living Our Commitments: A Pledge to All Children and Families," *Exchange* (March/April 2017): 34. (See www.childcareexchange.com for downloadable versions in English and Spanish.)

CHAPTER 2

Constructing and Understanding Social Identities and Attitudes: The Lifelong Journey

Carmela (age 4) asks, "Is Mexican my color?" Her teacher replies, "No, Carmela. 'Mexican' is not a color. It's the name of a big group of people to which your family belongs."

• • •

Abby (age 3) puts on a hard hat and goes to play at the woodworking table. "Look at me!" she announces. "Now I am a boy. Later I'll be a girl again."

• • •

Carly, a family child care home provider, notes, "First and foremost I am a Christian, a mother, and a teacher. But I'm beginning to understand I am also White and working class and able-bodied. I never thought about those things—but I've begun to see that they matter."

Throughout life, from early childhood on, all people actively construct a sense of self, a combination of social identities and individual, personal identities. This journey involves a continually evolving understanding of oneself and others and a recognition of how identity is impacted by how others see you and how you see others. Social identities are both externally imposed and internally constructed. They powerfully shape who you are, and you powerfully shape your response to them.

Personal and Social Identity

All people have multiple social identities, as well as individual, personal identities, each of which contributes to their sense of who they are. *Personal identity* is what most early childhood teachers think about when they consider ways to nurture children's positive self-concept. It includes factors such as a person's name, personality, talents, interests, age, and the specifics of and relationships with family members. These attributes are what give each person a sense of individuality. Personal identity is primarily fostered by a child's temperament, home, and extended family, and then by community and school experiences.

In contrast, *social identity* refers to the significant group categories that are created and defined by the society in which people live. These include culture, economic class, family structure, gender, language, race, religion, and more. In addition, societal attitudes toward physical attributes such as body size and shape make them part of people's social identities. For example, one child's *social* identities might include being male, East Coast urban, African American, Muslim, and from a two-parent, middle-class family. A second child's social identity might include being female, White, rural, Christian, English and Russian speaking, and from a working-class, grandparent-led family. A third child might be gender fluid, West Coast urban, Jewish, and from a professional, blended family. Some of these social identities receive support and approval within the dominant culture. Some are diminished and defined as "other." *Every* social identity has societal policies, stereotypes, and attitudes connected with it. These may affect how teachers view the children and families with whom they work as well as how they think of themselves.

At various times in one's life, some social identities may play a more important part than others. A person might also have shifting feelings about various social identities—being proud of some identities and downplaying or denying others depending on the circumstances of that person's life. Some social identities may shift throughout life: Economic class may shift. Marital status and family structures may evolve. Religious identities may change.

When one or more of a person's social identities are made visible in positive and powerful ways in classrooms, movies, media, and so on, that person may seem just to "be" and to be "normal" or "regular." It is not unusual to hear White adults say, "I don't have a culture. I'm just regular," or "I'm just human. I don't have a racial identity." Educators whose social identities are visible in society often find it easier to recognize their social identities by thinking back about times they experienced some doors being closed to them based on those identities or times they experienced feeling "different" in another country.

Why Social Identities Matter

Social identities carry various statuses, assumptions, and biases that affect how people are perceived and treated. These can powerfully enhance or undermine an individual's access to opportunities and resources. They make successful life outcomes easier or harder for a person. They also impact beliefs about a person's capacities and limitations (Derman-Sparks, LeeKeenan, & Nimmo 2015).

For example, a family with low income may have limited access to many of the resources children need. Their children may interact with teachers and other community services professionals who lack awareness of and sensitivity to their family's daily realities. It means children may grow up having to maneuver in a world where this lack of understanding is common. Here's a story from Julie's childhood:

> One of my earliest shaping memories was when I was in kindergarten. Dad was in the army overseas; my mom was working long hours. My sisters and I got ourselves up and out to school in the mornings, making our own breakfast and lunches. We often didn't do a great job of appearing clean and tidy. Valentine's Day was coming. I had laboriously figured out how to read the calendar so I could sign up to be the cookie monitor at school. When the day arrived, I proudly got ready to pass out the promised heart-shaped cookies. My teacher stopped me, took my hands in hers, and said in a shocked voice, "Your nails are filthy! You can't handle food with hands like that." I still remember staring at my hands, feeling like I had left my body and knowing a deep sense of shame and embarrassment. I also remember my determination not to let my mother know what had happened, so she wouldn't feel ashamed too.

How individuals feel about their various social identities may reflect or resist the social realities of advantage and disadvantage. Families and schools can have an important impact in helping children feel pride and strength about a social identity even when the society as a whole disadvantages that identity.

As an early childhood education student of Julie's explains,

> I grew up in a very poor family where money was an issue. I never had new clothes or new shoes. My parents would always shop at the flea market. Growing up was hard because I never had "cool clothes," and the other kids would make fun of me. Now I can

say, "That was classism." I don't know why having a word makes it easier to think about, but it does! And it has helped me feel pride in how well my parents managed despite the hardships they experienced.

The Beginnings of Identity

From their first year of life, children pay attention to differences and similarities among the people in their lives. They use these observations to make sense of the world, to identify what does and doesn't matter, and to construct their self-identity and their concepts about others. As young as 6 months, infants demonstrate that they notice differences in skin color (Bronson & Merryman 2009; Katz & Kofkin 1997). By age 2, children notice and comment on gendered differences (see Chapter 9) using gender labels assigned by society: "I a girl" or "Me boy." They also make observations about racialized differences (see Chapter 8), learning the names of colors and beginning to apply these to skin color: "He's brownish, but I'm browner!" (Ramsey 2015).

By age 3, children begin asking questions about their own and others' characteristics, including those related to gender, language, physical abilities, and racial identity (Derman-Sparks & Edwards 2010; Ramsey 2015). For example,

"Why is that man's skin dark?"

"Why is that lady getting pushed in a chair?"

"Why does she talk funny?"

"My skin looks like yours, Mommy."

"Why do I have freckles?"

"I have the same thing as Daddy."

By age 4, children begin to show awareness of family structure and economic class differences (Ramsey 2015; Tatum 2017):

"Why does Shoshanna have two mommies? Where's her daddy?"

"I want new Nike shoes like Matthew's."

Between ages 3 and 5, children also become very curious about what parts of themselves are permanent and will stay the same and what parts will change. They ask questions like the following:

"If I like to climb trees, do I become a boy?"

"When I play with dolls, do I become a girl?"

"Why is my skin this color? Can I change it? Can I make my skin pink like Toby's?"

"Will I always need a prosthesis on my arm?"

Constructing a Personal Sense of Self and Multiple Social Identities

The significant adults in children's lives play a major role in helping children feel either proud, shamed, or conflicted about their identities and about their attitudes toward human differences. Learning about both social and personal identities begins in one's family. However, messages from the larger society soon filter in and become a central influence. These messages come from many places: children's family members and friends, movies and television, books and advertising, and early childhood programs.

Some of what children learn about their own and others' social identities comes from *overt, direct* lessons. For example, adults sometimes explicitly declare their ideas about boys and girls: "Big boys don't cry," "Be careful. She's a girl. She can get hurt," "You're a beautiful little princess," or "What a strong boy you are!" Some people explicitly declare their attitudes about children with disabilities: "I do not want those kids with problems in the same classroom as my son. They'll take up all of the teachers' time." Or they make comments about same-sex parents: "Children can't have two fathers. One of them has to be the *real* father."

Children often experience conflicting messages about identities. This occurs when the behavior of families, teachers, religious leaders, or people portrayed in the media does not match their direct messages about people's social identities. For example, children may hear adults say that people are all alike and that they should treat all people with respect, yet they never see their family develop friendships with people different from themselves or even interact with other social groups in their day-to-day life. A teacher may do a "Who We Are" unit each year to support children's self-concepts yet use materials that show only White children, thereby making some of the children invisible. Or children may hear adults say that looks are not important, yet the same adults continually comment on children's height, attractiveness, and clothing. When such double messages are frequent and pervasive in a child's life, which message do you think the child absorbs?

In addition to explicit messages, much of what children learn about their social identities comes from *covert*, *implicit* messages. For example, children absorb the messages they see in advertisements about what a family is supposed to look like. They experience how their family is treated by others, whether welcoming or wary. Even before they have words, they notice when a family is treated poorly, receiving slow service in stores or restaurants, for example, or encountering rudeness from social agency personnel, as can happen all too often to children of color and children from families with low income.

Invisibility Erases Identity and Experience—Visibility Affirms Reality

Young children are learning about who is and who isn't important in society. When children see themselves and their families reflected in their early childhood setting, they feel affirmed and that they belong. When children's identities and families are invisible, the opposite happens. Children feel that they are unimportant and do not belong. They may develop a sense of shame about themselves and their families. They may start wishing to be like those who are in the visible social identity groups.

Messages of invisibility and visibility communicate who matters and who does not. When young children look at the books or posters in a classroom and find only two-parent families, they absorb the message that the images they see reflect the one right kind of family and that all other kinds of families are wrong. When the dolls in the classroom are all White, or the pictures on the classroom walls show only White children, children can conclude that White is normal and other colors of human skin are not as desirable. When the positive images they see in their early childhood programs or the media are portraying people only in professional careers, they may conclude that other kinds of jobs are not important or to be valued.

Those messages are particularly powerful coming from the people who teach children, provide their medical care, lead religious rituals, and act in other positions of influence or power. Children absorb these covert messages every day, often with the adults who care for them being unaware of what they are modeling.

Stop & Think: What Kinds of Messages Are Children Receiving About Their Identities?

- When looking at children's picture books, what family structures do children see? (This includes books that have animal characters as well as humans.)

- When children are taken shopping for clothing, what do the images on boys' and girls' clothing tell them about what it means to be male or female? How many items of clothing do girls "need" compared with boys? What messages does that teach children?

- In children's movies and videos, which characters use standard English and which do not? Who are the good guys and who are the bad guys?

- When you were a child, which of your social identities were visible in your school environment? Which ones were erased, made invisible?

Children Try to Make Sense of All They See and Hear

As in all other areas of learning, young children try to make sense of their world by creating theories from what they observe and their experiences. This is true for the everyday events of their lives, such as believing that if someone needs money, it comes from using a magic card that they stick into a machine on the wall, or that cars are alive because you have to feed them before they can go. This constructing of theories, or *schemas* (Piaget 1953), is also what children do to help them understand their observations of culture, disabilities, gender, skin color, and other identities. It is useful to listen to children's explanations because it helps you understand how young children are trying to make sense of great complexity. For example,

> After hearing about melanin and skin color, Robin asks, "If I eat melon, will my skin look brown like Leticia's [Robin's best friend]?"

> • • •

> Nathan looks at both sides of his hand and tells his mom, "This side is my Black part and this side is my White part."

> • • •

> "When I grow up, I'm going to grow a baby inside me," says Joon-woo, whose mother is pregnant. His friend Tad objects, saying only girls can have babies inside them. "That's okay," Joon-woo says cheerfully. "I'll tell my mommy to reborn me and I'll be a girl when I'm grown up."

> • • •

> "I want a button [hearing aid] like Francina has, so I can hear her Spanish words and talk to her," says English-speaking Juliette.

Listening to children's theories shows where they are confused. While working with children to expand and correct their ideas, be respectful of the remarkable intelligence that underlies their attempts to make sense of what they experience.

Young Children Form Pre-Prejudices

Pre-prejudice describes children's inaccurate ideas and feelings as they begin to build theories about human differences. Children pay attention to subtle cues from adults, and they draw conclusions even about issues adults may not talk to them about. They absorb inaccurate ideas, stereotypes, and attitudes about a wide range of human identities (Ramsey 2015). Consider these children's comments, overheard by teachers and families:

> At home after bathing, a 2½-year-old Asian child tells his mother, "Now my hair is white because it is clean."

> • • •

> A 4-year-old girl tells a male classmate during dramatic play, "You can't be the nurse. Only girls can."

> • • •

> Emily has a red birthmark along her forehead and over one eye. Ceci moves away from Emily, saying, "She has a mean face."

> • • •

> "You can't have two mommies," says a 4-year-old to a child who does. "That's bad."

> • • •

> A boy playing with hoses and fire hats says of another boy doing the same, "He don't got new boots like I do! So, he can't be fire chief."

These expressions of pre-prejudice are seeds that can grow into actual prejudice if a child's family or other important people in the child's life ignore or reinforce them. Even though many adults believe that young children do not notice differences and are unaware of prejudice, research shows that this is not so (Clark 1963; CNN 2010; Lane 2008; Murray & Urban 2017; Ramsey 2015; Tatum 2017).

Young Children Develop Ideas and Feelings About Societal Power Dynamics

In addition to pre-prejudice, children's comments reveal their absorption of messages about the connection between social identities and who experiences power and position in their world. They pay attention to who is in charge, who is the boss, who gets to make decisions. While young children do not yet understand the full implications of power and resource differences, they notice them. Their observations can spark ideas that become the early steps of learning internalized inferiority or internalized superiority (Van Ausdale & Feagin 2001). For example,

> Four-year-old Liam's preschool program maintains two separate and unequal programs in the building—one privately funded for affluent, mostly White children, which has newer, more interesting climbing structures, and another with an older yard for children from families with low income, mostly Latinx. During the ride home one day, Liam suddenly says to his mother, "Mommy, I'm really glad that I'm White." (Adapted from Derman-Sparks & Ramsey 2011, 45)

All children, including White children, should feel good about their racial identity, and it is logical to be glad to be in a program with better equipment. However, making the connection between Whiteness and having better services is a seed that can blossom into a sense of entitlement based on racial identity. This will get stronger as a child observes and continues to encounter examples of more acceptance of and better resources given to White children.

This next example comes from Louise's family and became an instigator for her anti-bias work:

> "I don't want to be Black anymore," my 4-year-old son announced at dinner one evening. In response to our question about why, he said, "I want to be like the people on *Emergency!* when I grow up." (*Emergency!* was a TV program about paramedics and firefighters, none of whom were Black.)
>
> It didn't seem that this was an issue of personal self-concept or that our son was saying he didn't like himself. Rather, it seemed to us that he was trying to figure out what to do with a media message about his racial identity. We immediately responded, "You can be a firefighter when you grow up if you want to. There are already many Black firefighters." We followed up with activities to reinforce this message, including visiting a fire station with an African American firefighter and buying a puzzle showing dark-skinned firefighters.

Observing young children reveals their ideas about power relationships related to such identities as gender, economic class, and culture:

> Jackson and Mia are playing in a truck they have made from the big blocks and cardboard boxes. "I'm driving," Jackson announces firmly. "I want to drive!" protests Mia. "I'm the Daddy Man, so I drive!" he replies. After thinking for a moment, Mia moves over to the passenger seat.

· · ·

> "How come we got a new car and Sophie's mommy brings her on the bus?" asks Olivia on the way to school. "Sophie's family doesn't have a car. Your daddy and I worked hard to buy our car," her mother replies a little defensively. Olivia thinks for a moment and then says, "I'll tell Sophie to tell her mother to work harder so she can have a car too."

· · ·

> Elena, a child from a Spanish-speaking family, enters an English immersion (English-only) program speaking no English. None of the staff speaks Spanish. As Elena picks up the new language, she refuses to speak in Spanish when her mother comes to pick her up. When her mother speaks to her in their home language, Elena firmly places her hand over her mother's mouth. She also begins to refuse to speak Spanish at home, much to the concern of her family.

Is this the beginning of Jackson learning about male privilege, or Olivia forming the stereotype that poverty is always a consequence of not working hard enough? Is Elena learning to hide, be ashamed of, or reject her home culture and language—and perhaps on a path to losing the ability to communicate with her family members?

Here is an example from Julie's family illustrating how bias issues beyond the family shape children's sense of self. In this case, both children deal with the same issue but with contrasting outcomes.

> When my son was young, he had wispy, white "dandelion" hair sticking up all over his head. Sometimes children at his nursery school teased him about his hair, which hurt his feelings and took some intervention from the teacher and support from us. A few years later, my foster daughter, who is African American, was teased for her large, fluffy Afro hair, and again, the teacher and our family intervened.
>
> During his kindergarten year, my son's hair became blond, straight, and very much like the hair he saw on boys in books and movies and on television. By the time he was 5, hair was no longer an issue for him. Indeed, others saw him as an all-American boy, and the many images of boys like him in school and in media reinforced this message.
>
> My foster daughter, however, picked up all the messages about the types of hair considered desirable or undesirable and the covert messages from movies, television, and books about who is beautiful and who is not. Such social messages repeatedly reinforced the early teasing, and try as we might, we were unable to protect her from coming to think of herself as funny looking. It was not until we moved to a community where there were many other African American people, and a favorite teacher with a wondrous Afro, that my daughter was able to see her own beauty.

The hurtful role societal attitudes play in shaping young children's thinking about their identities profoundly contrasts with teachers' and families' desire to encourage children to know who they are without feeling inferior or superior. This is one of the central challenges facing teachers and families.

Stop & Think: Childhood Messages About Your Various Social Identities

- When you were a child, how might you have described a "normal" person? What color skin did they have? Where and how did they live? What about their language, family structure, economic class, and so on?

- What is your earliest memory of realizing that some people were different from you and/or your family (for example, in racial identity, ability, family structure, religion, economics)? How did you feel about yourself in relationship to the people who were different from you? How did you feel about them?

- What did your family say about people whose social identities were different from your family's? Did their behavior match their words?

- What did you see or not see about people who were like you in books, videos, movies, TV, and advertisements? What messages did this give you about your social identities?

- Did you know, or know about, anyone who didn't behave in the ways expected according to stereotypes about their social identities? What did you think about those people?

You Bring to Teaching Who You Are

Deepening your understanding of who you are now and how you came to be that person is at the heart of becoming a skilled anti-bias teacher. As Rita Tenorio, an experienced anti-bias teacher and administrator, explains,

> This work is as much about changing your own perspective as a teacher as it is about what you do in the classroom. If you're not willing to make a commitment to the four anti-bias education goals for yourself, the rest is not useful.

As you recognize and better understand how your own experiences shape and strengthen or limit your social identities and your views, you can work on understanding the lives of the families and colleagues with whom you work. For example, if you were raised to believe that being prompt is a sign of responsibility and respect, and your family always had the income to buy a car (and get it fixed when a problem arose), then it might be hard for you to understand the experience of families who chronically drop off their children late because they must get to school by using unreliable buses or by depending on others to give them a ride. If you grew up in a family with a sibling who is disabled and came to understand how individual and unique each person with a disability is, you may be particularly skilled in working with families like yours.

Knowing yourself will also help you understand why some changes in thinking and perspective are easy for you and others are more difficult, as this teacher experienced:

> I teach in the child care program at my church on Sundays and have always planned an Easter curriculum, with eggs and spring flowers and baskets as well as telling the story of Jesus rising. I knew I couldn't teach the religious part of the curriculum at the public preschool I now work at, but I thought the eggs and baskets would be wonderful. I was so surprised that there were families who were offended! And I have to admit, I was pretty hurt. I hadn't realized how important those symbols are to me. It was a struggle to rethink my role as a teacher and find ways to embrace *all* the children I was responsible for.

While it is sometimes hard work to uncover your ideas and feelings about your own and others' social identities, it is also very rewarding. One of Louise's anti-bias students put it this way:

> Tonight was our last class. I've been thinking why it affects people so much. I think it's because, in untying the knot, you're unraveling the web of lies [about our identities] that each of us has inevitably experienced. . . . These have taken their dehumanizing toll, and in unraveling even a bit of the whole, we feel tremendously excited. We have only to unravel more of it to reclaim ourselves more completely (Derman-Sparks & Phillips 1997, 137).

How Do You Name Your Social Identities?

The words people use to describe their social identities may shift as their thinking about themselves shifts. It's important to let people know what terms you prefer and to learn how other people define their multiple social identities. Here are a few examples from Julie's students naming their social identities:

Luz: Culturally, ethnically, I'm Mexican American, and probably Californian. And definitely Catholic! But I'm also Mixtecan (the indigenous people of Oaxaca and Pueblo). I'm only beginning to learn about the Mixtecan part of my history. Here in the US, I'm also a woman of color.

Leroy: People see me and think, "He's a Black man." That's all they see. They're right, I am, because my grandfather was Black. But I think of myself as Louisiana Creole. That's the part of my identity and heritage that is alive for me. I guess my culture would be Creole, Californian, and Christian. My citizenship is American. I haven't figured out yet what my class is.

Mario: I'm Italian American, but I mainly live my day-to-day culture as a gay man. On my mother's side we're pretty much Choctaw and Cherokee—and I love learning about those lives. But I haven't lived my life as an Indian, so I guess it's my heritage, not my culture.

Miriam: I think of myself as White American. I also am hearing impaired and participate in the Deaf community and culture. I think of myself as an activist, which has its own cultural values.

My Social Identities Portrait

1. In each row, read the social identity term in column 1 and write in column 2 whatever word(s) you used to describe yourself as a child and the words you use now. Then circle the identities in columns 3 and 4 that apply to your life.

   You may not always have words to describe these identities. That's okay. Write down your best thought at the moment. Don't leave a section blank. You can always redo this as time goes on.

Social Identity	Description of Self		Groups Defined as the Norm; Recipients of Societal Advantages	Groups that Are Marginalized and Targets of Institutional Prejudice and Discrimination
	Childhood	Currently		
Ethnicity or heritage			European American "melting pot"	All other ethnicities, including indigenous peoples
Place of birth			Born in the country you now live in	Immigrant
Language			English	Home languages other than English
Racialized identity			White	People of color; biracial; multiracial
Gender			Male	Female, nonbinary, transgender, etc.
Sexuality			Heterosexual	Asexual, bisexual, gay, lesbian, polyamorous, etc.
Religious beliefs			Christian or Christian tradition	Muslim, Jewish, Buddhist, Hindu, pagan, atheist, etc.
Age (currently)			Productive adults (ages 20–50 for women, 20–60 for men)	Children, adolescents, women over 50, men over 60
Education (currently)			College degree(s) Highly literate	High school education or less Struggle with literacy
Body type/size			Slim, fit Medium height for women Tall for men	Large, overweight Very short or very tall
Able self (physical, mental, emotional health)			Healthy, Functional No apparent disability	Any form of disability: physical, mental, emotional, learning, behavioral
Economic class			Middle to upper class	Poor or working class
Family structure			Male/female married parents with one to three biological children	Unmarried; single parent; gay or lesbian parents; no children; divorced; adoptive, foster, or blended family; more than three children

2. Look at the pattern of circled identities and think about the following questions, then discuss a few of your insights with a partner.

   In what ways have you experienced either prejudice and discrimination or privilege and visibility because of these identities? Which identities made life harder for you, and which ones opened doors?

   Which of your identities have had the biggest impact on you? In which identities do you feel the most pride?

　　　　　　　　　　　　　　Anti-Bias Education for Young Children and Ourselves

Uncover Your Multidimensional Social Identities Portrait

One of the complicated aspects of thinking about social identity is that no one has just one identity. Everyone is a member of more than one social identity group. This means that each individual's package of multiple social identities carries a combination of societal advantages and disadvantages. For example, Luz's status as someone who is dark-skinned, a woman, and an immigrant makes her "other" to the dominant society, and she often faces social disadvantages. Simultaneously, in her status as highly educated and middle class, she has certain social advantages. Eddie, who is transgender male, White, and Christian, works as an aide in a child care program. He lives with prejudice as a person who is transgender and experiences suspicion about his motives as a man working with children. Yet, the color of his skin grants him societal advantages as well.

The "My Social Identities Portrait" exercise on page 32 is an opportunity for you to name and think about the multiple social identities that make up who you are and to look at how you have come to think about yourself over the years. There are no right or wrong answers. The more you understand these parts of yourself, the more thoughtfully you will be able to work with families and children of diverse backgrounds and social identities.

Guidelines for Heart-to-Heart Talking and Listening

Here are some guidelines to help you successfully engage in honest, respectful dialogue about one or more anti-bias issues in this book.

Agree to be talking/listening partners with one other person, each of you relating stories that explore who you are, what you have experienced, and how you feel in relation to the anti-bias issue you are discussing. *This is not a conversation.* One person talks, the other listens. Then change roles so the speaker becomes the listener and the listener becomes the speaker. Share equally the amount of time you have (e.g., two minutes each, five minutes each, an hour each). Keep each other safe by agreeing that you will not share with anyone what you have heard. Commit yourselves to respect the speaker's story as true for that person. Do not judge or interrupt.

Guidelines for the Speaker

- Speak from your heart. Provide enough details so that what happened and what you feel are clear.

- It's okay to cry, laugh, shake, yawn, or whatever while you are telling your story.

- Don't be embarrassed if you go quiet. Just wait until the words form in your mind and then begin again. It's okay to repeat yourself.

- Few of us ever receive the gift of someone deeply listening to us. This is your time, so take it!

Guidelines for the Listener

- Totally respect the speaker's confidentiality. (Do not share with *anyone* what you have heard!)

- Listen as a believer. This means you must listen to hear why the story is true from the speaker's point of view, even if you can imagine alternate perspectives.

- Stay out of the speaker's story: no questions, interruptions, distractions, advice, or recommendations.

- If strong feelings come up for the *speaker* while you are listening, remember that you do not need to come to the rescue. Your job as listener is to stay present and attentive and be confident that your conversation partner can work through those feelings.

- If strong feelings come up for *you* while you are listening, remember that the feelings are about you—not about the speaker. They are useful information for you to have about yourself.

- If you are having these conversations in a class or staff meeting, and afterward there is discussion, remember you can report back only on what *you* said and what *you* experienced. It is up to your conversation partner to decide to share or not share his story.

Communicating About Social Identities

An important tool for the personal work of ABE is learning to put words to your thoughts and history and opening yourself to truly hearing other people's thoughts and experiences. The exercises in this chapter, like all the Stop & Think reflection questions throughout the book, invite you to bring to the surface how your experiences have shaped your sense of yourself and others. These exercises also invite you to share and think with others who are going through the same process of personal and professional growth.

Engaging in such conversations deepens your insights about yourself and others. It requires you to find ways to openly describe what you have experienced and to develop the ability to deeply hear the experiences of others. Sometimes this may be difficult. People who carry deep injuries from experiencing prejudice and discrimination related to one or more of their social identities may fear reopening wounds. Other people may find it hard to examine social identities that connect them to the unfair treatment of others. Or, it may be uncomfortable for other reasons. Still, it is worth having conversations about your own and others' identities. Use the ideas in "Guidelines for Heart-to-Heart Talking and Listening" on page 33 to engage in these powerful conversations.

Culture, Ethnicity, Nationality, and Race: What Are the Differences?

The dimensions of ethnic, cultural, national, and racialized social identities are often confused with each other. However, they actually refer to different kinds of social group memberships.

Ethnicity, or *ethnic heritage,* is about the place of origin and cultural heritage of one's ancestors— parents, grandparents, and beyond. Ethnicity refers to a group identity rooted in common ancestry and common political, historical, language, and social experiences. Names of ethnic groups often, but not always, reflect the group members' place of origin, such as Mexican American, Italian American, and Chinese American. *Native Americans* is a term for numerous specific indigenous groups in the United States, each with their own languages, beliefs, and practices.

Individuals are born into ethnic group membership but can choose which aspects of its culture they make their own and which they leave behind.

Culture encompasses the specific rules and patterns of behavior, language, values, and world beliefs of various groups. People who share the same ethnicity share some but usually not all of these aspects of culture. While you may know the ethnicity of an individual, you may not necessarily know specifically how she practices the cultural patterns of her ethnic group. You have to find out! This point is particularly important when your job is to foster children's development and learning in the context of their home cultures as well as the larger culture of the country.

Nationality refers to the country of which you are now a citizen, the country (or sometimes countries) that provides you with a passport.

If your family originally came from Italy, your ethnicity might be Italian. If you were born in the United States, your nationality/citizenship would be American. How important your nationality is to you may well be based on how long ago your family lived in the country of origin. Many US citizens consider their primary national identity, American, also as their ethnic identity.

What Is Racialized Identity?

Race is *not* the same thing as ethnicity or culture or nationality. (See Chapter 8 for a discussion of what race really is.) Yet, in modern society, everyone is presumed to be a member of a racial group, so everyone's identity becomes racialized. Individuals do not choose their racialized identity. However, they *can* choose how to live their identity (e.g., rejecting societal messages of superiority and inferiority and choosing to work to end racism rather than accept its power relationships). Chapter 8 discusses racialized identity in greater detail.

Some but not all racial terms identify geographic places of origin. However, many *different* ethnic groups are often assigned to the same racialized identity group. For example, one term for White people is *Caucasian,* used by an 18th-century professor of medicine to refer to the people of the Caucasus Mountains in Eastern Europe, whom he believed were "the most beautiful race of men" (Blumenbach [1795] 1865). People designated as

Caucasian or White usually belong to one or more national/ethnic groups originally located only in Europe (e.g., English, Irish, French, German).

Africans who were kidnapped and carried to the Americas came from many different ethnic groups in Africa, with diverse languages, religious practices, cultural beliefs, and rules of behavior. Their enslavers grouped them into one racialized identity focusing on skin color, called at different times *Colored, Negro,* or *Black.* During the Civil Rights movement, the term *African American* emerged as one way to reclaim and make visible people's ancestry and place of origin and as a movement to claim their own cultural group name. African American culture was forged from the varying cultures brought to the United States by enslaved Africans and shaped by their subsequent experiences.

What's in a Name?

Sometimes people are confused or intimidated by the question of what terms to use for various social identities. This issue and its answers are rooted in US history and social and political dynamics. Many names for social identity groups came from people outside the group who had the power to give the group a name. As people think about how they understand themselves, their history, and their work for human rights, it is not unusual for groups to change their externally imposed social identity name.

For example, the original inhabitants of the Americas were named Indians because Christopher Columbus thought he had arrived in India. However, they called themselves by many different names, such as Arawak, Pequot, and Taino. In the 1970s, the Indigenous people of the United States began asserting their preference and right to be called by their nation or tribal names (e.g., Comanche, Diné, Ohlone) or by the group name Native American. The preferred group name for Indigenous people in Canada is First Peoples. These name changes have nothing to do with what is disparagingly called political correctness. They reflect groups of people deciding to name themselves rather than being named by others.

In 1970, the US Census began using the term *Hispanic* for people from Mexico, Central and South America, and the Caribbean based on the assumption that Spanish is spoken in these regions. However, this term covers people who speak multiple languages and have highly diverse cultures and governments. More recently the group term has shifted to *Latino,* and there is a movement to restate that term as *Latinx* to emphasize that it is gender inclusive. Whether this term holds or not, almost all people much prefer specific words that identify their heritage countries (e.g., Costa Rican, Dominican, Peruvian).

The terms people prefer to use regarding disabilities have also changed. The term *handicapped* is now considered a disrespectful way of describing a person with a disability. Other terms considered disrespectful include *disabled person* and *wheelchair bound,* because both make a person's disability the overriding definition by putting the disability first. Phrases have evolved that instead emphasize the person first: *a person with a disability* or *a person who uses a wheelchair.* (See Chapter 11.) However, some people do not prefer person-first language for themselves; being referred to as an autistic person or a Deaf person is a recognition that being autistic or deaf is an integral part of their identities. If you are unsure, as noted elsewhere in this chapter, always ask.

Names and pronouns for gender are also in the process of change as newer thinking about a gender continuum and the fluidity of gender identity becomes more common (see Chapter 9).

Names matter. No one likes to be called a social identity name they have rejected. It can be hurtful to continue to use particular words simply because it is what you grew up with or are used to using. Leslie Cheung, an early childhood anti-bias teacher, put it this way: "My parents are from China. I am Chinese American. If you have to put me into a larger group, say 'Asian American,' but don't ever call me 'Oriental.' Oriental is a rug, not a human being."

It is always respectful to learn the current preferred ways groups name themselves. In addition, you need to know how the *individual* members of a social identity group choose to name themselves. As you develop relationships with children's families, you might learn that one family describes themselves as Mexican American, another as Chicano, and another as Latina. This means you have to ask. Ask, listen, acknowledge—and follow the family's lead.

You may worry that asking about identity terms might offend someone. But it is deeply affirming to people to be called by the name they feel is most rightfully theirs. It is helpful to talk with families about children's curiosity regarding the differences among themselves and tell them that you want to know what words a family would like you to use in the classroom when children ask questions. It helps if you have included the four core ABE goals in your program's philosophy statement so families are familiar with your vision. And it is essential that you ask all families, not just those you presume are somehow different.

Social Identities Create Complex Feelings

Feelings of being "less than" or "more than" or of being an outsider are among the harmful psychological effects of the isms and biases about social identities. These messages teach members of advantaged groups to believe that they have a right to and are more deserving of society's benefits. At the same time, these messages convey to marginalized groups that they are less worthy in the eyes of society, which can result in the undermining of self-belief and confidence.

Learning to Feel "More Than"

One aspect of being a member of an advantaged group is presuming that your social identity is the normal, ordinary, and correct way to be (Derman-Sparks & Ramsey 2011). If you grew up in a reasonably happy and well-functioning two-parent (mother and father) family, as did your parents and most of your cousins, and this is also the image of families you see in popular culture, books, and so on, it's easy to assume that two-parent families with a mother and a father are the best for everyone and are the definition of normal and healthy. This may lead to the assumption (and bias) that single-parent families are by definition lacking, stressed, and unhappy. (This is where the derogatory term *broken family* comes from.) This bias also tends to disguise the reality that some two-parent families with a mother and a father can be seriously unhappy, struggling, and dysfunctional.

Messages of entitlement come along with being a member of an advantaged group. These messages frequently block people from seeing the world as it really is. For example, some White people might assume that if a person of color is admitted to a desired college to which they themselves were not accepted, it must be because the college extended preferential, unfair treatment to the person of color. They may not consider that the admitted person had exemplary qualities or skills that led to their acceptance. They also may not consider the fact that many high-ranking universities save spots for the children of alumni and big donors—regardless of the individual students' qualifications. Rather than recognize this as preferential or privileged treatment of wealthy families, it is thought of as normal and acceptable for children of wealthy families to go to the best schools.

An entitlement viewpoint, sometimes called *internalized privilege* or *internalized superiority,* also prevents people in advantaged groups from seeing the obstacles faced by people in other groups (Barndt 1991; William 2012). For example, it does not occur to some men to think that earning more money than a woman doing the same kind of work is a form of male privilege, or that being able to stand at a bus stop late at night without fear of rape is a form of male privilege. Most Whites assume that a police officer will pull them over only if they have done something wrong, which is a form of advantage that many racial groups do not have. Some straight, or cisgender (see *gender* in the glossary), people may not notice that LGBTQ (an acronym for lesbian, gay, bisexual, transgender, queer or questioning, and more) people may pay a high social price if they display a picture of their loved one in their workspace. These blinders of internalized privilege lead to incomplete and inaccurate pictures of what is going on in one's own life and community and in the lives of others.

As a result, group privilege is often invisible to the members of the group. As an economically struggling early childhood teacher, Julie did not consider herself privileged. However, an article by Peggy McIntosh (1989) opened up a whole new way of thinking about her whiteness. At the time, Julie wrote in her journal about the privileges she had taken for granted:

- If I am hired at a new center, or receive a promotion, I do not have to wonder if other staff assume I got the job only because of my skin color.

- If I mess up at work, it is unlikely people will presume it is the nature of my entire racial group to make that error.

- If I speak up at work, chances are people will credit my ideas to the quality of my individual experience and intelligence rather than presuming that I am a spokesperson for White folks in general.

- If my kids get into trouble, their behavior is unlikely to be attributed to their skin color, and my parenting is unlikely to be called into question due to my skin color.

The problem with systemic advantage is not the good a person with that advantage gains. The problem is that people in other social identity groups are systemically kept from realizing the same benefits and experiencing the same rights. On an individual level, even when specific social identities give a person societal advantages or privileges, life can still be hard. For example, one can have White privilege *and* have a hard life. But that person's skin color is not one of the characteristics that makes life hard.

If you identified one or more advantaged identities in "My Social Identities Portrait" in this chapter, it is a useful exercise to select one and consider, as Julie did above, what privileges come with that identity. *Learning to recognize your privileges is not for the purpose of feeling guilty or shamed but to work toward ensuring that everyone is respected and treated with the same rights.*

Learning to Feel "Less Than"

The harmful effects of "less than" messages that individuals may experience because of their social identity groups may include shame, having to be constantly alert, unsure of what might happen next due to one's perceived social identity, self-limitations, setting oneself apart, and self-rejection. Sometimes called *internalized oppression* or *internalized inferiority* (Barndt 1991; William 2012), these negative effects may also include behaviors such as rejecting one's natural physical characteristics, name, language, cultural traditions, or values. It can mean believing stereotypes about one's own group. For example, children from families with low income may absorb the social message that intellectual careers are not for them, that they just aren't smart enough for academic work. Some people may choose to deny their racialized identity as they begin to recognize the prejudice and discrimination their group experiences. As one college student wrote when asked to reflect on childhood messages:

> I remember always wanting to have straight hair and being jealous in a way of my sisters because our mother used to straighten their hair. . . . Really, it just made you more like White people. Nobody ever said that—but we were all thinking it. (Derman-Sparks & Phillips 1997, 59)

And, as one female teacher learned, it can be startling to realize you are operating from hurtful mistruths:

> I was so excited when I found out our new director would be a man. It's very important to have men in early childhood programs. But then I heard myself saying, "Besides, men make better bosses." I couldn't believe what I had just said! I realized that, somehow, I believed the stereotype that women could not be good bosses—that we would be gossipy and untrustworthy or pushy and aggressive. In reality, the last two directors I had worked with had both been women and had been fine at their jobs. I guess this is an example of my internalized gender oppression.

To greater or lesser degrees, everyone is affected by the psychological dynamics of who belongs and who is an outsider. Thinking about structural classism, racism, sexism, and other isms with classmates and colleagues offers many opportunities to uncover and critically examine the messages you have absorbed and their impact on your life. Ridding yourself of their influence on your sense of self can open yourself up to more authentic work with and for children and families.

Intersectionality

In this book we discuss different arenas of social identity in separate chapters, yet in real life children are always developing in the context of many identities simultaneously and will experience social advantages or disadvantages based on their *multiple* social identities. The experience of multiple identities is called *intersectionality*. The concept of intersectionality deepens thinking about the dynamics of social identities. It explains how various systemic forms of prejudice and discrimination create multiple and overlapping levels of social disadvantage and social advantage (Collins & Bilge 2016; Crenshaw, forthcoming). Intersectionality highlights the "complex and cumulative effects of different forms of structural inequity that can arise for members of multiple marginalized groups" (NAEYC 2019, 18). For example, many women of color experience a trio of societal disadvantage—racism, sexism, and classism—whereas White women experience the damage of sexism, such as generally lower wages than White men for similar work, but escape being the targets of racism.

In addition to shedding light on the impacts of the interconnections among an individual's social identities, the concept of intersectionality can also help you identify the potential connections between groups of people with different social identities. Early childhood teachers' different perspectives and experiences, based on their social identities, can

lead to misunderstandings and disagreements, yet as you share your different life experiences you can work together to find solutions that work for everyone.

. . .

When you achieve a deeper understanding of how young children actively construct their social identities and the damage that arises from stereotyping and bias, you can provide children with more effective support and education. Achieving a deeper understanding of how *you* came to be the person you are today, and how your identity influences your work with children and families, open the door to more authentic teaching and working relationships.

Anti-bias work with yourself and with children is a call to action. As you read the chapters that follow, keep in mind that becoming an anti-bias educator has a learning curve, as does acquiring any new idea or skill. It takes time, practice, and opportunities to do ABE effectively. Along the way, you are invited to compassionately, deeply, and truthfully learn about yourself and the children and families with whom you work.

CHAPTER 3

Building an Anti-Bias Education Program: Curriculum Principles and the Learning Environment

Because early childhood settings tend to be children's first communities outside the home, the character of these communities is very influential in development. How children expect to be treated and how they treat others is significantly shaped in the early childhood setting.

—NAEYC, "Developmentally Appropriate Practice in Early Childhood Programs Serving Children from Birth through Age 8" (position statement)

A classroom environment rich in anti-bias curriculum and materials invites exploration and discovery and supports children's play and conversations in both child- and teacher-initiated activities. This chapter describes guidelines for planning curriculum and selecting materials in the anti-bias classroom. In particular, we offer suggestions for using two valuable classroom materials—children's books and persona dolls—that can have an important impact on children's identity formation and greater understanding of the similarities and differences among people.

Guidelines for Your Curriculum

ABE is not just doing occasional activities around the topics of diversity and fairness, although that may be how new anti-bias educators begin. To be effective, ABE works as an understanding, a perspective, that permeates everything that happens in an early childhood program—including your interactions with children, families, and colleagues—and shapes how you put curriculum together each day. Nearly every topic in an early childhood program has possibilities for ABE themes and activities. For instance, the themes of self-discovery, family, and community are deeper and more meaningful when you explore ability, culture, economic class, gender, and racialized identity as integral parts of the themes.

So, too, do issues of fairness (Goal 3) and acting for fairness (Goal 4) arise as children explore various curriculum topics.

Ideas for specific ABE content and activities come from three major sources:

Children's questions, interests, or interactions with each other that teachers see as important to respond to and develop

Teacher-initiated activities based on what teachers and families think is important for children to learn

Significant events that occur in the children's communities and the larger world that teachers believe need to be explored with children

Here is an example of an ABE topic arising from a child's comment at snack time in a classroom of 4-year-olds:

The teacher sets a small pitcher of water on the table for children to pour from. Lupe, whose home language is Spanish, looks up and asks "Agua?" Casey, sitting next to her, says with annoyance, "No! It's water—not ahhgwa" (exaggerating the pronunciation). The teacher stops what she is doing and turns to Casey and says, "Lupe is right. What you call 'water,' her family calls 'agua.' There are many words for water, for crackers, for oranges, for everything! We all have words. We have *different* words. It's pretty wonderful!"

At group time the teacher follows up by asking children about the different words they have for people in their family. As the children call out *Grandma, Oma, Pops, Daddy, Papa, Abuelita*, and more, she writes them on a chart. She assures them that none of the words are wrong. They are just different. And they all mean someone who loves them.

Meet Anti-Bias Goals in Every Area of the Classroom

The ongoing exploration of how people are simultaneously the same and different provides children with a conceptual framework for thinking about the world they live in. For example, children playing with blocks can learn that although some children like to build large structures with the unit blocks and some prefer to make more intricate structures with the smaller blocks, all the children like to build. When discussing children's artistic creations, you can show enthusiasm and admiration for black and brown shades along with all the wonderful colors of the spectrum. The common curriculum topic of harvesttime can include respecting and making visible the people who grow, pick, and transport food.

Use Both Child- and Teacher-Initiated Activities

Children's questions, comments, and behaviors are a vital source of anti-bias curriculum. They spark teachable moments as well as longer-term projects. However, it is not sufficient to plan anti-bias activities only when a child brings up a relevant issue. Teacher-initiated activities are also necessary—be they intentionally putting out materials and books to broaden children's awareness or planning specific learning experiences around issues that matter to families and the community.

Here's an example of how a teacher begins with a children-generated teachable moment and follows up with teacher-initiated activities:

Three 4-year-old boys are on top of the climbing structure. Jenna (4 years old) starts up the ladder to join them and the boys shout, "No girls allowed! No girls allowed!"

The simplest response from the teacher would be to remind the children of the rules: "The climbing structure belongs to the school. All the children can play there." An anti-bias approach, however, asks for more. It requires the teacher to recognize that the drama playing out in the yard not only reflects the personalities and feelings of the four individual children but also replicates a hurtful social attitude in which girls are excluded from large-muscle, loud play, and boys are encouraged to ignore feelings.

The teacher starts by finding out what the children are thinking: "Why do you think no girls are allowed?" She pays respectful attention to the children's responses: "Girls can't climb high," "Girls can't climb fast," "We don't like girls" (accompanied by nervous laughter). All three statements are commonly heard stereotypes that are hurtful to *all* the children.

Next, the teacher suggests that the children test the stereotype. "Come on down and let's see if girls can climb fast and high or not." She might invite a few other girls to join in the challenge so Jenna is not alone. "Anyone want to guess what is going to happen?" she asks. With much laughter the children run and climb. Some girls are faster than some boys, some boys are faster than some girls.

Afterwards the teacher puts words to the event. "It looks like both girls *and* boys can climb high and fast. Thinking that there are differences between boys and girls in climbing is a stereotype." (Oh, how 4-year-olds love big words!) Then the teacher states the program's values. "Stereotypes are unfair. In our school we want everyone to be treated fairly. What can we do so that we can be sure that playing on the climbing structure is fair?" The next steps are suggested by the children. One says they can create a sign that says "Everyone can play here." "How about," says one of the three boys who began this episode, "how about if we want to play alone, we just say 'You can have a turn in a few minutes'?"

In addition, the teacher plans and carries out further activities. She adds children's books in which girl athletes are strong and fast and books in which girls and boys play together in large-muscle games. She invites a female athlete to come and visit and talk about what it is like to be a runner and asks a classroom mom who plays soccer to teach the children to kick a ball into a net.

The teacher relates what she has done and why with the other staff in her program. They consider the frequency of gendered exclusionary play in the program and agree to take the important step of identifying how (consciously and unconsciously) they may be supporting a binary view of gender in their classroom (see Chapter 9). For example, do they gather the children together by calling out "Boys and girls" rather than "Children"? Do they regularly comment on girls' appearance and clothing and on boys' accomplishments?

They agree to observe each other as well as the children and see what changes they can make to avoid the damage that gender stereotypes have on children's sense of themselves and of others. (Adapted from Edwards 2017, 78–79)

Using a combination of child-initiated, teachable moments and teacher-initiated, planned activities is the most effective way to expand children's ability to grow in the four ABE goals and to talk about, think about, and understand the world around them.

Pay Attention to the Realities of Children's Lives

While the four core ABE goals are the same for all children, specific activities should be relevant to the children's background and their lives. Some children need support to resist messages of racial or cultural inferiority; others need guidance to develop a positive self-concept without absorbing social messages that they are the normal ones and children who are not like them are less-than, strange, or negatively different. Children of wealthy families may need help resisting the message that material accumulation defines their worth and that of others; children of families with fewer resources may need support to resist messages that undercut their families' worth. Some girls may need extra support to develop confidence and interest in experiences that are math and science related; some boys may require help to develop skills for having nurturing, cooperative interactions with their peers and to engage in play that reflects these attitudes.

As in all other areas of the curriculum, teachers tailor and scaffold anti-bias education materials and activities to match each child's cognitive, social, and emotional developmental capacities. They plan and choose learning experiences that stimulate children to explore the next step of new ideas and skills and allow each child to apply new understandings and behaviors in her daily life.

Avoid Anti-Bias Education Missteps

Even when your intentions are good, you can expect missteps as you grow as an anti-bias educator. Here are a few common ones related to curriculum and materials.

The "Tourist Curriculum" Misstep

In this erroneous approach, a program "visits" other cultures by exploring related books, food, clothing, and celebrations for a day or two (e.g., Japan Week, Mexico Day). Then the program returns to its normal daily curriculum, in which diverse ways of life may be invisible. This is like a tourist briefly visiting another country and then returning home having only scratched the surface of the richness of that culture and having formed limited ideas of what the people and life there are actually like. Ironically, the "other people" a program "visits" often are children and families who are in the program or members of the children's larger communities.

In a tourist curriculum, the real diversity of the children, families, and larger community is left out of the ongoing daily curriculum. Excursions into other cultures become one-time activities—such as learning about a holiday, eating an unfamiliar food, exploring a few objects from daily life, or perhaps listening to a one-time guest—rather than ongoing learning about how people are the same and different. Another aspect of a tourist curriculum is using activities about a specific group of people only at certain times each year (acknowledging the achievements, or even the existence, of African Americans only during Black History Month; making Asian Americans visible in the curriculum for a celebration of Lunar New Year). Or, a school may have a once-a-year cultural fair as the primary "diversity activity." While a day like that in itself can be lovely—families bring food to share, play music, and maybe wear traditional clothing—it becomes a tourist curriculum when that one day is the only time in the school year that families share their lives with the children and when learning about the diversity of each other's lives is absent from the ongoing curriculum.

A tourist curriculum communicates the bias that some people's lives are the normal way to be while others are worth only an occasional visit. It presents a limited, simplistic, often inaccurate view of people's lives and reduces rich patterns of cultures to one or two small bits of information that are taken out of context. An example is representing the diversity of Native American culture by having children make fry bread or make paper feather headdresses. Doing generic activities like these gives the impression that all Native American peoples have the same culture and that all individual members of a particular group are the same. This entirely obscures the great diversity that exists *within* Native American peoples. In this way, a tourist curriculum trivializes the cultures it supposedly is intended to help children appreciate.

The "Token Materials" Misstep

Tokenism occurs when a single teaching material or image is used to represent an entire group of people. For example, a teacher might provide one dark-skinned doll amidst many White dolls, display just one poster or book featuring a picture of a child who uses a wheelchair, or provide a single book featuring Asian characters. Even if the depiction is accurate, failing to show the diversity that exists within groups leads children to draw conclusions about a group of people that can easily become overgeneralizations. Here's one example:

> Three-year-old Liliana enjoys looking at *Mama Zooms*, by Jane Cowen-Fletcher, a delightful book but the only one in the program that depicts an adult in a wheelchair. When a father who uses a wheelchair arrives to pick up his child in Liliana's program, she insists he can't be the daddy. "Wheelchair *mamas* take care of babies," she says. "Daddies have to drive the car."

It's impossible, of course, at any given moment to have every type of human diversity represented and celebrated in a classroom or on a bookshelf. But over the course of a school year, it's important to provide children with multiple visions of the way human beings are both alike and different.

The "Misinforming/ Misrepresenting" Misstep

This misstep tends to happen in two ways. One is to use examples from a group's country of origin to depict their life in the United States, such as using images and stories about life in Vietnam to teach about Vietnamese Americans. A second way is to teach about a group by focusing mainly on their historic way of life or ritual dress rather than their current lives—for example, all Native Americans live in tipis and wear only ritual clothing. Another form of misinformation is mixing up ways of life among cultures that are actually different—for example, assuming that all people from Central and South American countries have the same culture and live in the same way.

An ABE approach is not a recipe that lists only one way of doing things. Rather, you include anti-bias issues in your planning by considering the children and families you serve, the curriculum approach your program uses, and the four core ABE goals. Here are key questions to ask yourself as you and your colleagues plan learning activities and set up the environment. Begin by asking yourself these questions for one or two activities a week, and see how they change what you do and how the children respond.

- Where do I best fit ABE goals and issues into my curriculum plans for the day and the week?

- Who might be left out of this curriculum? How will I use the topic to include *each* child, connecting to the diversity of social identities and to individual needs? How can I be sure no one is invisible or unnoticed?

- How do I use this topic to strengthen each child's social, emotional, language, and cognitive development?

- What ideas, misconceptions, and stereotypes might children have about this topic? How can I learn what these are and provide accurate information and counter misinformation and stereotypes?

- How can I use this topic to support and strengthen children's innate sense of justice and their capacity to change unfair situations to fair ones?

- What learning materials do I need to gather to incorporate an anti-bias perspective into this curriculum topic?

Guidelines for Materials

In the anti-bias classroom, visual images and learning materials are culturally welcoming for all the children and their families and immediately make clear that all forms of diversity are welcome and honored. Each classroom has its own unique look and sounds, reflecting the family cultures and daily lives of the children and families it serves as well as the broader community.

Anti-bias classrooms contain similar materials to those found in many other early childhood classrooms, such as children's books, dramatic play props, items for exploring and creating art, blocks, toy vehicles, puzzles, games for building literacy and math skills, musical instruments, makerspace materials, and more. With an anti-bias lens, however, teachers select and provide materials that expand children's sense of self and their appreciation of different people and diverse ways of thinking and doing.

Many visual materials in early childhood programs, such as books, photographs, and puzzles, reflect the dominant culture in US society. They mainly depict White, middle-class and professional, suburban, able-bodied people in two-parent families with a mother and father and one or two children. Using materials that reflect only this particular group of people teaches children who are part of this dominant culture that they are the norm and teaches children who are not that they are marginal or "less-than" (see Chapter 2). When children's social identities are not honored in a classroom, it sends a strong message about who matters and who does not.

In addition to the importance of seeing themselves in their learning environment, children also learn from materials that illuminate diversity both within and beyond their own identity groups. This includes learning materials that accurately and nonstereotypically reflect

- Children and adults from the various racial and ethnic identity groups in your program and larger community

- Families from a range of economic groups performing all types of work (e.g., manual labor, office work, work in the home)

- People with disabilities of various backgrounds working, playing, spending time with their families

- Diverse family structures

- People, past and present, who have enhanced the quality of life and worked for social justice in the children's own communities and in the larger society

A useful rule of thumb is that about half of the materials in the environment should reflect the identities of the specific children in that classroom. In programs that serve children whose lives are too often made invisible by the dominant culture, even more plentiful images of themselves, their families, and their communities help to counter the harm of invisibility.

On page 180 you will find the form "Checklist for Assessing the Visual Material Environment" to help you evaluate your classroom environment and determine what you would like to change and expand. In addition to the visual images displayed in your classroom, it encourages you to think about how the following support diversity and inclusivity:

- Dramatic play materials

- Manipulatives

- Language

- Dolls

- Books

- Posters, photos, etc.

Review this list at least once a year, preferably with your colleagues. The checklist is also a useful tool for observing and assessing programs you observe or are considering working in.

Children's Books and Persona Dolls

Children's books and dolls are two important materials in early childhood programs as well in many families' homes. You can use these common materials in new ways to introduce and develop the four core ABE goals in your curriculum.

Children's Picture Books: An Essential Resource

Good stories capture the heart, mind, and imagination. They entrance and engage children and give teachers an opportunity to be their most lively and creative selves. They also provide a wonderful, ongoing way for children to learn about diversity and fairness. As a result, books are one of the most important anti-bias learning materials.

However, books can also convey inaccuracies and perpetuate stereotypes about who people are and how they live. A story from Louise's family illustrates this dynamic:

> When our son was 4, his grandparents gave him an alphabet book that depicted a Native American in a stereotypical way, with buckskin pants, feathered headdress, and naked upper torso. About six months later, our family went camping and met a California Native American family, who were camping next to us. One evening we got together around a campfire and the adults shared stories and information about their respective backgrounds. When the father described his family's background, my son looked puzzled and asked, "But where is his feathers?"

Because books are so influential as both mirrors to see ourselves and windows to understand others, a thoughtful, balanced book selection is essential. The majority of children's books tend to show dominant-culture representations of people and how they live. Even stories about animal families usually show the animal characters living with two parents and in isolation from other animal families (which is almost always incorrect!).

As you build your anti-bias library, consider these questions:

- Can all the children in my classroom find themselves and their families in our book collection?

- Do the books I provide support every child's family, racial identity, cultural identity, and home language?

- Are the book's content and images accurate and authentic? Do they depict current life?

- Do the books show diversity within groups and in the community?

Finding and Selecting Children's Books

There are many wonderful books that combine fine storytelling, rich language, and beautiful artwork with a broad representation of human diversity. To find good children's books, start with these sources:

- Your local library: Become friends with the children's librarian, and have the children make thank-you notes for books the librarian selects that they particularly enjoy.

- Your local bookstore: Many give a discount for teachers, so ask.

- The children's families

- Your colleagues

- Your professional networks

- Many blogs and databases examine books with an anti-bias focus. Some organizations and websites offer guidance for selecting books, books to avoid, or books to consider reading to children. Look carefully to be sure that these lists contain books that are age appropriate; many such sites focus on resources for older students. One place to begin is with a post titled "Building a Diverse, Anti-Bias Library for Young Children: A Masterpost" on the blog *Equity in Early Childhood* (Megan Madison, August 12, 2015). This post provides links to resources for building your library and finding diverse, anti-bias books.

Here are some initial criteria for selecting books:

- Remember that any book you choose needs to be well written, age appropriate, and compelling. No matter how important the message is, if it isn't a book that will interest young children, keep looking!

- Look at who is made visible in the book and who is missing. No single book covers everyone and every identity, but your collection of books should show a wide range of people by race, gender identity, family structure, economic class, culture, age, ability, and more.

- Look for stories in which children are kind, make friends across lines of difference, solve problems, and collaborate.

- Include both storybooks and nonfiction books.

Financing an Anti-Bias Library

Children's books are an easy resource to raise money for. Virtually everyone believes that it is important for children to be read to and to become literate. Develop a short request letter and encourage families to ask their employers, their banks, their grocery store managers, their children's grandparents, and others to consider donating funds. The letter can include a copy of a book plate that says "Thank you _____ for donating this book." Social clubs (Lions, Soroptimists, sororities), churches, mosques, synagogues, and local businesses are often delighted to be approached for small donations that will put high-quality books into the hands of children.

Dealing with Stereotypes in Children's Books

A stereotype is any depiction of a group of people—and its individual members—that makes it appear as if all members of the group are the same and, frequently, less than fully complex, interesting people. Stereotypes portray a simplistic, inaccurate image or message about a group of people that reinforces misinformation. Certain stereotypes are part of the dominant culture narrative. For example, boys are portrayed as leaders and girls as followers; White people are in the majority (e.g., if there are five children in the story, four are White and one is Black); children with disabilities rarely appear as main characters in books about anything other than their disabilities.

Even when a book has many great features, it can lead children to form an incorrect idea about a group of people. For example, books by Ezra Jack Keats, such as *The Snowy Day* and *Peter's Chair,* are classics beloved by children, and for good reasons. But unless children are exposed to other books that include different images of African American women, they may be left with stereotypes such as that all African American women are overweight. The less experience children have had with a group of people, the more important it is to offer a variety of stories about that group to prevent children from forming incorrect generalizations.

Occasionally, it is useful to keep a book with stereotypes specifically for engaging children's critical thinking. For example, one kindergarten teacher helped children to think about sexism with a book in which a girl helps her mother cook and clean and a boy helps his father mow the lawn. She asked the children whether they knew any fathers or brothers who cooked or cleaned and any mothers who mowed lawns. The children decided that the book "didn't really tell the truth" and ended up making their own book about all the things that boys and girls do to help at home.

One School Begins: Starting with Children's Books

by Encian Pastel, head teacher at a parent cooperative preschool

In our parent cooperative preschool, families gift a favorite book to the classroom on their child's birthday. It's a lovely tradition. But, as a parent and teacher began to analyze our book collection using the guidelines for selecting anti-bias children's books on SocialJusticeBooks.org, we had to deal with a glitch in the tradition we loved. Many of the books donated by families contained hurtful stereotypes or misinformation about various groups of people. Staff discussed these findings and our concerns about them. We then sent out an email with a book list of what the school needed and requested that families select books from it.

At first, families responded negatively: "Censorship," "Why are you changing our tradition?," "You're just being 'politically correct.'" We took a deep breath and started over. We talked to the families as they arrived or picked up the children. We sent out a new email explaining the full process of how staff came to our decision, with examples of the stereotypes found in our books, and discussed how those messages hurt children. We spelled out our commitment to providing children with books that accurately and respectfully represent the diverse world in which they live. We invited families to participate in thinking about the books with the staff.

To our delight, the families not only came to appreciate the changes, they began recommending wonderful books to us. They told us how much more thoughtful they were being in their choices of videos and books at home.

Persona Dolls: An Interactive Approach to Anti-Bias Education

Many anti-bias educators use storytelling with a special set of dolls called persona dolls. For each doll, which can be purchased or handmade, the teacher creates a name and unique identity, which stays constant throughout the school year. These dolls are kept separate from those that children use for play. The teacher slowly builds a collection of persona dolls, some reflecting the specific children and families in their classroom and others introducing new kinds of diversity. The teacher makes up stories about each doll with three objectives in mind:

- Reflect and relate to the lives of the children in the program

- Broaden children's awareness of various aspects of diversity

- Engage children in discussion about situations involving fairness and activism

The teacher invites the children to talk about the doll's feelings and to help the doll figure out what to do.

Julie Bisson, who has used persona dolls with children (and adults!) for decades, explains that

> Events in children's daily lives can be useful springboards for anti-bias learning through storytelling and discussion. In helping the persona dolls deal with issues of identity, diversity, and discriminatory teasing and exclusion, children can safely explore how to handle these issues in their own lives.

ABE teachers in many parts of the world, such as Australia, Ireland, South Africa, the Netherlands, and the United Kingdom, have found that persona dolls are a wonderful addition to a classroom, helping children engage in thinking about issues related to all four core anti-bias goals. For examples of how teachers use persona dolls in the classroom, see pages 57, 62, 131, 146, and 154.

Holidays in a Diverse World: Applying Anti-Bias Thinking to Curriculum

The role of holidays in anti-bias curriculum is a question often raised by early childhood educators. Most children's programs include various types of holiday curriculum. When grounded in anti-bias principles, learning about holidays can support children's cultural identities, help them feel valued, and enhance their and their family's feelings of belonging to the school community. It can also be a tool for broadening children's awareness of their diverse world, adding to their enjoyment of its cultural diversity and teaching them about people who make important social contributions across a range of civic and religious traditions.

Experienced anti-bias educators vary in the way they approach teaching about holidays in their curriculum. Some incorporate learning about a diverse range of holidays rather than focusing on the dominant culture holiday calendar. Some invite children to talk about how their families celebrate any given holiday. Others teach only about nonreligious holidays. Some choose to create celebrations throughout the year related to the school community rather than to societal or family holidays. Anti-bias educators in faith-based programs combine their religious holidays with the ABE principles of looking at diversity and justice. Some programs primarily focus on holidays that celebrate courage and social justice activism, such as Martin Luther King Day, International Women's Day, or Earth Day.

Holidays and celebrations carry important memories, both positive and negative, for most people. Catherine relates the following conversation she had with a preschool teacher working in a Head Start program:

> The teacher complained to me that using the anti-bias approach to holidays is so hard for her program because, according to her, "It is stressful not wanting to offend anyone." This was an "aha" moment for me. I shared with her that the focus of the anti-bias approach was not about not offending;

it was about including rather than excluding children and families. Children need to see their family traditions respected and to learn about other families' traditions. An anti-bias approach to holidays ensures that the children who do not celebrate a holiday do not feel inferior and that the children whose holidays are celebrated do not feel superior.

Stop & Think: What Do Holidays or Celebrations Mean to You?

When you were a child, what holidays or celebrations, if any, were significant in your family? What joys or pleasures did they bring? What tensions or stresses accompanied them?

To what degree did your schools reflect your family's way of observing holidays or holding celebrations? What did that teach you about the acceptability of your family?

How did your family's economic circumstances impact the holidays or celebrations you experienced?

What appeals to you and/or concerns you about the ways celebrations or holidays are done in early childhood programs?

Anti-Bias Outcomes for Children

Thinking through your program's approach to holidays will also lead to experiences that will have a powerful impact on children. For example, an anti-bias approach to holidays will help children to

See their family's specific approach to holidays made visible through learning activities (as compared to celebrations) in their early childhood program

Become aware of and grow comfortable with the reality that some people celebrate different holidays or celebrate the same holiday in different ways

Learn that some people do not celebrate religious or national holidays but do have other ways of having family celebrations and traditions

Recognize misinformation and stereotypes associated with specific holiday traditions

Learn about celebrations that honor people's work for peace, freedom, fairness, and justice for all people

Engage in family and school celebrations tied to the school year

Some Considerations About Holidays

Bringing an anti-bias lens to holiday events and curriculum requires consideration of several issues:

Although all cultures commemorate their significant beliefs, events, and people through special celebrations and holidays from daily work, there are no specific holiday or religious observances that are universal.

Even when many people observe a particular holiday, they do it in many different ways and for different purposes. In early childhood settings, the beliefs and traditions of one group or family may conflict with, or may complement, those of others, even within the same belief systems.

Secularized or commercialized aspects of holidays are not culturally or religiously neutral (e.g., Santa Claus at Christmas, dyeing eggs at Easter).

National holidays reflect the dominant culture and may not include all the people in your community.

Holidays have specific historic and/or spiritual meanings. For example, Dr. Martin Luther King Jr.'s birthday is a celebration of his work for justice, not simply an occasion to acknowledge that he was a peaceful person. Knowing the purpose and world view underlying a holiday will help you to make decisions about what role, if any, you want that holiday to play in your program.

Learning About a Holiday vs. Everyone Celebrating It

Learning about a holiday means teaching children what that holiday means to the cultural or religious groups who honor it and the varied ways these groups choose to celebrate it. With preschoolers, the focus is on how the different families in the program or the community choose to celebrate specific holidays. Teaching about a holiday calls on teachers to communicate accurate information appropriate to the children's levels of cognitive development in a clear and matter-of-fact manner. It also requires that teachers make very clear that the class can enjoy learning about each other's holidays while holding to their own family's beliefs and traditions. Teaching about a holiday may involve reading a book to children or inviting individual children and their family members to share what they do during one of their holidays.

Celebrating a holiday, on the other hand, engages children in holiday activities as full-fledged participants on the assumption that their families believe in the holiday's underlying purpose and meaning in the way that those who regularly celebrate it do. Celebrating a holiday is appropriate in faith-based programs or in programs in which the holiday is part of a belief system truly shared by every family in the program. Even then, remember that within a belief system, different families celebrate in different ways.

Anti-Bias Goals as Applied to Holidays

The four ABE core goals provide a framework for making decisions about holidays in the early childhood curriculum. Goal 1 (identity) and Goal 2 (diversity) focus on supporting children's healthy sense of self and family while embracing the human diversity of other families around them. Anti-bias teachers pay attention to not excluding or disrespecting any family's way of engaging in holidays. They do not impose holiday beliefs on families that do not celebrate them.

Goal 3 (justice) calls on teachers to think critically about the holidays they are considering using in their curriculum. This includes national holidays, which are official but which do not necessarily reflect the historic or current realities. Anti-bias educators ask themselves like these:

- Whose culture and history have shaped the messages of the holiday and the ways it is celebrated?

- Are certain groups of people invisible, misrepresented, or disrespected in that holiday narrative and material?

- Can I find ways to teach about a holiday that eliminates explicit and implicit biases while also respecting the core meaning of the holiday?

Goal 4 (activism) invites teachers to deepen children's awareness of and pride in those who have worked to make the world fair for everyone. Teaching about celebrations and special days that honor struggles for freedom, self-determination, and justice are one way to do this. For example, the Fourth of July commemorates the adoption of the American Declaration of Independence. Martin Luther King Day honors a man and a civil rights movement. Juneteenth celebrates the signing of the Emancipation Proclamation. Passover celebrates an ancient victory of the Jewish people over slavery. International Women's Day marks women's struggles to gain equality and decent working conditions. Cinco de Mayo commemorates Mexico's military victory over France. Earth Day honors the worldwide efforts to preserve the environment.

By age 4, although children cannot understand all the facts and complexities of history (or even how long "long ago" is), they can understand that many grown-ups have worked, and continue to work, to make the world a safer, fairer, and better place. Preschoolers can also connect activities about social justice holidays to their own experiences with unfairness and fairness—about which they care a great deal. Holiday activities engage children in critical thinking and activism that are appropriate to their developmental stage and their families' history and cultures.

Creating a Holiday Policy: Considering Different Perspectives

Having a written holiday policy for your program or classroom supports the ongoing decision making about which holidays will be included in the curriculum, why, and how. There is no one right policy, and policies change over the years with different staff, new families, and new issues in a community. A holiday policy should include objectives for holiday activities and school celebrations, the process for deciding which holidays to include, guidelines for addressing the religious aspects of holidays, and meeting different family holiday requirements (see Bisson & Derman-Sparks 2016 for further discussion of issues and facilitation strategies).

Ideally, the program director initiates and facilitates the collaborative process for shaping the program's approach to holidays. However, you can create your own classroom holiday policy with the teaching team you work with. What matters is that staff and families engage in conversations about holidays and their purpose for the children, sharing different perspectives, enabling everyone to grow in their understanding of their own and others' holiday traditions, and shaping the program's approach to holidays (Bisson & Derman-Sparks 2016).

One way to open these conversations is to brainstorm a list of holiday benefits and challenges, perhaps using the questions suggested above. Talk about what positive experiences children might have and what negative experiences. Work to clarify the purpose and meaning of the holiday. Consider the ABE goals. Some staff and families will welcome discussion of these issues, and others will not. Remember that working through the issues and emotions connected to many holidays is important and will help ensure that your program approaches holiday teaching and celebrations with an anti-bias perspective.

. . .

Building an anti-bias program for children is an ongoing process. Every day, children absorb and try to make sense of the world around them. An ABE learning environment and curriculum enriches everything that children do. It supports children to feel pride in themselves and delight in those who are different. It also teaches them skills to stand up for themselves and others against shaming, bias, or exclusion. It helps children—and you—thrive. It is hard work, but it is exciting!

CHAPTER 4

Building an Anti-Bias Education Program: Clarifying and Brave Conversations with Children

Everything teachers do—setting up the learning environment; planning the curriculum; observing, assessing, and thinking about individual children; and so much more—rests upon establishing strong, caring, and trusting relationships with children and families. Without such relationships with their teachers, children find it hard to open up, to learn, to grow, to feel safe. These relationships are built on

- Seeing each individual child as a member of a unique family with many, often complex, social identities that shape their learning and ways of being

- Respecting each child's individual way of learning and being rather than imposing an expected behavior

- Knowing how children learn to think and how they are, and are not yet, able to discern what is happening around them

- Understanding that children are in the process of learning at all times and that it takes many experiences before they master an idea or a behavior

- Listening carefully to each child to understand how each is making sense of experiences and/or behavior

An essential element in building strong relationships is your willingness to engage in conversations that support children's sense of self, that let them know they are safe and honored exactly as who they are. Children live in a world that sends multiple, stereotype-laden messages about their comparative value, their right to be visible, and how they are expected to behave based on their economic class, ethnicity, gender, abilities, racial identity, and religion. These overt and covert messages affect their own sense of self-worth and how they think about people who are different. Avoiding conversations about identity and fairness is a disservice to children who are developmentally dependent upon adults to help them make sense of the complex and contradictory societal messages they receive.

When programs do not demonstrate respect for and acknowledgement of human diversity, children and families cannot feel truly seen or honored. When a teacher avoids directly addressing comments or behaviors that can hurt another child, no child feels safe. Keeping silent not only does *not* help children, it actively hurts them. Learning how to break this silence, how to talk about anti-bias issues with clarity, courage, and caring, is an essential skill not only in the world of early childhood education but in the world at large. This chapter explores ways to build trusting relationships with children by directly talking about identity, diversity, injustice, and activism, which correspond to the four goals of ABE.

The Hurtful Power of Silence

It is hoped that children will turn to their trusted adults when they are confused or are hurt by their experiences. But to do so, children need a vocabulary to describe what they are thinking. Too often, adults ignore children's attempts to understand how people can be different from one another and yet the same. A White child asking about skin color is likely to hear something like "We are all the same. We are all friends here!" That child is left to figure out for herself why the people around her look different from one another and, with insufficient information, may

well decide that dark skin means dirty skin or that different skin colors mean different kinds of blood or different personalities.

Equally significant, *if adults go silent about things that children are seeing and trying to understand, children absorb the emotional message that the subject is dangerous and should not be talked about.* This leaves children with an undercurrent of anxiety and unease, which are the earliest lessons about bias and fear. Silence is a powerful teacher. What you don't say carries messages that are as strong as what you do say. Regardless of your intent, your unwillingness to openly talk with a child about the world sends serious, strong, and potentially hurtful messages. Consider:

- **Silence robs children** of a vocabulary to talk about or to ask questions about what is confusing or troubling to them.

- **Silence requires children** to figure things out on their own using their limited understanding of the world.

- **Silence teaches fear**—the subject is so unsafe the adults won't even talk about it.

- **Silence forces children** to rely on sources such as other children (another 4-year-old in the carpool, the 6-year-old next door, a 10-year-old cousin) and the media (TV, advertising, videos) for information, including how they should feel and think about what is happening in their world. These are major sources of inaccurate and often stereotyped information.

Talking about anti-bias issues can be challenging, especially if a person has not experienced the particular bias. If this is true for you, you may be reluctant to talk about sensitive subjects out of fear that you will offend someone or that the conversation will worsen a situation. You may have been explicitly or implicitly taught that nice people don't mention human differences or that noticing differences is the same as being biased.

If you experience prejudice and discrimination yourself, comments or behaviors from children that reflect society's biases may stir up painful experiences or anger. Your own experiences may hinder you from being available to children to help them understand

A Mother's Story

by Nadiyah F. Taylor, director of the Department of Early Childhood Department at Las Positas College

Anti-bias education is personal for me and for the well-being of my child. I am a Black woman in an interracial relationship and have a beautiful biracial son who is 4 years old. He has dark brown hair with rich red and golden-brown highlights. It is big, bouncy, and full of curls that spring this way and that and seem to move with a wind that comes from within. He wears his hair in braids, twists, ponytails, and cornrows, and his favorite style is "my curls, Mom."

One Sunday night I braided my son's hair in loose cornrows. He ran to the mirror to admire the hairdo and expressed excitement about the way it looked and that it would keep his hair from falling into his face while he practiced his new skills on the high bar at school. However, sometime between arriving at school with his father at 7:30 a.m. and his classmates' arrival at 9:00 a.m., my son concluded that "Even though it made me sad, Mommy, I needed to take out my braids so (one of his classmates) wouldn't tease me." One child teased him saying that he had "puffy" hair and was a "barnacle head." Other children thought

he looked like a girl. And, as we learned later, the teacher said and did nothing. My husband, who saw him later that morning, described to me the devastated and shamed look on my son's face as he explained to his dad what had happened.

During the following week, my son decided that it was safe to wear his hair in curls, but that he could add no other adornments and definitely could not have braids or ponytails. During the same period, he also started to talk to me about how he thought my hair was puffy and looked a little weird.

Can you imagine what it felt like for me to see some of my son's sparkle diminish that day and what might have been different had his teacher and his school followed through on a real anti-bias program?

We talked to his sweet, honest, overwhelmed teacher who, despite the school's written anti-bias statement, said she had no idea how to intervene or where to start or what resources might be available to her. As a result, all the children lost out. My son's sense of himself was injured, and all the children missed out on an opportunity to appreciate human differences and to recognize hurtful behavior.

the confusing messages they receive in the world in which they live. Whatever the reason, remaining silent in the face of bias helps keep it alive.

In Nadiyah Taylor's case (see "A Mother's Story"), what a difference it would have made for her son if the teacher and staff at his school had had the knowledge, skills, and courage to address that experience with him and the other children! How useful it would have been if the teacher had recognized that, even if the teasing was based on simple curiosity, it replicated a painful social attitude about African American hair and about boys' hair and girls' hair. What a gift it could have been if the teacher had used that moment to protect Nadiyah's son and to support all the children in learning about the wonder of the many ways hair grows, the beauty of

different kinds of hair, and the joy for boys *and* girls of wearing their hair the way they like! In addition, *if the teaching staff had been prepared to respond, the incident could have been an important moment of building trust and safety between the child and teacher and between the child's family and the school.* It could have reinforced for *all* the children the message that they would be accepted and honored for exactly who they were.

Stop & Think: What Did You Learn About Speaking Up or Keeping Silent?

- What do you remember from childhood about how you made sense out of the great range of human differences? Did you ask questions? If not, what stopped you? If you did, who did you ask?

- What are your earliest memories of noticing differences such as skin color or economic class? What words did you have to describe what you noticed? What feelings did you absorb from adults about those differences?

- What topics did you learn were not for children to discuss? How did you feel about those subjects?

- What keeps you silent today when you hear or see evidence of bias or prejudice?

Holding Clarifying Conversations About Anti-Bias Issues

What children ask, say, or do about any aspect of their own or others' identities and differences offers rich teachable moments for ABE, including their comments or behaviors that reflect discomfort, stereotypes, or rejection of an aspect of diversity. How you respond to these opportunities is a central part of effective teaching.

Anti-bias conversations begin in many ways. Sometimes a child is simply curious about human differences and wants information. Sometimes the behavior or questions indicate a child is struggling with pre-prejudicial thinking. Sometimes there is intent to hurt emotionally or physically. Sometimes there are indicators that a child feels shame or fear about a social identity. And sometimes,

world issues from the news or from terrible events in the community intrude into the life of the classroom. In each case, you can respond in developmentally appropriate ways, always directly acknowledging what is going on for an individual child or a group of children.

Fit Your Conversation to the Child's Understanding

Young children often do not have words to describe what is on their minds. They are just beginning to develop vocabulary to describe how they feel. Observing their body language and behavior for cues about what they are feeling and what they understand provides you with more accurate information than their words. When you talk with young children, do the following:

- Listen carefully.

- Ask questions.

- Respond with simple, straightforward answers.

- Check to see what the child has understood and is feeling.

- Proceed in small steps.

Here's an example:

Three-year-old Tobin, who wears a brace on one leg, is watching three other children near the sandbox load wagons with small pumpkins that are near the sandbox and pull them around the yard to a table market they have set up.

Teacher: Hey, Tobin. Looks like you're interested in the pumpkins.

Tobin: (*Shakes his head.*)

Teacher: Do you want to play with the other kids?

Tobin: (*Nods.*)

Teacher: Would you like me to come with you to ask them?

Tobin: Too fast.

Teacher: Too fast?

Tobin: (*Nods.*) Too fast.

Teacher: Are the kids moving too fast for you to play?

Tobin: (*Nods.*)

Teacher: We could ask them to go slower, or you could load the pumpkins for them to take to the market table.

Tobin: I could load the pumpkins?

Teacher: Yes, you could offer to load the pumpkins.

Tobin: (*Suddenly seems determined, pushes the teacher away, and walks over to the children.*) I can load the pumpkins. You can take them to the market.

This is a pretty straightforward conversation. The teacher pays attention, asks questions, checks in with the child, and offers small amounts of information. If there had been more than one child involved, the teacher would have helped the children hear and understand each other. If it was a situation where a child was being hurt, or potentially could be hurt, the teacher would stop the action and then continue with the conversation.

Respond to Children's Curiosity or Puzzlement

Children rely on adults to help them figure out what things mean. Their questions create teachable moments, unexpected opportunities to respond to their attempts to understand what they observe. Your response is to give accurate, developmentally appropriate, matter-of-fact information that helps children develop their understanding of diversity and also to communicate the feeling that differences are interesting and wonderful, something to be appreciated and celebrated. Here are some examples of such responses:

Child: Why does Anil's grandma wear that costume?

Teacher: That's not a costume. Anil's grandmother is visiting from India. She is wearing a dress called a *sari*. It's her everyday kind of dress—it has so many beautiful colors, doesn't it?

• • •

Child: Why does Jeremiah have braces on his feet?

Teacher: Jeremiah's feet and legs need help to work together. So the doctors gave him braces to help him walk and stand.

• • •

Child: How come Olivia has two mommies?

Teacher: Some families have one mommy or one daddy, some have a mommy and a daddy, some families have grandparents who raise the children. Olivia's family has two mommies. Our families have different people in them, and they love us and take care of us. Each family is special!

Although questions like these appear to be uncomplicated requests for information, an anti-bias teacher files the question away and waits to see if there are bigger, more complex issues behind the questions. If so, those may need to be addressed through the curriculum, with classroom visitors, and/or with special activities.

Guidelines for Clarifying Conversations

1. Find out what the children think. Listen, ask questions, pay attention to the ideas and feelings expressed. Think about the issues of fairness and unfairness (justice and injustice) that are part of this moment.

2. Tell the truth. In simple sentences that children can understand, give them accurate information about the issue. And, of course, check to see what they understand, how they feel, and what they think about this information.

3. State the justice issues. What is fair or unfair, kind or hurtful about this situation? How do they know?

4. Speak your values. "In our program, we . . ." or "This is what we believe . . ." or "Here's how we treat people in our school . . ."

Clarify and Extend Children's Ideas

Clarifying conversations go further than offering correct information. They engage children in thinking critically about issues and provide them with new, accurate information. Be aware that you may need to think through your own confusions and biases and revisit the issue, but you still have to do something at the moment.

Here's an example of a clarifying conversation:

Three-year-old Gloria asks the teacher why Cici's hair is black and her own hair is yellow. At first, the teacher handles this as a simple matter of a child being observant and curious. She responds by saying, "We get our hair colors from our birth families. People have lots of different color hair. Even in the same family, people can have different colored hair. It's so interesting!"

However, reflecting on that interchange later in the day, the teacher thinks about societal attitudes about hair that reflect prejudices related to racism and sexism. She thinks about the powerful stereotypes that exist about hair: the length of hair considered appropriate for boys and for girls; the degree of acceptableness of texture and curl based on ideas about race; who gets to wear barrettes and ribbons and who doesn't; and the unspoken cultural norms about whether or not it is okay to touch a person's hair. This seems like an important set of attitudes to address in the curriculum to help the children avoid developing biased ideas. So the teacher plans activities to further clarify and extend the children's thinking about hair and to introduce anti-bias values about this topic.

First, the teacher takes two photos of each child: one of the back of the head and another of the face. She uses the photos to make cards for children to try to match the hair to the child. The children have a wonderful time playing with the cards. The teacher listens and offers alternative vocabulary if the children's words are potentially hurtful. When a child remarks, "She's got funny hair," the teacher replies, "What makes you think it is 'funny'? What other word could you use instead?" All kinds of conversations come up as the children use new, appreciative, and descriptive words: *fuzzy, pointy, shiny, curly, everywhere flying, smooth.*

The theme about hair then leads, as the teacher thought it would, to the children wanting to really look at, appreciate, and touch each other's hair. This is okay with some children and not at all okay with others. This leads to an opportunity for the teacher to set a guideline for how the classroom community respects differences: "We are all alike—we have hair on our heads. And we are all different—we have lots of beautifully different kinds of hair. In our classroom, if you want to touch someone else, first ask that child. If that child says yes, you can touch their hair. If that child says no, you say okay and just look."

You will find many more examples of clarifying conversations and curriculum follow-up in each of the social identity chapters of this book (Chapters 6–12).

Address Signs of Pre-Prejudice

As noted in Chapter 2, sometimes children's questions, comments, or behaviors indicate an underlying stereotyped idea about, discomfort with, or rejection of human differences. These are signs of pre-prejudice—beginning ideas and feelings that can develop into real prejudice. They may be based on a child's limited experiences or be an attempt to make sense of a new reality using new cognitive abilities that reflect the child's developmental level. Pre-prejudices may also reflect imitations of adult behavior. Even if young children are making fun of a specific identity only by repeating words or ideas they have heard from others without knowing what they fully mean, use of such language still has the potential to cause real pain to another person and to turn into real prejudice.

Indicators of children's negative ideas about a particular human difference come in various forms. For example, a child might exclude certain classmates from play because they don't speak English well, insist to a peer that he cannot have two daddies, or make a negative comment to a new child who comes to school wearing worn-looking or soiled clothes. Each of these behaviors reflects a hurtful societal attitude that, unless addressed, sows the seeds of prejudice and bias.

It is essential to *always* respond clearly to comments or behaviors that indicate pre-prejudice. They are important teachable moments. Ignoring them gives the child permission to hurt another child and is a lost opportunity to help that child learn to think differently. Remember, name calling, put-downs, or discriminatory behaviors can break children's hearts. Whatever the origin of such indicators or the diversity issue they raise, ignoring them can lead to ingrained prejudice and acceptance of prevailing stereotypes and misinformation.

Here's an example of how Eric Hoffman, a long-time anti-bias teacher of 3- to 5-year-olds, responded to a pre-prejudice situation:

> One morning, four 4-year-olds were talking and giggling and repeating a jingle that made fun of Chinese people. Although I was pretty sure their interest was in the silly sounds and their pleasure in playing together, I felt it was important to intervene. "I hear you saying a rhyme that makes you laugh," I said. They started to repeat the words, but I stopped them. "Do you know what the word *Chinese* means?" They all shook their heads. I explained that it referred to "people who are Chinese" and that a Chinese person would be insulted by the jingle, that their feelings would be hurt. The children looked concerned. I also started to talk about "people coming from a faraway country called China," but I could see I wasn't making any sense to them.

> One child said, "We want to say silly words." I agreed, saying, "It seems like you're not trying to hurt anybody's feelings. So, let's think of some rhymes that won't upset anyone." We came up with a great list of ridiculous rhymes that left them rolling on the floor with laughter.

> I felt good about how I handled the situation until later in the day, when I heard one of the children say to another, "You shouldn't say Chinese. That's a bad word." Ouch! I decided to use the persona dolls to explore the issue in greater depth. I had one of the dolls talk about her loving Vietnamese family, and how much she hated being made fun of for her physical differences. The doll talked about how wonderful her family was and how much her feelings were hurt when people made fun of the way they looked. That opened the door for many classroom discussions about racial/ethnic labels, countries around the globe, ancestors, and how much it hurts to have someone make fun of the way you look, speak, or act. (Adapted from Derman-Sparks & Ramsey 2011, 134–136)

Whether a teachable moment arises from children's direct questions or more indirectly as it did in this vignette, talking to young children about fairness and unfairness means taking abstract ideas like racism or classism and translating them into concrete, child-friendly language. Developing your skills for doing this takes practice and reflection about what works and doesn't work and what you might do next time. Don't be discouraged! Fortunately, children create many opportunities for you to keep practicing your responses to their teachable moments.

Brave Conversations: When Bias Undermines Children's Development

Sometimes children display a pattern of ideas and behavior that indicates that they have negative feelings about one or more of their own social identities or have internalized bias against others. This signals a worrisome influence of prejudice on children that goes beyond their attempts to make sense of the messages they are absorbing about who they are and about various kinds of human diversity. In this situation, you must respond. You may feel uncomfortable or anxious about opening up these issues with children or with their families or both. You may worry that you will not say the right thing or that family members will be angry. If so, it is essential to ask another teacher, your program director, or colleagues outside of your program to help you sort through your feelings and plan how you are going to take action.

Respond to a Child's Negative Self-Identity

What if a child's behavior indicates that she has negative feelings about one or more of her own social identities? Such feelings are wake-up calls that require action—with the children, with the families, *and* within the program. Ignoring children's denial or shame about their identities has the same effect as agreeing with their denial or shame.

Here are two examples:

> It is December and all the hoopla in the stores and in the media is about Christmas. Many of the children in your program are eagerly talking about gifts, tree decorations, and Santa Claus. You notice Sarah, a 4-year-old Jewish child, listen to the talk around her, walk away, come back and listen again. One day she announces that her family has gotten "the biggest Christmas tree ever!" and that she has "a hundred lights and toys" to put on her tree. When you ask her about this, reminding her that her family celebrates Hanukkah she says firmly "They're all Jewish. I'm not!"
>
> You realize with a shock that you have ignored the classroom Christmas buzz as "ordinary December excitement," and that you have permitted at least one child to be made an outsider who is now denying her identity.
>
> • • •
>
> Demarco and Will are washing their hands before lunch when you hear Will, who is White, say to Demarco, "Hey, the insides of your hands are white like mine." Demarco, who is African American, looks at his hands and says, "All of me is White, I just look dark."

Moments like these are sudden windows into what is going on in a child's mind. In the moment, you can clarify that you think differently about the matter. You can support and reassure Sarah, who expressed negative feelings about her identity. "Sarah, you have a warm, loving Jewish family!" You might say, "You can still like trees and lights and be Jewish at the same time." To Demarco you might say, "You know what, Demarco, all of you is Demarco, every part. Part of your skin is darker and part is lighter, and all of it makes a wonderful Demarco."

Then you need a longer-term plan:

- **Think about how your classroom does and doesn't support Sarah's social identity and the social identities of all the children in your class.** Do you have books in which all children see their families represented? Are you carefully teaching "We are all the same—we are all different" in *everything* you do? Are children playing out stereotypical attitudes or behaviors without a response from the adults?

- **Check your perception with other staff.** Ask if they have heard similar remarks from the child. Also ask them to pay attention to the child over the next few days with your observation in mind. What do they see and hear that sheds light on how the child thinks about this particular social identity?

- **Check in with the family.** Describe what happened in a tone of affection and concern for the child. For example, "Demarco and Will have just started a new friendship that seems very satisfying to both. But this week I heard Demarco tell Will he was actually White, like the inside of his hands, and that his skin only looked dark. I was concerned because, like you, I want him to feel proud and happy about his skin color." Explain how you immediately responded to the child's self-negating comments. Ask if the family have ever heard similar comments at home and welcome their suggestions for ways to work on this at school. If you sense that the family would be willing to share, ask what they are teaching their child about who he is and what, if anything, they want their child to know about dealing with prejudice.

- **Take responsibility for what happens in your program.** This is very important. It is easy to assume that children's problems all come from the home. But however unintended, the dynamics at school may be the source of the problem.

- **Listen to the family carefully, nondefensively, and supportively.** Topics of social identity are often loaded with strong feelings for families who want their children to feel strong and proud about who they are. A family may not trust your sincerity about wanting to support their child, particularly if you do not share the family's social identity that you are discussing. This means you need to listen even more carefully than usual and assume you have much to learn.

- **Make an action plan with the family.** Depending on what you and the family have observed, try to figure out together what you can do at school and what the family can do at home to build the child's self-awareness and self-esteem. Take the family's advice seriously and, where possible, use it. Talk about your ideas to support the child's identity at school. If they ask for your suggestions on follow-up at home, come up with some ideas together.

● **Assure the family you will keep them informed. Make a plan about when to check in again** in the coming weeks about what you did and how their child responded. Then, follow up!

Act on a Child's Ongoing Discomfort, Fear, or Bias

Sometimes a child demonstrates a pattern of behavior that indicates a deeper internalization of negative, prejudicial feelings and ideas about another's identities. You may notice a pattern after you have intervened a few times in incidents that looked like pre-prejudice, but the child's behavior persists. Perhaps the child continues to refuse to play with a classmate because "her skin is dark" and escalates the behavior by telling other children not to play with her or repeatedly uses a racial slur against some of the children in the group.

This is upsetting behavior to observe and it can be challenging to face. It can bring up feelings for you as well. However, it is vital that you address it thoughtfully and thoroughly. When a child is

causing distress for another child, stop the action, listen carefully, and provide comfort, limits, and explanations. Here are additional steps you can take:

● **Document the child's specific behavior.** Having written notes will help you explore what is going on for the child. Also note the contexts in which the child's behavior occurs.

● **Talk with other staff.** Check your perception that a pattern exists by talking with other staff. Tell them what you have observed and ask whether they have seen similar examples. If they have, together identify the contexts in which the child's behavior typically occurs. If they haven't, ask them to observe the child. However, it is important to follow through with your own observations and perceptions. Some teachers may be in denial that young children can have internalized prejudice at their age.

● **Think about what the child may be feeling and thinking** and what factors may be triggering the behavior you see. Keep in mind that a child's discomfort or bias may have a variety of underlying sources, such as influence of media or peers, a dynamic in your program, beliefs taught in the child's family, an unpleasant experience that the child is inappropriately generalizing, or a combination of such reasons. Consider your own program. What have or haven't you done that might be reinforcing the child's behavior?

● **Develop a draft plan of action** for working with the child at school.

● **Work with the child's family** to gather further information and finalize your plan of action.

When you notice and document a *pattern* of incidents indicative of a child's discomfort, fear, or bias, having more in-depth conversations with the family is essential. You may want to ask another teacher or the program director to join you. The goals of these conversations are to figure out *with the family* what might be behind the child's negative behavior as well as how to promote the child's own positive identity and capacity for interacting with others across various kinds of diversity in unprejudiced, respectful ways.

Remember, you are the child's *and* family's ally. You are there to support and help, not to judge or condemn. Remind yourself and the family of the program's anti-bias mission. Speak from a place of caring and thoughtfulness. Find a way to reiterate that the child is important to you as well as to the family.

- **Open up the conversation by sharing your concerns** about what is happening for the child and to other children in the group. Present this from the point of view of caring for and wanting to support the child, not as bad behavior of a problem child. Also, do not assume that the child's behavior reflects negative attitudes taught by the family. That may be a factor, but there may well be other reasons. (See Chapter 5 for addressing situations in which family prejudice is a factor.)

- **Share your observations** about the child. Be specific, providing anecdotal data. Explain the reasons for your concern.

- **Ask the family to share their observations** about the child's behavior regarding the aspect(s) of diversity under discussion. If they have seen the same pattern, how did they respond? How do they feel about the child's behavior? What do they want the child's attitude to be toward the aspect(s) of diversity under discussion? What do they think might be influencing the behavior?

- **Agree on strategies for intervention at home and at school.** Let families of the children who were the targets of hurtful, prejudicial behavior know that you are working with the other child's family. However, keep confidential the discussions you are having with that child's family.

The next chapter provides more in-depth discussion about working with families when anti-bias education and families' biases and values are in conflict.

Conversations When Community and World Issues Affect Children

Much as we all want children to live in a kind and gentle world, the reality is that almost all communities, and certainly all countries, struggle with terrible events that come from nature and from people, such as fires, floods, hate crimes, pollution, shootings, and wars. Communities and countries also struggle with people's conflicting beliefs and political struggles on a whole range of issues. These events affect everyone

directly and indirectly, and many people carry intense feelings about them. Many world and community events also intrude on and affect children's lives. Some of the children you teach are directly affected. Children who are not directly impacted still see community and world events in the media or overhear adult conversations about these issues. What do you do when children bring the effects of what is happening in the world into your classroom or program? As you know, remaining silent leaves children with no support. But what do you say? And how?

Early childhood teachers give children ways to think about what is going on through play and thoughtful discussions. It can be challenging to feel capable of acting when the subject is tied to, or based upon, bias, fear, and especially hate. Political issues, religious intolerance, racism, homophobia, sexism, and other biases should have no place in the world of young children. But they do exist, and when children hear about them or experience them, suddenly those issues are in your classroom or program.

The guidelines on the next page will help you hold meaningful conversations with children in the face of difficult events and situations.

The following stories illustrate brave conversations with children about diversity and equity issues that reflect events in the children's larger community and in the world. Each story begins with unexpected comments from 4-year-old children, raising sensitive, challenging issues. These spontaneous conversations reveal children's limited understanding of the subjects and comments they make that can be hurtful to other children. They also reveal that teachers may have strong feelings about topics the children bring up.

Guidelines for Brave Conversations with Children

Make it safe for all the children involved. As always, the first thing to do when children are distressed is to intervene and to be a safe and reassuring presence for all the children.

Find out what the children know. Without judgment, find out what the children are feeling and thinking and how they make sense of the situation. Listen carefully and reflect the children's thinking back to them. Name their feelings.

Identify and manage your own feelings about the issues the children raise. You may want to talk further with colleagues to further sort out these feelings.

Tell the truth. Clarify misinformation as factually and simply as you can: "Here's what I know about what has happened."

Give the children something to do to make it better. State the safety issues. Think about what the children need for processing their feelings as well as for clarifying the misinformation. Let the children know there are people who work to fix problems. Create ways for the children to do something age appropriate about the situation.

Talk with the families. Once a sensitive issue comes up with a few children, most of the children will hear about it in a short period of time. It's important to alert all the families about the issue (without using individual names, of course). Offer a brief explanation of what you have done to address the issue and ask families for their ideas as well.

Brave Conversations in Action

The Good/Bad President

The children are engaging in conversation at snack time. Melisande, their teacher, overhears two children:

> **Casey:** I love the president!
>
> **Saul:** I hate the president. He's a bad man.
>
> **Casey:** You can't say that! He's a good guy.
>
> **Saul:** Is not, is not.
>
> **Casey:** You're bad for saying that.

Melisande is very surprised when Casey and Saul start arguing about the president at the snack table. She's pretty sure neither child has any idea what a president does or why it's important. But they clearly know who he is and have heard someone talking heatedly about him. Several other children at the table are drawn in, all equally sure they love or hate the president and all of them convinced it is important and urgent. Melisande asks the children to take turns telling her what the president did or didn't do that they like or don't like and that she will write down their ideas. She writes them down regardless of whether their ideas are correct or incorrect. Then she asks them how they know those things. "My Momma says it," "It was on the television," or "Everyone knows that!" are some of the answers.

Melisande feels it is time for some facts. She talks a little about what a president is (avoiding the word *boss*) and that people choose someone for that position by voting. She tells the children, "Almost always, some people get the president they choose, and some don't. We are all part of the same country where he is the president. Just like at school, people's job is to listen to each other and to stay friendly." She sends a note home to the families telling them what happened and that the class is going to do some voting activities so children can begin to understand what voting is.

Melisande's reflection: The hardest part of this conversation was that I have strong feelings about the president too and I knew I had to keep my opinions to myself. I also knew that the families in our program are on all different sides of political issues, and I was afraid anything I said would offend someone. I struggled with how to make the conversation age appropriate and decided to try some voting activities with the class. This was a big flop! I realized the issue for them was aligning themselves with strong feelings from home. So, we went back to the all-important idea of anti-bias education. We are all the same. We have the same president. Grown-ups vote for presidents. We are also all different. Some of our families like the president, some of our families don't like the president. In our school it is okay have different ideas.

Bad Guys Go to Jail

In the play yard, Ariel, the teacher, observes the following incident between Elijah and Charles. Elijah is gleefully pushing several children toward a big square he has built of blocks.

Elijah: All you bad guys go to jail. Go on. Go on.

Charles: (*Crossing his arms and planting his feet.*) Will not. Will not. And my brother is *not* a bad guy.

Ariel: Whoa, let's stop this game. Charles does not want to go to jail. And remember our school rule—anytime someone doesn't want to play, they don't have to play.

This stops the action, but Ariel realizes that Elijah's statement about bad guys still hangs in the air and that Charles looks defiant and scared at the same time. She knows he is very upset about his older brother being in jail. She also knows that he doesn't like to be touched much, so instead of putting her arm around him she pulls a chair over to where he is standing and has this conversation with him:

Ariel: Charles, I know you really love your brother and he is *not* a bad guy.

Charles: Elijah is dumb. He doesn't know nothing.

Ariel: Do you miss your brother?

Charles: No! (*Storms away.*)

Ariel knows she has to work with Charles about this incident. She also needs to address the issues this incident has raised at group meeting time, but she doesn't want to focus on Charles and Elijah. She waits a bit and then tells Charles that one of the persona dolls, Pilar, has an uncle in jail and wants to talk about it at group time. "I don't care," Charles replies angrily, and then he asks anxiously, "Is her uncle a mean guy?" Ariel takes that for permission.

At group time she brings out Pilar and describes how she visited her uncle in jail. Riveted, the children are full of questions: "What did he do?," "Was he a bad guy?," "Did they lock up Pilar too?," "I wouldn't go to a jail, un huh." The class has a great conversation about why they think people are sent to jail and what they think happens in jails. Ariel clarifies their ideas where she can, promises to find out things when she doesn't know answers, and gives them words for the feelings they have expressed. She emphasizes that "the prisoners" are people, with families and friends outside of the jail. She talks about how sometimes people make a big mistake that hurts other people and how much Pilar loves her uncle and hopes he will come home soon.

When she talks with Charles's family later in the day, she assures them that she did not focus on their family during this discussion and asks them what else they wish she had said about Pilar's story. They are relieved that she did something to keep Charles from feeling shamed and ask her to help him put some of his artwork or pictures of him at play into an envelope to send to his brother.

Ariel's reflection: I don't know why I didn't expect this. A number of children have a relative or family friend in jail, so of course it's going to come up sooner or later. It wasn't too much of a surprise to me when Elijah started calling his block construction a jail. He likes to play games about heroes conquering bad guys and who has power over whom. I had been trying to work with the children about people not being good or bad but hadn't thought about the question of jails and prisons.

Anti-Bias Education for Young Children and Ourselves

I wasn't all that happy with how I handled this. Personally, I don't agree with the way folks are being sent to jail and the inequity about who ends up in prison and who doesn't. And I didn't really address Elijah's need to be a hero and feel safe by building jails. This is one of those world issues I need help thinking about in terms of helping young children to understand and to feel safe.

What If You Can't Think of What to Say?

Being an anti-bias teacher doesn't guarantee that you have ready, perfect answers to challenging and troubling topics. You have feelings and opinions too. Your life is affected by the same difficult issues with which the whole society struggles. Sometimes the words just don't come. Regardless, it is essential to not let the moment slip away. Stop the action. Make sure all the children involved feel safe. And then use phrases like the following:

- "This is really important, and I need to think about how we can talk about it."

- "I'm not sure what words to use right now. But I'm going to ask Jamal to help me, and we will all talk about this tomorrow."

- "Let's go ask Chitra to help us think about this . . ."

- "You know, when I was your age no one helped me think about this, so I'm not sure what words to use. But I'll think about this and we will talk later."

After you've made the situation safe for the children, take care of yourself. Talk with a colleague. Email a friend. Recognize that you have feelings too and need support. And be sure to follow up with the children! You may need to do some homework to get more information and to talk with colleagues about how you want to approach the topic. In addition, it is useful to reflect with your colleagues about how you did (or didn't) respond to the children in the moment and what you think worked or what you might do differently another time. Use the guidelines for heart-to-heart listening on page 33 in Chapter 2 to guide this conversation. What's really wonderful is that every time you engage in this kind of conversation, you, the children, and the families all get better at listening and talking about hard topics.

. . .

In an ABE program, teachers find themselves engaging in a variety of conversations about identity, diversity, and fairness every day. Some are between a child and teacher, some become the topic for a full-class discussion, and some become the kick-off for further curriculum activities. One of the wonderful gifts of your commitment to children is that, for their sake—for their sense of acceptance, safety, and learning—you push yourself and grow your skills every day. It is, as teachers regularly report, one of the benefits of doing anti-bias education work. Lupe Cortes, who started out as an infant and toddler teacher and is now director of a regional Head Start program, explains:

> Anti-bias work constantly pushes me to self-reflect, to do the personal work that is necessary to be the best teacher I can be at that moment. I have to ask myself, "Why is this so big for me?" I get discouraged sometimes that there is still so much work to do with myself, that I have all sorts of stumbling blocks, that the onion has too many layers. However, I end up growing from the experiences—and they keep my work fresh. There is still so much to learn, and the meaning of the work makes it worth all the struggle and risks.

Caring, open relationships with children are vital to quality ABE. Building and sustaining them takes time, persistence, work, and creativity, because there is always more to learn, to rethink, and to put into action. Be sure to identify your successes and your moments of joy and to share them with your colleagues and the families in your program.

CHAPTER 5

Building an Anti-Bias Education Program: Relationships with Families and Among Teachers and Staff

In a caring, cooperative workplace, human dignity is respected . . . and positive relationships are developed and sustained. . . . The same ideals that apply to children also apply as we interact with adults in the workplace.

—NAEYC, *Code of Ethical Conduct and Statement of Commitment*

Respectful, open, collaborative working relationships among teachers, staff, and families in an early childhood program enable ABE to thrive. When the adults are working well together, even the most complex tasks feel doable.

Building Anti-Bias Relationships with Families

The NAEYC Code of Ethical Conduct affirms that "we acknowledge a primary responsibility to bring about communication, cooperation, and collaboration between the home and early childhood program in ways that enhance the child's development" (NAEYC 2016, 11). In an anti-bias program, this responsibility is central. As Lisa Lee, a longtime leader in early childhood work with families, eloquently explains,

> Families honor us with the care of their children. Our daily interactions promote or discourage cultural pride, empowerment,

and a sense of self-worth and belonging in the children and their parents. Instead of seeing "deficits" and cultural differences as the problem, teachers who are allies with families appreciate the strengths and gifts that families bring to the children's and staff's learning experience. When we bring depth to implementing an anti-bias approach, we uphold their trust.

Your ability to engage families in ABE issues rests on forming mutual relationships with them. As families begin to trust that you care about and believe in their child, they will be more willing to open up to you about their hopes, beliefs, and concerns. Families that feel accepted and respected are also far more open to listening to you when you talk about what you are doing in the classroom and why you are doing it. The respect you show families creates the opportunity for true conversation and discussion—and for support.

You are a much more effective teacher when you understand each child's unique family. There is so much that you can learn from families: their expectations and hopes for their child, their childrearing strategies, how they handle challenging behavior, what they see as their child's strengths, and concerns they may have about their child's development. You can also learn about a child's daily routines and rituals; the family's religion and the special days and ways they celebrate; their home language; and the child's interests and how the child approaches new experiences. The more you know, the more you come to appreciate the context of a child's life and the more effective you are as a teacher.

Stop & Think: Self-Reflection About Relationships with Families

Your personal experiences of school–family relationships influence your ideas about what your relationship with families should look like and how you should connect with them. Past experiences also affect how comfortable you are interacting with families.

- What did you learn about school and family when you were a child? What did you learn about teacher authority? Were you taught that the teacher is always right? Did you ever talk to your family about problems at school? If so, what was their reaction?

- How do you want children to feel about their family's connection to you and your program?

- What experiences, skills, and personality strengths do you have for connecting and building partnerships with families? What attitudes might stand in your way? What skills do you need to develop further?

- What is your best hope for what teacher–family relationships might look like?

Like all other aspects of becoming a teacher, developing skills and confidence in your relationships with families is a step-by-step journey. There is tremendous satisfaction in establishing trust and communication and being able to problem solve challenging issues that come up in the course of the school year.

Applying Anti-Bias Education Core Goals to Relationships Between Adults

- Teachers, directors, and all program staff will develop skills and confidence to reflect on and talk about their own anti-bias journeys and about ABE. **(Goal 1)**

- Teachers, directors, and all program staff will make sure that all families are welcomed, visible, respected as a major resource of information about their children, informed about the program, and provided opportunities to contribute to the anti-bias education of their children. **(Goal 2)**

- Teachers and program directors will regularly reflect on and discuss the planning, implementation, and assessment of an anti-bias learning environment and curriculum. **(Goal 3)**

- Teachers, directors, and all program staff will develop skills and confidence to engage in courageous anti-bias conversations with each other and with families about issues related to the children and to the program in general. **(Goal 4)**

Create an Inclusive, Secure, and Supportive Environment for All Families

Depending on where you teach and the administrative and legal structure of your program, some interactions with families that create a supportive environment are the responsibility of directors and administrators or of head teachers. Ideally, the entire staff shares this responsibility. Regardless of what position you hold, a clear picture of ways to welcome, show respect for, and support families will help you bring strong school–family relationships into being. Here are some ideas teachers have developed for making all families feel welcome:

- **Share information about who you are.** Families are generally more open with you if sharing information is reciprocal. Post pictures of yourself and the staff with short descriptions of your families, hobbies, and hopes for the year. Let families know about important events in your lives.

- **Create spaces in the classroom for families** to post personal photos and thoughts. Create a family wall where each family can add information about various aspects of their lives, such as photos of the family at work or play, birthdays, births, and maps showing a family's place of origin. Post questions on the family wall and encourage family members to respond.

- **Create a comfortable space where families can informally meet.** If possible, have water, coffee, and tea regularly available. Be sure your classroom is accessible to people with disabilities.

- **Create an inclusive family library** of resources and referral materials. Set up a print or digital family resource bulletin board with information about what is going on in your classroom. Include articles for families and listings of support services and community advocacy organizations for all kinds of families and family circumstances. Create a borrowing library of family-friendly books about childrearing, early childhood education, and other topics families might be interested in learning more about. Make sure there are materials in the families' home languages.

- **Make sure the family handbook clearly states and reflects the program's inclusive approach** to all families. Acknowledge all family structures. For example, the phrase "Dear Parents" can imply that every family has two parents in the home. Use "Dear Families" or another inclusive term. If the handbook includes photos, be sure that they reflect your program's anti-bias commitment. Develop additional handbooks in families' home languages as needed.

- **Create an equitable enrollment form.** For example, replace *Mother* and *Father* with *Parent/Parents, Co-Parents, Guardians, Family Members,* or simply *Family.* Use families' and children's correct last names; children may not share the same ones as the adults filling out the forms.

- **Share your program's ABE mission statement** with each family. In addition to explaining the ABE goals of the mission statement, it is helpful to also describe some of the specific ways you do ABE activities with the children.

Learn About Each Family During the Initial Intake Interview

If someone other than teachers does the initial intake interview, be sure that the information from the interview gets to each child's teacher immediately. Teachers can then follow up with their own first conversations with families. For most families, face-to-face conversations are more effective than written questionnaires. Ask the family about their hopes for their children and their expectations of the early childhood program. Find out what behaviors they consider most important in their children. It's also useful to find out who the child thinks of as family (e.g., does it include grandparents and cousins) and what terms the child uses for each person.

Keep in mind that families will vary in how much information they choose to disclose to you at the beginning of the school year. Some information may feel too personal or unsafe to share. For example, a family that has one or more undocumented immigrants may be fearful of deportation if the school has too much information about them. Family members may not want to disclose their sexual orientation. If a family chooses not to answer a specific question, let it go for the time being. You can return to the topic after you have built a trusting relationship with the family.

Find and Promote Common Ground with Families

As a teacher, you already share the most important common ground with families—wanting to foster their child's development and learning. To build on that common ground, look for ways to create dialogue with each family, where you listen and learn as well as talk. Some families are at ease talking with teachers and are comfortable raising issues of concern about the educational program. Some families, at least initially, wouldn't consider raising issues of concern, much less challenging a school policy or a teacher's practice, because they believe that a teacher is to be respected and obeyed. Most families experience teachers as being in a position to judge their child and their parenting, rather than as partners in fostering their children's development and learning.

When you speak regularly with each family, it makes an enormous difference to share their child's progress and talents and not just problems that arise. When families hear that you like their child, care about what is happening to their child, and make the effort to talk and connect with them, it builds trust.

It is important to talk with families in their home language. There is always a way to do this, although it may take effort on your part. Some strategies include hiring staff members who speak families' home languages, asking another family member who speaks English to translate (it's usually best not to ask a child to interpret), recruiting community volunteers, or using a language translator app. If you do not speak a family's language, make an effort to learn some words and phrases in that language to help the child and family feel welcomed and to model that learning is for everyone—even the teacher!

Use Varied Communication Methods with Families

The more frequently you chat with each family, even for a brief time, the more your relationship will grow and the more effective you will be as a teacher. You may find, as many anti-bias teachers have, that the

relationships you develop with families are one of the great joys of your work. Here are some ideas teachers have found effective for communicating with families:

- **Engage in frequent, short, informal chats with families** at children's drop-off at the beginning of the day and pickup at the end of the school day. Be sure to pass on information from these conversations to the rest of the teaching team who are not there at the times families come in. Some families will want to engage in small talk together to get to know each other; others will be more interested in talking with staff about their child. You can talk with all of the children's families every couple of weeks through phone conversations, texts, or email. For families who don't have a phone or email, it's even more important to make time for face-to-face conversation at drop-off or pickup times. You can also write short, friendly, notes to send home with children.

- **Hold regular family–teacher conferences.** These are useful, more formal ways to talk with families about what their children are learning and doing, but they are not sufficient as the only or primary way to communicate. Most programs schedule these during specific times in the school year. In addition, a teacher may call a family conference about a specific concern. It's important to invite all the people involved in parenting a child to participate, and it can help to let families know ahead of time what you would like to discuss so they can be thinking about it.

After greetings, state the reason for meeting, such as the concern you have about a child's behavior or development, and then ask family members questions that will help all of you understand the situation better and develop some plans. Does the family see similar behavior with the child at home? In what situations? What do they do? If a behavior happens only at the program, what may be causing that? What suggestions do they have? Listen carefully to the answers. Then raise your ideas about what may be happening and what you might do, and ask for their feedback Encourage input and perspectives from each person involved. *Spend as much, if not more, time listening as you do talking.* If a conflict comes up about what to do, use the Acknowledge, Ask, Adapt strategy described on pages 70–71.

- **Make home visits.** When children first start in your program, a home visit can be a wonderful bridge of familiarity and safety for the child. The purpose of these visits is to connect with the child, not to evaluate or judge the family. During these visits children share information such as their favorite toys, where they sleep, the family pet. This begins a one-on-one connection with you that helps the child and the family begin to trust you. Some families may feel uncomfortable meeting in their home, so be open to meeting the child and family at a park or some other location the family suggests.

Reach Out to and Include Families in Anti-Bias Education

The idea of ABE will be new to most families. It's important to let families know from the beginning that you consider the four core anti-bias goals to be a fundamental part of your program. Nothing will support anti-bias learning for a child as much as their family supporting the same goals.

Invite families to join you in thinking about and implementing the anti-bias goals with the children. Listen to their ideas and use that information to help plan activities. You might have a program-wide meeting to focus on what the goals are, what they mean, and how you use them to develop plans for the children. Share with families the anti-bias issues that come up in children's play and keep them informed about how you build curriculum around the topics.

Send home children's work with an explanation about the purpose of the activity and what their child did or said. Let families know about the children's anti-bias learning during informal conversations, in class newsletters, and through posted documentation in the classroom.

Encourage Families to Engage in the Daily Program

Find ways for family members to interact with the children in daily activities. Be sure to reach out to male family members, many of whom want to be engaged but are not sure how or have not been invited or made to feel welcome. Family members can read with the children or teach them everyday words in their home languages (e.g., *mother, father, grandparent, baby, milk, toy, bed, play*). They can tell stories about family experiences or share specific skills like cooking a favorite dish or fixing a car. Ask if they are interested in making learning materials for the classroom, such as puzzles that use photos of the children. Find out what other ideas they may have for interacting in the classroom. Document all of these experiences by taking photos; share the photos with families by email, on your classroom's secure webpage, or on a family bulletin board.

Involve Families in Thinking About and Planning Anti-Bias Topics and Activities

As you introduce and work on anti-bias issues with the children and get to know families, invite family members to share their ideas with you. What do they want their children to know about who they are (talents, personality, interests) and who their families are (race, ethnicity, beliefs)? What do they want their child to know about people who are different from their family? How do they teach their children to handle hurtful moments and slurs about who they are and who others are? In addition, invite all the families to meet as a group to discuss their ideas and feelings about children's identities and attitudes toward others. In a group discussion, people have the opportunity to hear different perceptions and may be more open to communicating their own. Don't worry if only some of the families come. If they find the meetings useful, they may encourage other families to come.

Help Families Connect with Each Other

As you become more experienced and as families get to know you as an anti-bias educator, activities such as the following become wonderful times of community building that can have a lasting effect.

- **Hold family get-togethers and potlucks.** Shared meals are wonderful occasions to help families connect. Use some of the Stop & Think questions in this book to help families get to know each other and to guide in-depth discussions among families.

- **Offer targeted discussions.** Plan small discussion groups around specific topics families express interest in, such as multiracial families, nonsexist parenting, or name calling among children. As each family provides their own perspective, these discussions build further connections among people.

- **Consider group activism.** In programs with established anti-bias curriculums, families sometimes take on community projects or other activist efforts related to their children. One group of families decided to meet with the toy stores in their neighborhood to present an alternative list of quality children's toys and books that countered classist, racist, and sexist stereotypes. Families at another center traveled by train with their children and the teachers to the state capital to meet with their legislator about the importance of bilingual education for all children. In a third center, families took an interest in a national campaign to limit advertising of products during children's television programming.

When Some Families or Staff Disagree with Anti-Bias Activities

Even among families who fully support ABE, disagreements may arise over a specific topic or strategy. How you handle a disagreement is even more important than whatever solution you come up with. The following example demonstrates a teacher listening carefully to a family's concerns, showing genuine interest in their ideas and their dreams for their child, and respecting their perspective. Even though the father's concern differed from the teacher's, her anti-bias approach opened the door to finding a productive solution.

> Cecilia, a family child care provider, notices that the older boys are playing roughly with the babies and toddlers. Her response is to plan a "Taking Care of Babies" curriculum, which includes a visit from a father showing the children how he diapers his infant son and feeds him a bottle; reading books such as *William's Doll* (Charlotte Zolotow); and setting up opportunities for the children to bathe dolls. When Oliver's dad arrives to pick him up, he is very upset to see Oliver cradling a doll. His father is adamant: "No son of mine is going to play with dolls!"
>
> Cecilia responds that she will honor his request but would like to better understand why he feels as he does so that she and the family can work together. Oliver's dad reluctantly agrees to come back and meet with her. At the conference, Cecilia listens carefully as the father shares that his own dad roughed him up as a child for "not being tough enough" when he was bullied at school. He is very fearful that Oliver might be similarly bullied. As Cecilia carefully listens, Oliver's dad begins to feel that she really understands how much he loves his son and how much he wants to protect him.

At this point, Cecilia explains her curricular objectives: to teach Oliver to play more gently with the little ones and to help prepare him to become a good dad someday—goals the father agrees he can support. With some mutual understanding and trust established, the two agree that it is okay if Oliver cuddles and pretends to feed stuffed animals instead of dolls.

Adapting is a balancing act, whether between teachers or between a teacher and family member. Cecilia sees the solution she and Oliver's father agreed to as a step in the right direction. She knows that changes in attitudes take time. Even though the agreed-upon solution is not what she would have preferred, the respect she built resulted in the father being far more open to her anti-bias work on gender in the months that followed.

To find solutions to disagreements with families, you need to figure out what you are willing to change and what you are not. You also need to determine the line between what is workable and what could hurt the child or the program. For example, it is relatively easy and painless to grant a family's request that their child keep his shoes on even though you allow children in your program to take off their shoes. On the other hand, if a parent says, "I don't want my child to be around the Spanish-speaking children," agreeing to the parent's request would harm children's emotional and cognitive well-being and conflict with basic principles of honoring diversity and of anti-bias education.

Acknowledge, Ask, Adapt: Facing Conflicts About Anti-Bias Issues

Acknowledge, Ask, Adapt is a method for engaging in discussion and generating solutions when disagreements arise. Such disagreements might arise between teachers, between teachers and staff, between teachers and families, and among families (Derman-Sparks 2013). Engaging in the Acknowledge, Ask, Adapt process is both an intellectual and an emotional experience in which the participants create fresh understandings and solutions. It requires people to be willing to enter into dialogue with respect for each other and a willingness to learn (Derman-Sparks, LeeKeenan, & Nimmo 2015).

The Acknowledge, Ask, Adapt strategy rests on the principle that problem solving requires self-reflection and open, nonjudgmental listening to other people's perspectives. The goals are that neither party wins or loses; rather, each person is heard, does some shifting, and participates in creating a new solution. One of the satisfying surprises of facing and working through disagreements is how much less energy is spent avoiding the issue and feeling irritated and how much closer people become as they learn to trust each other and work together respectfully.

There are three objectives of this strategy: to identify and clarify the common ground among the participants; for the program to show responsiveness to cultural practices; and to find a solution that still aligns with your program's anti-bias mission. Here are the steps in this process:

Step 1: Acknowledge

- Acknowledge to yourself that a cultural or values clash exists with a family member, a family, or a colleague.

- Communicate your awareness to the other person(s) that a problem exists and needs attending.

- Avoid becoming defensive or making a quick judgment about what underlies the conflict.

- Engage in self-reflection, examining your own feelings. Be clear about your own values and position on the issue shaping the conflict. Ask yourself, "Am I willing to solve this conflict or do I just want to do it my way?"

Step 2: Ask

- Collect information that will give you a better understanding of what underlies the conflict. Talk to the parties involved and to any others you think can provide additional information.

- Ask questions such as these: Why do they feel as they do? What is at stake for them? What would they like to do? Listen carefully and repeat what you have heard.

- Respectfully share your perspective and hoped-for outcomes without describing them as the way experts do things or the only right way to act.

- Make sure that everyone is heard and then clarify the key points in the disagreement.

Step 3: Adapt

- Consider the information gathered in the Acknowledge and Ask steps.

- Look for and identify where you and your colleagues or a family have common ground. Listen to alternatives from all who offer them, and then consider the ideas.

- Consider regulations your program must adhere to, although you might decide that a long-term action is to try to modify a particular regulation. Also consider current staffing and material resources and what else might be needed.

- Agree to try a new solution—and do so!

Adapting what you are currently doing and creating new practices is a balancing act. Sometimes, after engaging in the Acknowledge, Ask, Adapt process, you may not be able find a solution that honors the different perspectives on an issue. One option is to agree to continue exploring the issue at another time. This works if you do not have to come to a decision about what to do right away. A second option is to agree to a temporary solution and reopen the discussion after a trial period.

Find a Third Space

The Acknowledge, Ask, Adapt strategy opens the door to a "third space" solution. Seeking a third space calls on each party in a conflict to first understand the other's position and needs and then to use this new knowledge and empathy to craft a *brand-new*

solution that works for all parties. This is an alternative to one person winning and one person losing in a conflict and to both parties agreeing to a compromise where everyone gives in a little but no one quite gets what they think is right. The third space concept is especially desirable for disentangling and resolving differences in cultural perspectives and anti-bias values. It calls on everyone's creativity and openness to generate a solution (Derman-Sparks, LeeKeenan, & Nimmo 2015).

When a Family's Wishes Conflicts with Anti-Bias Values and Goals

Sometimes figuring out a solution using the Acknowledge, Ask, Adapt process does not seem possible. For example, you may work with a family who requests actions that directly violate anti-bias values. Here are some examples:

> "I do not want my child sitting next to or playing with any Arab children."

> "I don't want Kelly thinking that a family with lesbian or gay parents is a real family. Please don't say that."

> "I don't want my daughter playing with a Black doll. I know she's only 4, but that can lead to interracial dating and marriage."

> "I think it's a waste of my children's time hearing stories or songs in Spanish, so I don't want these activities in the classroom. We are an English-speaking country."

> "You need to make sure that child with cerebral palsy doesn't get more of your attention than Ethan."

How you handle requests or comments like these depends to some extent on your role in the early childhood program. In some instances, the lead classroom teacher or the program director may need to be part of the discussion with the family. The easiest (and often most tempting) response is to assert immediately that "in this classroom, we encourage all the children to sit and play with everyone, and we respect all kinds of families. If this is not acceptable to you, then you can decide if you want to take your child to another class or program." While this bottom-line approach ultimately might be necessary, *it is not the way to begin.*

An anti-bias commitment calls on us to respect others enough to open up conversations about bias and prejudiced behavior in ways that respect the individual or family who raises the issue, optimize the likelihood of finding some common ground with the family, and possibly encourage more open attitudes.

Invest some time and energy with the family. Find out what factors precipitated a family member's comment. Listen carefully and with an open heart. Remember that none of us is free from bias. Sometimes bias is based on a lack of—or incorrect—information. Sometimes a negative experience is overgeneralized into bias against a whole group. Sometimes a lack of validation in the person's own life contributes to a strongly held prejudice. Remember also that some people use ableism, racism, sexism, or another ism as an outlet for their own frustration, anger, and fear. These factors do not make the bias acceptable, but recognizing their influence can help you see the whole person and not just the biased behavior. So listen deeply.

Share with the family why you think it is vital to children's healthy development and future life success to develop comfortable and respectful interactions with all kinds of people. Engage the family in exploring their concerns about how ABE may change their child. Remember that this is a dialogue, not a monologue; make sure that family members have ample opportunity to express their views and that you are open to learning from their views, just as you are hoping they will learn from yours.

Talking with a family about their prejudiced views and discriminatory behavior may not always end in agreement. Some people will not want to talk; some, even after a number of conversations, will hold fast to their original stance. When this is the case, the bottom-line approach is appropriate: "We will not allow prejudice and discrimination in our classroom. If this is not acceptable to you, we can help you find another program for your child." Then it is up to the family to decide what they want to do. If it becomes clear that a family cannot stay in the program, it is important that the director help them identify other resources in the community and handle their departure as respectfully as possible.

Building Collaborative, Anti-Bias Relationships with Colleagues

As an ABE early childhood educator, you need other people who can help you work effectively—to help you think, laugh with you, share your struggles with you, show you new ways of thinking, and celebrate small changes. You can't do this work alone. You have a responsibility to establish open, respectful, and collaborative relationships with your colleagues and others in the early childhood education field.

Meet Regularly with Colleagues

In the best of worlds, all program staff members meet together regularly to talk about anti-bias issues as they relate to the children, themselves, and each other. These meetings are opportunities for teachers to share ideas, to discuss what has been effective and what needs work, and to plan what comes next. Many directors include some information about anti-bias principles and practices at each staff meeting.

Since it is an important part of being an effective anti-bias educator, creating time for staff to be together to talk must be a priority. There are a number of ways to do this. One program includes funding for staff to meet one Saturday morning a month. Another approach is to hire part-time staff to cover nap time so teachers can meet during that time. Some programs have a biweekly half day for the children, which allows time for planning and staff development. Still another approach has been for school district offices, social services offices, or community colleges to offer monthly equity and diversity discussion groups leading to in-service or college credits.

Anti-bias topics at teacher meetings vary. Sometimes an individual teacher or team presents a case study. A group might engage in heart-to-heart conversations (see page 33) using the Stop & Think questions in this book. Sometimes the group discusses a previously assigned reading about ABE to jump-start working on a new anti-bias topic. The group might plan together how they will address a specific anti-bias topic. Ideally, a whole staff takes on the journey of integrating anti-bias goals into their work.

Many individual teachers, however, find themselves having to do anti-bias work on their own with just the children in their class. If this is your situation, it is essential for you to find at least one other person with whom to regularly reflect, share ideas, and assess your work. You may find another teacher in your program who is also committed to ABE. There may be another student in your anti-bias college course who shares your passion. Perhaps a colleague outside your program is as committed as you are to the importance of children learning to live with strength and skill in a diverse and inequitable world. With this person, take turns raising issues and problem solving. If you can't meet in person, communicate by phone or email. Just be sure to make that support a regularly scheduled part of your work life.

Notice How the People in Your Program Treat Each Other

Early childhood educators are not immune to the power dynamics endorsed in society. Staff members earn different amounts of pay, are given different tasks to do, are provided more or less of a voice in decision making, and are offered more or less access to professional learning and respect. In addition, there is always diversity among the people who work

in any given program. However well-intentioned the members of a staff may be, deep-seated biases and prejudices have a way of seeping in to work relationships. Learning to work respectfully with your colleagues requires you to consider how social identities impact your interactions.

To reflect on your interactions with colleagues, ask yourself the questions in the Stop & Think below. Consider whether you do the listed actions frequently, sometimes, or rarely. Next, focus on those you answered with *rarely* and plan for how you will move to *sometimes* and eventually to *frequently*. Reflecting on these questions and making plans for improving your practice should be an ongoing effort throughout the school year.

Stop & Think: How Do I Interact with Others on the Staff?

- Do I treat all staff—teaching assistants, teachers, the program cook, the staff who clean, the director, and others—as important contributors to the program?

- Do I treat others respectfully, recognizing and appreciating their cultural styles and belief systems? Do I ask about, openly talk about, and appreciate the differences between us? Do I model open and respectful listening?

- Do I model and encourage colleagues to share all responsibilities regardless of any gender stereotypes among staff?

- Do I recognize my own discomfort or biases I have about any specific aspects of diversity? Do I work on overcoming these feelings?

- Do I constructively talk with other staff about any actions that I think undermine respect for diversity? Do I support our efforts to identify biases and change practices that do not encourage fairness?

- Do I work with others to find ways to ensure a diversity of skin colors, languages, gender identities, abilities, and family structures among staff at all levels?

- What did you learn as a child about dealing with disagreement and conflict? Have you developed other ideas as an adult?

- When a conflict arises with a colleague or a family member of a child in your program, what are your first emotional responses?

- What techniques do you use when you find yourself in a situation of disagreement or conflict over what to do as an early childhood professional? The disagreement might be about a child, a specific activity or part of the curriculum, or an area of ABE you think is important.

- What kinds of disagreements or conflicts are more difficult for you to address? Why do you think that is so?

- What techniques would you like to be able to use in situations of disagreement or conflict?

. . .

Treat Disagreements and Conflicts as Opportunities for Growth

The Acknowledge, Ask, Act process described in this chapter and the guidelines for heart-to-heart conversations described on page 33 apply to staff relationships as well as family relationships. Conflicts and disagreements about practices and ideas are inevitable given the diverse perspectives of staff and families as well as societal events and viewpoints. However, an anti-bias learning community is open to embracing and handling this complexity.

Conflict is a productive part of the learning process. The disequilibrium created by conflict is a prelude to sharing information and solving problems, creating opportunities for people to expand and shift their perspectives and behaviors. With this in mind, ABE leaders can embrace conflict as a healthy dynamic in the pursuit of change (Derman-Sparks, LeeKeenan, & Nimmo 2015).

Collaborative, trusting working relationships with families and among colleagues require time, effort, and persistence to develop and sustain. Remembering the vision of what you want to accomplish provides the energy for applying anti-bias goals to your work as a teacher and to your program. Taking time to periodically assess your work with your colleagues and to plan further activities improves and sustains your program. Successes and moments of joy are concrete examples of your best hopes becoming a reality—so celebrate them!

CHAPTER 6

Fostering Children's Cultural Identities: Valuing All Cultures

At group time, Britta's teachers play the country music CD that Britta brought to her Head Start class. When her mom, Beth, comes to pick her up, one of Britta's teachers returns the CD to Beth. Looking a little embarrassed, her mother explains that she hadn't realized Britta had taken the CD to school. "But, Mom," says Britta, "that's my Culture Share." The teacher chuckles and explains that she encourages children to bring things from home that reflect their daily life. "We call it 'Culture Share,'" she says, "and we all enjoyed listening to the music that Britta loves."

• • •

A new child, Bashar, has recently come to the United States with his family from Pakistan. He speaks some English but never responds to questions addressed to all the children during circle time or snack time. The teacher is concerned and asks his mother if Bashar is shy or afraid. The mother says, "Bashar isn't shy! He is polite. He is waiting for you to call his name before he speaks."

Cultural identity is fundamental to how people live, speak, and interact in the world. Beginning in infancy, everyone forms a cultural identity in the context of their families. As young children move into the larger world, such as early childhood programs, they

encounter the dynamics of cultural diversity. They are faced with learning how to interact with people who operate with differing cultures. By the time children are preschoolers, they also begin to become aware of and absorb positive or negative attitudes toward their own and others' cultural identities (Ramsey 2015).

Children's evolving cultural identities and awareness of cultural diversity intertwine as they grow. Early childhood educators can do much to support individual children's cultural identities and help them learn about cultural diversity and fairness. Supporting children's cultural identities is the focus of this chapter, and the next chapter continues the discussion by focusing on working with children to learn about cultural diversity and fairness. You'll benefit most from first reading and digesting the content in this chapter before going on to the next, because fostering children's healthy cultural identities strengthens their learning to respect cultural diversity and fairness.

Anti-Bias Education in Action: Every Child's Family Culture Matters

Rosie Quintero operates a family child care home. She has thought a lot about how to help children in her program feel that they belong, that they are at home even when away from their own homes. One of her approaches is to ask each new family to tell her about some of the child's favorite foods and how they are cooked in their home. On 3-year-old Devyn's first day, she serves him a familiar, favorite dish at lunch. She also tells Devyn that his mother told her how to make it. Devyn went home that day and told his dad, "I like Rosie's house. It smells right!"

Applying Anti-Bias Education Goals to Cultural Identity and Diversity

- Children will show pride in their family's cultural identity, language, ways of practicing daily life, traditions, and heritage. **(Goal 1)**

- Children will comfortably use their home culture knowledge and home language within their early childhood program. **(Goal 1)**

- Children will feel that they belong and are valued, whatever their home culture. **(Goal 1)**

- Children will develop the skills to thrive in the culture of the school and in the larger society. **(Goals 1 & 2)**

The Big Picture: Culture Is Who You Are

When you honor all children's cultural identities and incorporate them into the daily life of your program, children come to understand that they are safe and welcome—just the way they are. When you value cultural differences while appreciating the similarities everyone shares as human beings, you create a foundation for children to thrive in a culturally complex world. To effectively support children's and families' cultural identities, teachers need to strengthen their understanding of the characteristics of culture.

Everyone Has a Culture

Carol Brunson Day (2013), an internationally known expert on the central role of culture in children's development, identifies six essential elements that make up a culture:

- Culture is a set of rules for behavior.

- Culture is a characteristic of groups.

- Culture is learned.

- Individuals are embedded, to different degrees, within a culture.

- Cultures borrow and share rules.

- Members of a cultural group may be proficient in a cultural behavior but unable to describe the rules. (6)

The concept of culture includes many rules and beliefs about behavior: about how members of the culture eat, sleep, talk, play, care for the sick, relate to one another, think about work, treat the elderly, and remember the dead. Culture also encompasses the religion or spirituality people practice, or not, and the clothing, housing, food, rituals, and holidays with which they feel most comfortable.

One very important aspect of every culture is how children are raised. Through everything they do, families communicate their cultural values, beliefs, rules, and expectations to their children. Children bring to their early childhood programs the knowledge, language, and behaviors they have been learning since birth. These are their tools for interacting with, understanding, and navigating the world around them. A fundamental part of fostering children's cultural identities is to enable children to use the cultural knowledge they bring to school as a valued tool to build their competence and sense of self in that setting (NAEYC 2019).

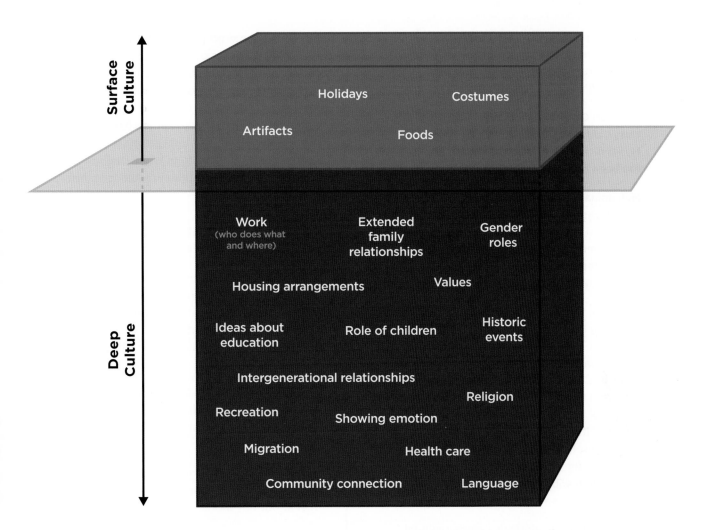

Surface Culture

Holidays Costumes

Artifacts Foods

Deep Culture

Work (who does what and where) Extended family relationships Gender roles

Housing arrangements Values

Ideas about education Role of children Historic events

Intergenerational relationships

Religion

Recreation Showing emotion

Migration Health care

Community connection Language

Teachers also bring their cultural knowledge to the early learning setting. They continually navigate their own cultures (how they were raised), the cultures of their early childhood education programs (such as the expectations of developmentally appropriate practice), and the cultures of the families in their programs. The more you understand the specifics of your own culture, especially as it relates to raising and teaching children, the more aware you can be of the family cultures children bring to your program.

Striving to integrate these various cultures in your work can be complex and confusing at times. It is also, however, a rich source of fascinating new experiences and learning. Being open to learning about and respecting each child's culture empowers your teaching, gives meaning to children's experiences in your classroom, and provides support to the families who have entrusted you with their children.

Culture Has Many Elements

It is easy to think about the exterior expressions of culture—things that you can see, taste, and identify. This is called *surface culture* and includes household objects, foods, music, art, and holiday traditions. However, encounters with deep culture are how you learn about and honor who people are. *Deep culture* includes individual and family interactions, behaviors, beliefs, and values that are directly and indirectly observed. (See the diagram above.)

Cultural Identity Is Dynamic

While everyone has a cultural identity, the way they define that identity and their way of living within their home culture and the larger culture varies from person to person. People's cultural identity is likely to be connected with other aspects of their social identities, as noted by these educators:

Peggy: I'm Black, and that's both my racial identity and my heritage. My culture is Black, rural Arkansas, with more and more California city girl thrown in.

Jennifer: Culturally, I identify as working class Californian. I guess I'm also White. My ethnicity is a mystery to me. My family has been here forever. I am a US citizen.

Mohammad: I identify as Iranian, and American, since I was born in Los Angeles. I speak both Farsi and English. I am also a member of the American Arab Anti-Discrimination Committee, a national advocacy organization. That's another important part of my identity.

Christina: My father's family lived in the Tucson area long before it became part of the United States. He called himself Mexican American. When I was in college, I began calling myself a Chicana (much to my father's annoyance!). Later, as I began to feel connected with other groups of people from throughout Latin America, it felt more natural and accurate to call myself a Latina. I'm not sure how I feel about the new term Latinx. It sounds strange to me. But I understand why people would look for a word that isn't gendered.

An individual may identify with a specific cultural group without embracing *all* of its aspects. For example, a person may identify as Jewish yet not attend a synagogue. Another may identify as Mexican American yet not speak Spanish. Some people may also identify with specific elements of more than one cultural group. A person may deeply treasure their childhood culture but decide that certain aspects of that culture are no longer useful or were hurtful and decide to raise their child with other values or behaviors. For example, as one early childhood education student explained,

Respect was important in my traditional Indian family. For my parents it meant children could not have a different opinion from an adult or speak up for themselves. I want my children to respect their elders, but I also want them to know their ideas matter too and that their dad and I will always listen.

Culture also evolves as people adapt to new environmental or economic situations, as new generations modify their childhood beliefs, and as people encounter ideas from other cultures. It is essential to learn how people define their own cultural identities rather than make assumptions based on stereotypical ideas about a cultural group's way of life. Remember that children from White families also have family cultural identities in addition to their racialized social identity.

Stop & Think: Understanding Your Own Family Culture

- When you were growing up, what values were most important for your family about your behavior at home and in the community? What mattered to your family about your behavior as a girl or a boy?

- What were your family's expectations and rules for adult–child relationships and teacher–child relationships? Which expectations do you still agree with?

- What messages did you receive from your family about money? Being on time? Speaking up in a group? How did they feel about questioning accepted ideas?

- To what extent did you feel that your family culture aligned with, or was significantly different from, the larger society, and in what ways? How did you feel about that?

- In raising children of your own, what values, behaviors, and attitudes from your family of origin have been or would be most important to you to pass on—or to not pass on?

Young Children Construct Ideas and Attitudes About Cultural Identity

Long before children are aware of or have words for what they are doing, they internalize a profound sense of rightness and familiarity with the particular way the people in their family behave (Day 2013). This sense of "how it is" lies at the core of the child's evolving positive self-concept and cultural identity.

Cultural Identity Begins at Birth

From the beginning of life, infants absorb their families' culture. How the family talks, sounds, touches (and doesn't); the tones of voice they use to express love, comfort, displeasure, anger, and other emotions; how they comfort each other; how individuals sleep, eat, dress, and bathe; and how the family's language sounds are all part of each child's cultural learning. During the preschool years, children begin to sort out which practices are flexible (noisy play is okay at one relative's house but not another's) and which ones are absolutes (spitting at someone is never okay). These messages about what is and isn't acceptable are rarely simple.

Language Is a Fundamental Part of Cultural Identity

Long before children can speak, they begin to absorb the language(s) they hear at home, including tone, pronunciation, and the patterns of conversation. Language becomes a critical skill for navigating the world and for providing deep feelings of connection and identity. Even when their home language is the same as that of the dominant culture, most children encounter different communication styles and sometimes other languages when they become part of groups outside their families. This causes not only a linguistic shift but also a shift in the child's sense of self, connection, and identity. For children who speak a language other than English at home and are dual language learners, it is often a major shift. This affects not only their identity but also their connection to their family and their long-term capacity for learning (see "Language Matters: Nurturing Dual Language Development" on page 84).

An anti-bias approach to facilitating dual language learning includes finding ways to support children's home language as an essential component of integrating home cultures into your program. It also asserts that the development of bilingualism is important for *all* children who are growing up in an increasingly multilingual world. In sum, a welcoming, affirming, anti-bias learning environment makes visible all languages and supports bilingualism as an important aspect of cognitive and social and emotional development (see "Additional Resources for Working with Dual Language Learners" on page 86).

Cultural Continuity or Discontinuity

Young children feel that the way their family does things is natural and normal. They bring that feeling with them when they enter your classroom or program. They also bring rules and tools for being in the world that they learned from their families. Should children look the teacher in the eye when they talk to him? Should they call the teacher by her first or last name? Should the child wait for the teacher's explicit invitation to use a toy or material or plunge right in? How should children respond to conflict with another child?

When the practices you use in your classroom—talking, encouraging, comforting, guiding, explaining and reinforcing rules of play, choosing food for snacks and meals, napping, handling peer conflict—are similar to what a child's family does, the child experiences *cultural continuity* and a sense of competency and safety. In contrast, children experience *cultural discontinuity* if the practices in your program differ from those in their home culture.

While most children experience some degree of cultural discontinuity between home and school, for some the gap is enormous. Children who come from the dominant cultural group are most likely to find a high degree of home-to-school continuity, and thus to feel most at home, because the curriculum, materials, and teacher interactions in most early childhood programs reflect dominant culture norms. The children know how to act and can use the tools they have learned for being competent in the world. This continuity supports their positive feelings about their home culture and therefore about themselves.

However, other children experience cultural discontinuity—some so much so that their early childhood setting undermines their sense of competency and security. Some children feeling cultural discontinuity may withdraw from classroom activities, not participate in conversations with classmates or teachers, or exhibit behavior that puzzles teachers.

> A 3-year-old child, new to the program after spending time in a refugee camp, went outside to go to the bathroom. When the teachers showed him the toilets and told him he needed to use them, he simply stopped urinating at school. His bladder would get so full that his stomach ached, but he persisted. The staff was careful to not shame or judge him, and after talking with the family they arranged for an older brother to introduce the child to the sounds and processes of the bathroom at school. A few weeks later, the issue disappeared.

It takes thoughtful, sensitive support to help children develop strategies for maneuvering worlds that are disconnected. In such programs, children learn and thrive because they "feel supported, nurtured, and connected not only to their home communities and families but also to teachers and the educational setting" (NAEYC 1995, 2).

Dominant Culture Attitudes and Children's Cultural Identities

Forming one's cultural identity is not simple in a diverse society such as the United States. How teachers and families help children manage contradictions between home and school cultures has a profound effect on children's development.

Invisibility of children's home cultures in their program's visual images and materials undercuts their evolving sense of self and social identities. Invisibility also conveys a message that there is something unimportant or even wrong about the family and therefore about the child. *Visibility* of a child's culture, in contrast, conveys the message that the child and the family are "real" and that they matter. How you treat children's family members also conveys either positive or negative messages. These behaviors can be overt or subtle (see the discussion of implicit bias on page 11 and microaggressions on page 13).

Over time, some children may begin to feel ashamed about their home culture in response to how an early childhood program manages cultural discontinuity. Some may reject their home culture, wanting to act only like the dominant culture, which may include refusing to continue speaking (and developing fluency in) their home language. In contrast, children whose family culture is more congruent with the school culture may come to believe—often at a subconscious level—that the way their family does things is the real, right way. They may begin to think of unfamiliar family cultures as distressing, strange, undesirable. Such feelings, backed by prevailing societal biases, can turn into prejudice.

Families trust that the ways you interact with their children—the things you choose to teach, the behaviors you foster and those you work to change—will support their children's growth and help them succeed at school. At the same time, they expect that you will not create a divide between their children and the family's way of living and their cultural identity.

Stop & Think: Building Your Capacity to Foster Children's Cultural Identities

- What experiences have you had in which the way you and your family did things was not acceptable to a school, hospital, employer? What was that like for you?

- Which specific beliefs from your own cultural background about working with children are most important to you? Which aspects of the early childhood education culture in the United States are most important to you?

- What skills can you bring to adapting your principles and beliefs to home cultural beliefs that are different from your own?

- Which early childhood education culturally based practices are you unwilling to bend or adapt?

Curriculum Guidelines for Nurturing Children's Cultural Identities

This section describes a set of guidelines for implementing learning environments and curriculum that enable children to use *both* their home and school knowledge for learning. Teachers who create learning environments that incorporate and build on children's home cultures promote children's healthy social, emotional, and cognitive development and academic achievement. This principle is vital to the healthy development of children's cultural identities and to their appreciation of differences and similarities among people. "We shall care for and educate children in positive emotional and social environments that are cognitively stimulating and that support each child's culture, language, ethnicity, and family structure" (NAEYC 2016, 9).

Begin with Families

As you consider your classroom environment and the experiences you provide for children, keep in mind that for young children, cultural identity and diversity exist in the context of their home cultures—not in abstract cultural groups. When young children enter any early childhood setting, their circle of experience widens beyond the cultural rules and practices of their own family. This happens in many ways. At home they may play with older siblings and cousins while at school they play only with children close to their own age. At home they may nap on the couch snuggled with their cousin, with the television on and busy family life all around them, while at school they must nap alone on a cot in a darkened, quiet room. They may speak a language at home that no one knows at school. They may not be familiar with some of the learning materials in the early childhood program and may need permission and assistance to use them at first. They may expect to be cued when it's their turn to participate in a discussion rather than speak up spontaneously.

Teachers and families have a common goal. All want children to be secure, happy, and able to learn and succeed in their school lives and beyond. Yet too often, both groups feel judged by and anxious about the other. It is important for teachers and families to develop mutual respect—with families recognizing that teachers may well know more about children in groups and children's development in general, and with teachers recognizing that families know far more about their child in particular. Both types of knowledge are necessary for children to flourish. As a teacher, it is part of your professional responsibility to build this type of relationship with families and to reassure them that you are on the same side they are.

Learning about the rules, traditions, and expectations of children's families is a process, not a one-time interaction or interview. When you develop meaningful relationships with families, they can help you create classroom environments and approaches that are culturally consistent with children's experiences at home. Equally important, you can help families learn the necessary skills of negotiating differences between the home and school cultures.

Explore Ways Families Are Both the Same and Different

Each child's family culture and every family is in some ways both different from and the same as every other family. Here are some ways you might explore this with children:

> **"In your house children watch a video before bed, and in Micah's house children listen to a storybook."**

> • • •

> **"Tomás asked for una manzana, and Xion asked for an apple. You both wanted the same thing!"**

> • • •

> **"Aramaan's father isn't wearing a bandage around his head. It's a special headdress called a turban. He wears it every day. It's part of his family's beliefs."**

> • • •

"You went to the gay pride parade with your family this weekend. Mai and her family spent Sunday at a church picnic. And I was at home making playdough! We all do such interesting things on the weekend!"

Always avoid putting the spotlight only on children whose cultural backgrounds differ from the dominant culture or from the rest of the class. Children whose family cultures are different from the majority of the children in a class are in a vulnerable position; they may not want to be different from their peers. Find ways to make learning about these children's families part of learning about *every* child's family.

Use Families' Home Cultures to Individualize Your Curriculum

A fundamental principle of developmentally appropriate practice is that decisions about curriculum, environment, experiences, interactions— every aspect of the early childhood program—must be considered within individual children's social and cultural contexts (Copple & Bredekamp 2009). This, along with providing experiences that are appropriate for children's ages, individual abilities, interests, and developmental levels, ensures that learning is meaningful and respectful for each child and family. Individualizing the curriculum requires striking a balance. In the example below, the teaching staff devised a plan that was both responsive to the family and consistent with the principles of their early childhood program:

Two sisters, ages 3 and 4, have moved frequently with their mother as she looked for work. The program they attend, like many centers, has separate classes for children of different ages. Day after day, the older child keeps coming into the younger child's classroom. Each time, the teacher sends the older child back to her own classroom. The reason, their mom explains when the teacher asks, is that the older sister has always watched over the younger one as they moved from one unfamiliar place to another. Neither girl, the mother adds, feels safe when the two are separated. After brainstorming together, the teachers from both classrooms agree that the older child may join the younger

one at specific times during the day and whenever the younger sister asks for her.

By using information about the children's home culture to individualize its age-based policy, this program went a long way toward reassuring the family, who had no friends or family in the community yet. The decision also helped the girls adjust to their new setting.

Carol Brunson Day shares an example of creating a new way to set up nap time in an infant and toddler program that incorporated elements of how families cared for their children:

Licensing rules require that children nap in their own cribs. However, some of the babies, whose families are from Southeast Asia, sleep in hammocks at home, and they will not go to sleep in the cribs. So the staff get creative. They tie hammocks diagonally from the crib posts. The result: The infants sleep and licensing requirements are satisfied, because the infants are still "in the cribs."

This program's solution worked for everyone because the teachers were able to provide what the infants were used to and comfortable with while still meeting the licensing requirement. Each child was indeed in a separate crib. And the licensing agency could see the advantage of allowing the infants to sleep in a way consistent with their families' practice that was still healthy and safe.

As Carol Brunson Day notes, ultimately, it is vital to understand that

We can learn principles for creating culturally consistent programs. However, there is no recipe for being there. The "there" is built by you with families and staff. It is always a dynamic process and depends on the people who are together in a program at any given time. It calls on everyone to be willing to negotiate and compromise if necessary. If you stay open to the fact that your way is not the only right way, trust in the ability of people to figure out differences, and really work on it, you can get to where you want your classroom to be. When everyone has access to deciding on a solution that works for them, then there is real equality.

Anti-Bias Education for Young Children and Ourselves

Support Children from Immigrant Families

with Luis Hernandez, early childhood education specialist

Most early childhood programs include children who are members of families who are new immigrants. Their families have come to the United States for multiple reasons and from all over the globe. They represent multiple economic groups, religions, experiences and expectations, and diverse languages. And they are here, members of communities and early childhood classrooms. Teaching and caring for these children with respect and skill is a fundamental responsibility for early childhood teachers.

A study of immigrant families in several US cities found that they often feel a mix of hope and apprehension when they enroll their children in early childhood programs (Adair & Barraza 2014). Their concerns "can be connected to disparaging and discriminatory comments and attitudes circulating in the larger society about immigrants and immigration. In addition, some teachers have limited experience with or education about the immigrant communities they serve" (32).

Although the impact of cultural discontinuity is considerable for all children, for those in new immigrant families the impact is more intense and has more potential to damage the relationship between children and their families. Consider that the word *familiar* is based on the word *family*. When the world young children find themselves in is *unfamiliar*, where they make their way for the most

part without their families present, think how hard it must be for them to trust their own perceptions, to feel competent and sure of their capacities.

The following strategies can help support children and families who are immigrants:

- **Nurture a sense of welcome, belonging, and safety.** Showing children that you care about and want them in the group is even more fundamental to your role than teaching specific content, including English. Counter negative attitudes toward immigrants in media, other children, and elsewhere. Not feeling safe and cared for undermines children's learning. Immigrant parents often mention hugging, comfort, and patience as most important for their children before they talk about learning (Adair & Barraza 2014).

- **Help children feel competent by building on the strengths they bring—but do not overwhelm or rush them.** Intentionally and sensitively work to identify each child's funds of knowledge, interests, and skills. In addition, give children time to open up at their own pace. Be patient and encouraging, giving children time to learn. Do not label a child as having a lack of intelligence and ability for not yet speaking English easily or for being reserved (Adair & Barraza 2014).

- **Use instructional strategies and materials that specifically support dual language learners.** Make learning visual and hands-on. Narrate what you are doing and what the child is doing so he hears the connections between a new language and what he sees, feels, and does every day. Make it comfortable for children (and families) to take the risks of learning a new language. Model correct use of language rather than correct a child's language mistakes while he is speaking; you risk interrupt the child's thinking and can make the child wary about using the new language.

- **Stand up for honest assessment.** Identifying where a child is in her development and learning yields accurate results only if assessment is carried out in the child's languages (NAEYC 2005). Assessing a child in a language she does not know is, by definition, an inequitable and therefore inaccurate vision of the child's skills and understandings.

- **Make a special effort to welcome the children's families and help them feel that they also belong.** As much as possible, make connections with other families in your program or in the community who speak the families' language and can help you communicate with them. Set up an initial meeting in a place that is convenient and comfortable for the family, such as a place of worship or a community organization that supports immigrant families, and bring someone who speaks their home language if you do not. Talk about what their child will experience in your program and listen to what the family has to say about their child. Find out what their child enjoys doing and learning, and ask how things are different in the United States from what children experience in their country of origin (Adair & Barraza 2014). Encourage family members to come to your class with their child for the first few days so they see how your program works.

- **Learn about the dreams families have for their children.** Hoping to create a better life for their children is one of the most consistent and strongest motivations for people to immigrate to the United States. Acknowledging this can start an ongoing series of conversations with families about their children and home cultures.

Language Matters: Nurturing Dual Language Development

by Laurie Olsen, founding director of SEAL (Sobrato Early Academic Language Preschool–3 Initiative)

Young children are linguistic geniuses—their brains are wired to acquire language, absorbing the sounds and rhythms of the language(s) that surround them. By the time they arrive in your program, they have spent years soaking up language, developing vocabulary, learning to pronounce and form the sounds of their home language, and internalizing the language's structure and use. They absorb the sounds, words, and structure of that language from the songs and stories of their families, the intimate loving murmur of grandparents, and the negotiations and play with siblings. By age 2, they have an emerging competence to understand and label their world and express what they need and want in their home language. That language is both functional—used for communicating—and emotional and personal—deeply entwined with thought, culture, and identity.

When they enter an early childhood program, young dual language learners—children who are learning their home language and English—are exposed to a broader world, a place beyond their home and family. Children who enter English-only programs must leave their home language at the door. Their world disappears. Despite your warm smile and reassuring touch, they find themselves in a place in which their language, their means of communication and understanding, has no relevance, no power, no function. It is profoundly disorienting. Children experience a loss of self, resulting in disequilibrium and invisibility. How you respond and support them as they face this significant transition has a profound impact on their long-term language development, their sense of belonging and identity, their future educational trajectory, and their relationship to their family and culture.

In the United States, everyone needs English. It is the language of school, commerce, political participation, and access to other systems. Every child also needs the language of her home, heritage, and culture to maintain relationships and connection and develop a strong identity. Mastery and ownership of both languages, therefore, is essential. And a strong grasp of the home language is the best foundation for developing strong English skills (Burchinal et al. 2012; Cárdenas-Hagan et al. 2007). Many view bilingualism as a great benefit for everyone; it is linked to stronger executive function, increased social interaction, strengthened literacy and academic outcomes in both languages, and greater economic opportunities (National Academies of Sciences, Engineering, and Medicine 2017).

- **Learn how the child's family thinks about the role of teacher.** Families bring a range of ideas about and experiences with teachers. Do not make assumptions about how the families you serve think regarding a relationship with their children's teacher. Instead, as you get to know each family, talk with them about their experiences and hopes for relating to teachers, and share the kind of family–teacher role you hope to achieve with them. Over time, figure out a relationship that meets both your needs and the family's.

- **Connect new immigrant families to each other and to other families in your program.** It is important for people to know that they are not alone, that they have allies to help them learn to negotiate life in a new country. Ask family members of other children to familiarize new immigrant families with community resources, such as the library, parks, medical help, and immigrant support advocacy groups. Bringing new immigrant families together also allows them to connect and help each other.

Children have the capacity to learn two languages simultaneously. This reality contradicts the myth that simultaneously learning two or more languages confuses children and is detrimental to their development (Paradis, Genesee, & Crago 2011). In fact, considerable research concludes that simultaneous development of a home language and English is the strongest approach to fostering dual language learners' linguistic, cognitive, and social and emotional development (National Academies of Sciences, Engineering, and Medicine 2017). Devastating rejection and loss of the home language often occurs when young children are in English-only programs, with clear long-term negative consequences for family relationships, cultural connection, identity, and academic success (Oh & Fuligni 2010).

Wherever possible, dual language learners should be in early childhood programs in which both their home language and English are actively affirmed, engaged, and supported—where there are bilingual adults who talk to them, read to them, and model language for them and where they can develop increasing competence in both languages (Cummins 2001; Cummins & Early 2011). This is not always possible, however. Many programs do not have staff who speak the languages of all the children and

their families. But every program can find ways to make room for a child's language, actively affirm that language, support the child's connection to and exposure to his home language, and help him develop pride in his bilingualism. Early childhood educators must recognize the urgency and stakes if they fail to provide this support.

Supporting dual language learners' linguistic development and identity can only be done in partnership with families. Teachers must find ways to communicate with families in their home languages. Every program can also express the importance of maintaining children's home language while learning English and support families' efforts to do so. Because families' desires for their children to learn English can be so strong, and because there are still lingering damaging effects of harsh English-only policies in the United States, teachers are an important source of clarification and information about supporting children as *dual* language learners (Ovando 2003).

Early childhood educators must act with clear intentionality. During the early childhood years, children's linguistic capacity is open and receptive. Whether children learn shame or pride in their bilingual capacity is very much in the hands of their educators.

Address Differences Between Home and Program Cultures

The field of early childhood education has its own set of beliefs, values, and acceptable behaviors—in other words, its own culture. Some aspects of the field's cultural convictions about what children need do not necessarily match what is valued across all cultural lines. Developmentally appropriate programs must consider not only a child's age group and individual characteristics but also the social and cultural contexts in which the child lives (Copple & Bredekamp 2009). "Children's learning is facilitated when teaching practices, curricula, and learning environments build on children's strengths and are developmentally, culturally, and linguistically appropriate for *each child*" (NAEYC 2019, 13, emphasis added).

Here are examples of practices commonly found in early childhood programs in the United States that may conflict with the practices of some cultures. As you learn more about each child's home culture, you will find that some early childhood practices must be adapted or rethought. Respectfully consider how you might incorporate elements of families' cultural practices into your own teaching. When you cannot incorporate certain aspects, you can still respectfully acknowledge that "this is the way we do it at school and that is the way you do it at home. There are lots of ways to do things."

● Early childhood practice tends to promote children's independence, autonomy, and initiative. However, in some cultures it is important for the adult to first model how to perform a task or how to use materials before children put their own ideas into action. Families who share this cultural value want their children to become competent and develop their own gifts—but believe this is best done by learning to use materials carefully.

● Many early childhood teachers acknowledge individual children for their efforts and achievements as a motivation technique. However, some cultures emphasize the importance of *inter*dependence among peers and do not agree with singling out one child for praise, as if that child's activities existed outside of the group. In this case, families want their child to learn and achieve—in order to contribute to the *group's well-being* as well as the child's own.

- Early childhood practice tends to focus on individual rights. For example, if one child is using a toy and a classmate also wants to play with it, teachers often set up a schedule of turns or help children come up with a solution. However, some cultures feel strongly that learning to share with others is far more important than a child getting his own way—and some families may prefer that teachers have the two children play together right away, instead of waiting to take individual turns.

- Teachers usually expect a child to speak directly to them, look them in the eye, freely ask questions, and express their thoughts or desires. However, some cultures expect children to wait for the adult to acknowledge them before speaking and to be thoughtful about what they say. These families want their child to feel safe and assured around adults—but to also be respectful according to their family rules.

- While early childhood programs are more attuned to dietary needs than in the past, they may not be aware of food traditions and practices that are important to a family. A family might not eat meat, might avoid dairy in the same meal as fish (tuna salad can be a problem), or might eat with the right hand only. Ask families about their wishes and also find out if there are special behaviors expected around toileting or sleep.

Each of these examples asks you to think about ways to incorporate and respect family cultural beliefs *and* remain true to the foundational principles of developmentally appropriate curriculum. These are both/and opportunities, *not* either/or choices. They require finding ways to incorporate and blend different perspectives. (Review the Acknowledge, Ask, Adapt strategy and the search for a third space on pages 70–72 in Chapter 5.)

. . .

Children learn best when they feel safe, valued, and that they belong. This requires honoring their cultural identities. Making the children's family cultures visible and integrated into your daily plans is essential. It is also necessary to honor the *diversity* of cultures in your program. The next chapter discusses this subject. No matter who people are, how they speak, their place of origin, or their way of living, together you are a community.

CHAPTER 7

Learning About Cultural Diversity and Fairness: Exploring Differences and Similarities

At snack time, 4-year-old Colin announces that he got shampoo in his eyes when his dad gave him a bath last night. Molly looks puzzled and says, "Daddies don't give you a bath. Mommies give you baths." Miriam adds, "My mommy and my big sister give me baths." Miguel adds that in his family, "We take showers, not baths." Tiffany joins in too: "My nanny scrubs my hair."

If you look for diversity, you will see it everywhere! Even when all or most of the children appear to come from the same cultural group, there are differences within the group. For example, the children in a classroom may all be White but come from different economic classes and family structures. The program may serve all Latinx children, but their families come from different parts of Mexico or Central America; they may have different religions or hold different attitudes about discipline or respect.

While human beings share basic needs—everyone laughs, cries, eats, works, and plays—they do these things in different ways. Support children's understanding of culturally different ways by intentionally weaving the theme "We are all the same; we are all different" throughout your ongoing curriculum. Highlight that both similarities and differences exist: All people eat, but they eat different foods; all babies are carried, but they are carried in different ways; all people sleep, but they sleep on different things.

Anti-Bias Education in Action: Everyone Gets Scrubbed!

After listening to the children's spontaneous conversation about who takes baths and who takes showers, the teacher joins the conversation. "It sounds like everyone's family gets scrubbed! That is an important way families take care of children. In some families daddies bathe the children; in some families mommies bathe the children. Sometimes grandparents or brothers or sisters help keep you clean. And in some families you get clean in the shower, in some it's in the bath, and in some you use a washcloth at the sink. Isn't that interesting!"

The next day the teacher engages all of the children in talking about how they get clean and who helps them, and together they make a chart showing all the different ways families take care of getting scrubbed.

The Big Picture: We Are All Cultural Beings

As discussed in Chapter 6, everyone has a culture. Culture is what gives each person the rules and tools for living and acting in the world. And, while children the world over accomplish the same tasks as they grow and develop—like learning to walk, communicate, and interact with others—the way they meet these developmental tasks happens in the context of the rules and tools of their family's culture. For example, cultures differ in the way adults support children's efforts and when they expect children to start and achieve a developmental task. Also, certain behaviors that are acceptable in one culture may not be in another.

Young Children Construct Attitudes Toward Cultural Ways of Living

As they form their own cultural identity, young children also begin to become aware of other cultures. When they enter an early childhood program, many young children meet peers from families quite different from their own. Even if their classmates come from similar cultural backgrounds, each family will not live in the same way. How the important adults in their lives feel and act about cultural differences deeply affects children's attitudes toward cultural diversity. It also affects their construction of their sense of self in relation to others.

Discovering Cultural Differences

Young children intuitively feel that the way their family does things is natural and ordinary and right. When they encounter people who behave or speak in unfamiliar ways, they may be curious, confused, or wary.

> "Teacher Marisa," calls Mia loudly from the playhouse. "Abby says you got to go to bed if you're sick. I want to lay on the couch with a blankey and she says 'NO.'"

> • • •

> Darik looks carefully back and forth at the family pictures the teachers have posted on the wall. In a puzzled voice he asks, "How come Robin and Jackson don't have no grandma in their house?"

> • • •

> It's a hot day and the children have taken off their T-shirts and shoes and socks and are playing in a plastic wading pool. Tam, fully dressed, sits next to the pool pouring water in and out of cups. Jada frowns and says, "Tam, take your shoes off and come on in!" "No," says Tam. "Mama says I will get sick if I don't stay dressed warm."

Children are also often confused when they learn cultural identity terms and try to figure out who belongs in each ethnic and cultural group and what characteristics define each group. They make comments and ask questions such as these:

> "Lupe can't be Mexican. She doesn't speak Spanish!"

> • • •

> "Are we Jewish? Josh says we can't be 'cause we have a Christmas tree."

> • • •

> "Is this my Black blood or my Japanese blood?" asks Kenji, who is biracial, as he stares at his skinned knee.

Absorbing Stereotypes and Fears About Differences

As young children try to figure out human differences, they also begin to learn stereotypes and attitudes about other ethnic and cultural groups. Children may begin to fear, often at a subconscious level, people who live differently than they do. Such ideas can grow into powerful prejudices—especially if the messages from the dominant society reinforce them. These messages may convey invisibility, misinformation, or explicit biases.

Clarifying conversations (see Chapter 4) provide accurate information and are one necessary strategy for interrupting a child's development of a bias. Here's an example:

> Jane's mother, Ann, tells one of the classroom teachers, Meagan, that Jane has said she doesn't like Erlinda, a Salvadoran teacher, because Erlinda "talks funny and is too dark." Ann reports that she explained that Erlinda is from a country where many people have dark skin and that Erlinda is learning English. She also told Jane, "I like all of your teachers, and I want you to like all your teachers, too." Jane listened but continued to insist that she didn't like Erlinda. Ann tells Meagan, "I don't know what else to do!"
>
> Meagan suspects that Jane is uncomfortable because Erlinda is different from anyone else the child knows. She talks with Erlinda and Ann, and together they develop a plan to help Jane learn more about Erlinda, both at home and at school. That night, Ann talks to Jane about El Salvador and shows her some picture books about the country. Jane seems interested.
>
> In school, Erlinda talks to Jane's snack group several times about her life, showing them photos and objects from her daily life in El Salvador and in the United States. Ann follows up by inviting Erlinda to their home for a meal. This plan works. Both Ann and Meagan notice that Jane feels more comfortable interacting with Erlinda.

The second example describes a child's learned bias that hurts another child. It also illustrates the impact of societal biases on young children.

> Margaret, who is 4 years old, refuses to play with Mariam, who wears a traditional Muslim headscarf. "Go away, you no-good Arab," she yells. Mariam backs off, looking first surprised and then near tears. Their teacher immediately intervenes. She puts her arm around Mariam and hugs her, then firmly says to Margaret, "That is a hurtful and unfair thing to say to Mariam." Margaret insists, "My dad told me not to play with her. People who wear scarves all over their head are no good and will hurt us."
>
> The teacher puts her other arm around Margaret and says, "Margaret, in our classroom everyone plays together. I have a different rule than your father. I don't think the same thing he does about people who are Arab." Margaret looks uncertain, and the teacher adds, "I'm going to talk with your father about our different ideas and rules. Right now, Mariam is feeling very sad about your words, and I'm going to read a book to her. You may join us if you want." Margaret looks confused and turns her back on the teacher. The teacher quietly asks another teacher to check in with Margaret and then takes Mariam by the hand. "Mariam, I am so sorry that Margaret said such an unfair, untrue thing to you. I'll remind her again that in our classroom we take care of each other and do not leave anyone out."

This teacher chose to support Mariam immediately because she was most concerned about the hurtful effect of Margaret's words and behavior on Mariam. The teacher also planned to get in touch with Margaret's parents later that day. She knew from previous conversations with them that they had strong prejudices toward certain groups of people. After school, the teacher phoned Margaret's parents, briefly related what had happened, and described how she handled the incident. She set up a time for a conference with them to increase her own understanding of what was behind the family's bias and to discuss the anti-bias principles and practices used in her classroom and in the program.

The teacher also met with Mariam's family. At that meeting, she explained what had happened and how she had responded, and she asked them to let her know if Mariam showed any further distress. In addition, she shared ideas for educational activities she planned to do with all the children to share accurate information about Muslims and about Arab American people, which might help them to resist stereotyping. She assured the family that she would not put the spotlight on Mariam but rather would use children's books and persona doll stories (see pages 44–47) to accomplish her objectives. She also made clear that she would monitor any further incidents and continue to support Mariam.

Strategies and Activities About Cultural Diversity and Fairness

Here are several strategies to plan longer-term activities to support children's exploration of cultural differences and similarities and to address specific misinformation and early biases and fears—pre-prejudices—that children show about specific cultural issues or groups. These ideas and activities were gathered from ABE teachers working in a range of settings. Use them as they fit your ECE program, and adapt them to the specific realities of the lives of the children you teach. Planning activities based on what you know and learn about the children, their families, and their communities is most effective. Remember that fostering children's learning to be comfortable with the ways people are different and the same goes hand-in-hand with nurturing children's own cultural identity development, as discussed in Chapter 6.

Weave the Theme "We Are All the Same; We Are All Different" Throughout Your Learning Environment

This basic concept in anti-bias work is a useful tool for teachers to use in their interactions with children.

- **Infuse comments about human sameness and differences as teachable moments arise throughout the day.**

  "All the children are painting, but you each made different pictures."

  "Everyone at the table wanted a drink with your snack, but some of you liked the orange juice and some wanted water."

  "We all have words for people and things we love, but we have different words and some of us have different languages."

  "Santiago wants to play firefighter, but Matias wants to cook in the restaurant. You both want to play, but you want to play different things."

- **Create a family culture shelf.** Every two or three weeks, invite a different family to put special objects on the shelf that represent who they are. Place the shelf high enough that the children won't take down the objects but low enough for them to easily see. A little bulletin board behind the shelf will let families put up snapshots. Over time, make sure to ask each of the children's families to participate. A good way to start is to have one of the children's teachers do the first display as one example.

  Each time a new family shelf is set up, take a picture with the child next to the shelf. At circle time, ask the child (and a family member if possible) to talk about what the objects are for and how they matter to them. The family shelf activity is interesting to children and one effective way to help families learn about each other.

Build on Teachable Moments

Here is an example of how one teacher built on a child's comment about nap time to explore the different ways children nap with their families.

As the children get ready for nap time, Ivan says, "At home I get to sleep with Grandma. It's nice. She keeps me safe from dragons." Krista, in the cot next to him, responds with feeling, "I'm big! I sleep in my own room. *I* don't need nobody to keep me safe!" Rafael adds, "I don't like dragons. And I don't got a grandma."

Teacher Nathan quiets the children, saying only, "It's nap time now and not time for talking. There are no dragons here, and I'm here to keep you safe." But it is clear to him that he needs to address three topics—grandmothers living with families, children sleeping with others, and dragons and other scary things that make children anxious when they go to sleep.

Nathan discusses this with his coteacher. They plan a curriculum theme called "Everyone Sleeps" that might last several weeks depending on the children's interest. That afternoon Nathan adds to the library corner several books that show families sleeping in a variety of settings and ways.

At group time Nathan asks the children how many of them sleep with someone else in their room or in their bed and makes a chart of their answers. He keeps the tone of the conversation exciting and interesting as they discuss many ways that people sleep. When he asks whether the class should make their own book called *We All Sleep,* the children enthusiastically agree and eagerly dictate their own sleep stories over the next few days.

With the help of some family volunteers, they collect pictures from magazines showing families of different cultural, racial, and economic groups sleeping in many settings and glue them into the class book as illustrations. Throughout the book the adults print the phrase "We are all the same. We all sleep! And we are all different. We sleep in different places and with different people." The children love the book because it contains their stories and their friends' stories. This study of sleeping also opens a new discussion about fear of dragons or monsters, which leads to another curriculum plan and more conversations.

Learn About the Many People in Children's Families

Talking with children about their families is a good place to start when exploring similarities and differences. While the structure of families within and across cultural groups varies greatly, all families carry out similar tasks.

- **Make a display of the people in children's families.** If possible, borrow or take photographs of all the people who live with or take regular care of each child, even if some people do not live with that child. Do not second guess or correct the child. Be open and sensitive to the fact that some families may not have or be willing to share photos of family members. Engage the children in talking about the similarities and differences in their various families. Make no judgments about which kinds of family are better, and do not accept judgments from children. Emphasize that families of all kinds take care of children.

- **Make a class book titled *Our Families* for children.** Make a page for each child *and* each teacher. Include who lives with them and the ways different family members and people beyond the family's household take care of them. Include the terms children use to name their various family members. For example, Kaito's page might say: "This is Kaito's family. He lives with his dad and his grandma. His aunt and uncle sometimes take care of him, too. Kaito's dad cooks dinner for Kaito and puts him to bed. Kaito's grandma brings him to school and works as a secretary. A dog named Yori lives with Kaito and his family." Discuss with the children the many different family members who take care of them and the various names children use for their family members. Make copies for the children to take the book home to share with their families.

- **Read children's books about families that reflect the ethnic and cultural groups in your class.** *Always* use more than just one book about a group. Talk about the differences and similarities between the lives of the children in the books and the lives of the children in your class. For example, read *Who's in My Family?,* by Robie H. Harris. Ask the children what they eat for breakfast. You can also use books with animal families, like *Goodnight Moon,* by Margaret Wise Brown. Ask the children who they think the "little old lady" in this story might be. Who puts the children to bed in their own families?

- **Tell persona doll stories.** Have the dolls' stories support the many kinds of families in your program and provide opportunities for the children to continue to explore similarities and differences among families. For example, you might ask, "How is Luisa's family like yours? How is her family different? Isn't that interesting!" See Chapter 12 for more information and guidance about discussing diversity in family structure.

Learn About the Many Ways Children's Families Speak

Children can understand that even though languages sound different, they all serve the same basic purpose of communication. At this age, children easily learn new words and phrases in languages other than their home language. This is not only fun but conveys the message that hearing accents and new languages is interesting rather something to be afraid of. All children are growing up in a multilingual world, and they can all learn respectful ways to interact with people who speak a different language or speak English differently than they do. It is never acceptable for children to tease or make fun of someone about how that person speaks.

The following activities can also be done in programs where everyone speaks only English by introducing words spoken by other people in the children's larger communities. None of the suggestions requires you to know another language well, although it does help, and learning a second language as an adult will give you a wonderful way of connecting with families who themselves are learning English. Even if you are monolingual, you can model your delight in and comfort with the many ways humans communicate. Ask the families and staff in your program, or people in your community, to help you with the languages you don't speak. It not only supports you as a teacher, it tells children and families that you respect and honor their culture.

- **Learn common words and phrases** that preschool children typically use in their daily communication, such as *hello, friend, I like it, please,* and *thank you.* Start with the different home languages spoken by the families and staff in your program. Learning even a few words models your respect for and enjoyment of the many ways people speak. Ask friends or staff who speak other languages to teach you how to sing a simple song in those languages. A preschool teacher asked the children's families to help her learn to sing a favorite song, "Where, oh where, is our friend [child's name]? / Way down yonder in the paw paw patch," in English, Spanish, Croatian, Russian, and Japanese. The children would call out the language they wanted her to sing and would then sing with her, adding their names in the appropriate place.

- **Make a poster and a book titled *The Words We Speak,*** featuring four or five words children commonly use and what they are in their home languages: names of family members and pets, classroom words (*story time, let's play, snack time*), common objects, days of the week, and so on.

- **At snack time, refer to foods in more than one language.** Ask families to help you learn the words they use at home.

- **Be sure that the labels you use in the classroom (*dramatic play, blocks, art table*) are written in the languages children speak.** Show children examples of different writing systems, such as English, Chinese, Arabic, and Cyrillic.

Learn About the Many Ways Children's Families Eat

Anti-bias education programs practice openness and flexibility about the food served for meals or snacks. This means finding out what families want their children to eat for snacks and meals and what they do not eat for religious, health, or other reasons. Asking children to eat only foods with which they are not familiar—or worse, those foods they are forbidden to eat—is hurtful.

> In one program, several children's families had recently arrived from Southwest Asia. Rice was central to their diet, and they were used to eating it every day. Without rice, the children felt hungry—even though other food was available. The cook in their early childhood program felt that cooking rice every day was too difficult and argued that she could serve it only two times a week, as she was used to doing. Feeling strongly that rice be available to the children every day, the program director purchased an electric rice cooker to make it easier for the program cook to make rice. Some of the children in the program objected to having rice every day, but the teachers remained flexible and encouraged the children to eat something else that was offered if they didn't want rice.

Inviting children to try the foods of other families' culture may seem like an easy way to teach about cultural diversity, but it can backfire. Many young children are not open to new foods. Invite, but do

Showing Respect for a Dual Language Learner

I used to go in early [to the center] to pick up Amanda-Faye [my daughter] so I could stay to observe. . . . One day I decided to stay for story time. Mohammed, one of the teachers, was reading a book and mispronounced some of the words. When the preschool-age children started giggling, he put the book down gently and said, "I want to tell you that I come from a country called Iran, and we speak Farsi there. English is my second language, and many of the words are difficult for me. When I make a mistake and people laugh at me, it hurts my feelings. It's okay if you help me say them right."

He was so gentle in his delivery. From the look on the children's faces, I could see that they understood. From then on, when I would hear Mohammed reading and making a mistake, I would also hear the children say, "Mohammed, that's not the right way. This is how you say it." Then he would thank them for their help. I realized that it didn't matter that I was born in America and still mispronounced words. I decided to try Mohammed's technique with adults and children and found that it really generated respect and understanding.

Adapted, by permission, from L.I. Jiménez, "Finding a Voice," *In Our Own Way: How Anti-Bias Work Shapes Our Lives* (St. Paul, MN: Redleaf, 1999), 32–34. ©1999 by Linda Irene Jiménez.

not force, children to try new foods. Help them understand that sometimes children and adults like new things and sometimes they do not. Intervene immediately if children make fun of other children's food or call it yucky, explaining that it is hurtful to make fun of the food another child likes. Teach them to respectfully say, "No, thank you. I don't want any today."

Learn About the Many Ways Families Sing, Dance, and Make Music

Play music from the cultures in your community and from children's home cultures at movement and dance times and for relaxing at rest and nap times. Make this music available to children at other times as well. To make sure that the music is what the families actually sing and listen to, ask them for suggestions. Choose songs that reflect concrete aspects of life that interest young children: food, families, adventures, funny stories. Gather a collection of rhythm instruments used in children's home cultures. Sharing music not only helps children enjoy other cultures, it also contributes to building a sense of community in your classroom.

Every Culture Has Important People and Heroes

Children thrive on stories about heroes, past and present, who have made and are making important contributions to society. Begin with the people closest to the children's lives and families. Find out who the children in your program think of as their heroes, which will likely include family members and people in their neighborhoods who help their families or who join with others to improve their community. Here is an example of a simple story you might share:

> **At story time the teacher told the children about Rhea's mom. Rhea's family lived where there were no parks or playgrounds. So her mom talked to many of the other people who lived near them and got them to write lots of letters and to go to meetings to talk with the people who made decisions about parks. And now . . . they are going to build a park right near Rhea's house!**

Children also love to hear about heroes in the larger society. When discussing well-known people, be sure to select those from diverse groups across races, ethnicities, genders, physical ability, and classes. Tie their contributions to children's interests and everyday lives. For example,

> **"Maria Montessori was a doctor and a teacher, and it was her very good idea to have chairs and tables that are just the right size for you to use!"**

> **"Dolores Huerta works hard to help farm workers and their children have better homes, food, toys, and education. She tells everyone if they work together, they can make the world a better place."**

> **"Stevie Wonder is a composer and singer. He is also a person who is blind. He has made many people happy with his music. He wrote a special birthday song for Dr. Martin Luther King Jr., and now many Black families sing it on their children's birthdays."**

Learn About Cultural Diversity in the Larger Community

Once you have established a classroom culture that honors the diversity within your class or program, you might decide to add learning opportunities about people in ethnic and cultural groups in the broader community. Focus on cultural groups with whom the children are most likely to interact. Know the ethnic and cultural backgrounds of people who make up the children's wider community, including the people they may regularly see on television (who become part of their world).

- **Find out children's ideas about people** in their larger community whose cultural identities are not represented in your classroom. Show the children pictures that accurately portray people from that culture and ask questions like these: What do you know about this person? What do you think this person eats? Where do you think this person lives? Where does this person sleep? Does this person have a family? Do you know people who look like the person in this photo? Based on what you learn, plan a series of activities to counter children's mistaken ideas and to teach them accurate information.

● When possible, **invite individuals to your class to tell stories** about their lives and to join in activities with the children more than once. You might also interview people and make a class book or wall about them. Connect with a teacher in a local high school and see if her students will read to or do other activities with the children. Ask the high school students to make a video about their neighborhoods that includes interviews with local leaders from various places in your community.

● **Read children's books about cultural groups that are present** in your larger community or visible in the media. Put together a selection of accurate, up-to-date books about children and families from the community group you are introducing. Look for books that discuss everyday themes that children can relate to, such as getting together with family friends, visiting the doctor, and welcoming a new sibling. Help children identify similarities and differences between the child in the story and themselves. Ask them, "What did you like about the story?," "What is the child doing that you like to do?," "What is different from what you do?," and "How is the child's family [home, bedtime ritual, etc.] the same as or different from yours?" Focus on current life in the United States (unless the children travel back and forth between the United States and their home country on a regular basis; then look for stories that show both).

Including Holiday Activities as Cultural Events

Family celebrations and/or holidays are part of nearly all families' cultures. Some of these events reflect the religious beliefs of the family or the traditions related to life events, such as births, birthdays, coming-of-age celebrations, weddings, and deaths. Some reflect historic events connected to the family's ethnicity (e.g., Mexican Independence Day on September 16; Lunar New Year in late January or early February). In addition, families from diverse cultural traditions

participate in US holidays (Independence Day on July 4, International Women's Day on March 8, Memorial Day on the last Monday in May). However, *how* they participate in these celebrations varies. Some families may not celebrate holidays at all, although they have family celebrations and gatherings on a regular basis.

As noted in Chapter 3, secularized or commercialized versions of holidays are not culturally or religiously neutral. While some families within the Christian tradition see Christmas trees and Santa Claus as "just fun," others, even within the same tradition, see them as a pagan appropriation that trivializes one of their two most important holy days of the year. For many families of other faiths, the activities are inseparable from the underlying religious meaning of the holiday.

Other designated holidays reflecting dominant culture traditions—and often included in early childhood program activities—may include beliefs or practices that are not shared by all families. For example, celebrating Mother's Day and Father's Day, in the traditional narrative, recognizes just one type of family. Most early childhood education programs serve a wide range of families, and many differ from the one-mother and one-father family structure. Both the NAEYC Code of Ethical Conduct and the ABE approach make respecting family diversity a cornerstone of quality early childhood programs.

As discussed in Chapter 3, it is helpful to have a holiday policy for your class or program to provide a context to make choices about holiday activities for the children in your class.

Criteria to Consider for Choosing Specific Holidays as Learning Activities

Remember the difference between learning about a holiday and celebrating a holiday discussed in Chapter 3. If you choose to include learning about holidays in your curriculum, look for ways to include at least one holiday observed by each family, without holiday activities taking up too large a portion of your curriculum. The following questions can help you decide which holidays to honor in your program:

- Which holidays matter most to the children's families and the staff in your program?

- What underlying beliefs are central to the holiday? Is it a sacred or holy event, a historic or secular event, or a rite of passage (such as a birthday, wedding, or memorial)?

- How many families celebrate a specific holiday—all, some, none? What are the different ways the families celebrate that holiday?

- Which holidays could present problems to any of the children's families or the staff in your program, and why? What will you do if a problem arises?

- Thinking in terms of their development, what can be wonderful about the holiday for children? What might be difficult for them? What, specifically, do you want the children to learn from the holiday(s) you choose to bring into the curriculum?

- To which of the four anti-bias goals would you connect the activities?

Respect All Families' Holiday Traditions and Their Specific Ways of Celebrating—Or Not Celebrating

Respecting the cultural diversity among the families you serve means recognizing that all have the right to their traditions. It is hurtful to children and families to impose the holidays of one group on all the children and staff, or to make the holiday traditions of some groups visible while others are invisible. For example, Louise still remembers how unpleasant it felt every Christmas when teachers expected that she celebrated Christmas and knew all the songs, while her family actually celebrated Hanukkah. Recognizing that no family's traditions should be disrespected means thoughtfully and respectfully figuring out how you and your program will use holiday activities as one part of your curriculum. It also means paying attention to the principle of inviting children to learn about other children's holidays rather than asking them to celebrate the holidays in the classroom.

Pay Attention to the Language You Use in Holiday Activities

This is an important element in learning about, rather than celebrating, a holiday grounded in a specific faith or a particular historic event. The words you use support or undercut the concept of religious diversity and each family's freedom of choice. Choose words that focus on the history of the special day and that also make clear the diversity of beliefs.

For example, you might explain Christmas with words such as "Christmas is special to some families because it celebrates the birthday of the God they believe in. Some families celebrate the day with gifts and their family members eating a meal together. Some go to church to celebrate." Phrases such as "Christmas is the birthday of the Lord" should be reserved for Christian families to use in their homes. Likewise, telling the story of Hanukkah could focus on how "Jewish people got together and fought to be able to practice their religion. Some Jewish families light candles for eight nights to honor the event, and some give their children a present each night." Religious Jewish families might tell the story in their homes as "God sent a miracle and the temple's oil lamp burned for eight nights."

Learn About Different Ways to Honor Birthdays

All cultural groups do not recognize and celebrate birthdays in the same way. Learn how the families in your program do or don't celebrate their children's birthdays. Carefully think through how, if at all, you will address differences. For example, some families may honor the child but not with gifts or fancy decorations. Families who have adopted children may choose to celebrate adoption days instead of birthdays—or both.

Birthday celebrations held by families outside of school can pose problems. For example, some children from the program may be invited to the party but others are not; some families cannot afford gifts or do not ascribe to commercial gift giving. Encourage families to think about ways they can support anti-bias principles of respect and caring for each child and family as they plan a birthday celebration. They may agree that all children in the class will be invited or that a family comes to school to celebrate with the child's classmates. At the least, consider having a policy that if all children are not invited, birthday invitations cannot be distributed at school. Stress that respect for everyone underlies this policy. In addition, encourage families to emphasize caring rather than materialism with regard to gift giving.

Help Children Understand When a Staff Member or Child Does Not Participate

Teaching respect includes helping children understand that in some families certain behaviors are acceptable and in others they are not. Consider the following holiday example:

> A mother brings a special lunch to school for her child's birthday. She does not realize it is Ramadan, when observant adult Muslims fast between dawn and dusk. She is upset when Edward, a student teacher, doesn't eat anything. She complains to the teacher that both her and her daughter's feelings were hurt. The teacher explains Edward's practice of fasting. She also tells Edward that the child was puzzled that he did not eat the special lunch. Edward makes sure to talk with the child that the next day, explaining why he hadn't eaten, and assures the child that he is happy for her birthday.

When Families Do Not Want Their Child to Participate in Holiday Activities

When a family does not want their child to participate in classroom holiday events, which may include birthdays, respect their preferences regardless of the reason. Work together to find a third space (see page 71). The first step is to find out the family's specific concerns. Many families are comfortable with their children learning about other people's holidays if it is clear the holidays are not being *celebrated* in the school. You may find that through committed, respectful dialogue with families, you can adapt how you plan specific holiday activities to allow all children to participate. Here's one such adaptation:

> As each holiday approached, the program had a regular circle time discussion with children to talk about their holidays. One of the program's new families, who were Jehovah's Witnesses, did not want their child to attend when the class talked about holidays. After talking with the family,

the staff decides to continue the circle time but to ask the children to talk about their "special family time." This approach worked.

When families object to a holiday that your program is considering celebrating, listen carefully to understand their views. It is not only respectful to do so, it is also often highly educational. Columbus Day is a case in point. Many families with Native American heritage experience the holiday as a day of mourning, not only due to the loss of their traditional homelands but also because it is a celebration of a person whose treatment of indigenous people was violent and destructive. Here's a story from a school that altered their practice after such a discussion with families:

> Our school district required us to acknowledge Columbus Day but did not require that we *celebrate* the day. After talking with the children's families, we decided we'd have a circle time where we talked about Columbus's courage to cross the ocean and his coming to the Americas. But we also talked about his incorrect idea that he could say that now the place that he landed was his! We sang Nancy Schimmel's wonderful song "1492," which names dozens of the peoples who were "already here!" We were surprised by how easily the children learned the chorus [see www.sisterschoice.com/activitysss]. As a result of our conversations with the families, it was clear that we also needed to develop a curriculum that honored the local Native Americans.

Thanksgiving: Rethinking a Dominant Culture Holiday

An ABE approach does not require eliminating traditional national holidays. It *does* require critically rethinking how to teach children about them. Consider Thanksgiving. An official national holiday and day off for schools, Thanksgiving is widely celebrated by people in the United States. Many schools tell and enact the dominant culture's version of the Thanksgiving story. While it is not necessary to stop teaching about Thanksgiving in an ABE program, it *is* necessary to think through how you will do so in a way that teaches accurate information and reflects anti-bias values.

As with all holiday curriculum, it's important for you to understand the story the holiday is built on. This is particularly important when the story is about people who are still present and members of our communities. The common Thanksgiving narrative largely reflects the perspective of the European colonists, not the indigenous people who had been living on the continent for many generations. And while the dominant culture narrative honors the social struggle of one group who immigrated in search of a better life and religious freedom, it does not recognize the cost to the Native Americans they displaced. For this reason, many Native Americans have a different narrative about the history of Thanksgiving (Dunbar-Ortiz 2014; Turkewitz 2017), which includes the concept that the day makes some people sad. It is useful for children as well as adults to recognize and give voice to the understanding that Thanksgiving is a holiday that makes some people happy and some people sad.

In addition, many commercial and school decorations used for Thanksgiving reflect damaging misinformation and stereotypes about past and present Native Americans. It is as if children are exposed every year to a theme week that misinforms them about Native Americans.

Anti-bias teachers who decide to include Thanksgiving activities in their curriculum use a range of alternative approaches to the holiday. Here are some examples.

Teach About the People Who Help Supply Food to Others

Since meal rituals are such a focus in Thanksgiving traditions, some teachers plan a series of activities that teach about honoring the people who grow, harvest, and deliver food.

- Find out what foods farmers grow in the area where you live. If possible, visit the fields with the children and meet some of the people who grow and pick the harvest.

- Ask families who celebrate Thanksgiving to let you know what seasonal foods they use for the holiday. Make displays and read books about the people who do the work of growing and harvesting those foods.

- Invite visitors who box, ship, load, or sell food in your community. Ask them to share with the children what they do. Help the children make the connection between the visitors' work and the foods their families buy and eat. Encourage the children to make thank-you cards for the visitors.

- Plan a cooking project where children make some food that they can take home for part of their family dinner (cranberry relish or applesauce, for example). Together, research and learn about where the ingredients come from and who provided them.

Connect Thanksgiving and Immigration

Since Thanksgiving honors the first European immigrants to come to what would become the United States, it is a good time to highlight positive learning about new immigrant families (although it should not be the only time you do this). One idea is to talk to families to learn the stories about how each came to the United States. Then hold storytelling times in the weeks before Thanksgiving in which the children hear these stories. For some children this will be a story about their immediate family; for others it will be a story about their grandparents, great-grandparents, or earlier ancestors. For Native American children, it will involve stories about their ancestors being in the land long before people of other racial and ethnic identities came. Develop the theme of how wonderful it is to have people from so many places.

Help Children Understand What Being Thankful Means

Young children have a relatively easy time understanding the idea of something that makes them happy. The concept of thankfulness is considerably more difficult. They may need help thinking about how to appreciate people and experiences that bring them joy and good health.

- Ask children to dictate a message to someone who makes them happy. Have them include what that person does and how thankful the child is. If the person is not someone in the child's home, help the child put the message in an envelope and ask the family to mail it.

- Create a thank-you class book that you add to for the rest of the year in which the children can record their appreciation of visitors, special events, and so on. Read it frequently at group times.

Teach Accurate Information About Native Americans Before, During, and After Thanksgiving

It is not uncommon for young children to hold incorrect and negative ideas about Native Americans. Deborah Menkart relates the following conversation a mother had with her 5-year-old son:

> C: Mom, who was the first person born in America?
>
> Mom: Good question. It would be a Native American who lived on this land first, but I don't know the specific person.
>
> C: No, I mean the people who look like me—White people. Who was the first? The people who built the good houses.
>
> Mom: What do you mean by good houses?
>
> C: You know, the ones like ours with walls and a roof, not the pointy ones.
>
> Mom: You mean tipis?
>
> C: Yeah, those can easily fall. I'm talking about people who made the roads and towns and had better medicine.
>
> Mom: Honey, Native Americans did many things better than we do now. They protected the earth when they grew crops. And their houses made sense for how they lived because those who lived in tipis moved around a lot. Things can be different but not better.

Children should know that there are many, many native peoples in the Americas. They speak many different languages, and they live in cities as well as in remote places. They are proud of and work hard to retain their culture (NMAI 2018). Here are some ways you can help children begin to understand this:

- **Collect accurate, current images and information that counter the children's stereotypes and misinformation.** Several children's books and adult picture books offer authentic images. Websites such as www.firstnations.org provide suggestions for accurate books about Native Americans. If your community has a museum about Native American life, its gift shop may have useful materials. Focus on the daily contemporary life of specific nations. It is best to choose a nation from your own geographic area.

- **Use accurate, respectful terms.** *Native American* is widely used to refer to indigenous peoples in the Americas, particularly those in the United States. The terms *American Indian* or *Indigenous American* are currently preferred by many Native American people (NMAI 2018). Even more respectful is to use the specific name of the nation you are talking about (e.g., Choctaw, Haida, Shoshone). If you have Native American families in your program and you do not know which names they prefer, ask them.

- **Find out what the children in your program think** they know about Native Americans. Where do Native Americans live? What do they do? How do they look? Are any of the children Native American? Do any know someone who is? Make a note of the children's misconceptions and stereotypes—for example, that all Native Americans live in tipis, shoot with bows and arrows, or wear feather headdresses. Create activities that counter the children's incorrect ideas and stereotypes.

- **Make a class book** with accurate, current images that enable children to explore the contemporary life of Native Americans in all its diversity—for example, in the country and in the city, in the Southwest and Northeast.

- **Read children's books that accurately portray contemporary Native American life.** Examples include *Niwechihaw / I Help,* by Caitlin Dale Nicholson; *On Mother's Lap,* by Ann Herbert Scott; and *Sweetest Kulu,* by Celina Kalluk. Do not substitute traditional Native American folktales for books about contemporary Native American people. (See www.oyate.org for dependable information about stereotypes and criteria for choosing children's books.)

- **Tell stories with persona dolls about current Native American life.** As with all persona doll stories, be sure to use authentic-looking dolls and accurate information. Create a specific doll child and family who are from a specific Native American nation. Tell stories about different aspects of their daily life as well as stories that strengthen both children's empathy for the hurt of prejudice experienced and their skills for standing up to counter it.

Do Not Ever Allow Children to Pretend-Play Being "Indians"

While pretending to take on a specific role such as father, doctor, truck driver, or superhero is common in young children's play, pretending to be a member of an ethnic group that is not one's own is insulting to real members of the group. Explain to children why pretend-playing "Indian" or any other identity group is disrespectful and hurtful. A young Navajo-Laguna-Kiaoni-Pueblo girl named Monica explains that

> It makes me mad when children make fun of my culture. . . . When the children grow up I don't want them to think that Indians put feathers in their hair and dance around the fire. We don't do that. . . . One day I saw a kid running around with a feather in their hair and putting their hand to their mouths and making weird noises and I cried when that happened. So, what I want you to do is . . . learn about our real history. (Oyate, n.d.)

Consider Creating Unique Class or School Celebrations

In addition to, or instead of, celebrating the holidays observed by children's families, some teachers create their own celebrations for various parts of the school year. This approach makes it possible for every child to participate in shared special days with the rest of the class. Celebrations can be respectful, for example, occasions for honoring families, thanking the people who make the school work (cooks, custodians, bus driver, etc.), or recognizing family and neighborhood heroes. Celebrations can also be whimsical and playful: Bring Books Alive Day (make and wear costumes from books, eat foods from favorite books, act out favorite stories); Pajama Day (wear pajamas and slippers to school, tell bedtime stories, share family bedtime rituals); or Backwards Day (wear your clothes backwards, do things in reverse order of an ordinary day). Celebrations can also be used to mark the passing of the year with an annual end-of-year picnic or potluck dinner. These events help give the year a sense of ceremony and time passing and often become favorite memories for families and children.

Action Projects

Choose an issue that directly affects the children's lives and that relates to a social justice event or celebration. Engage in an action project related to the special day to help the children gain a sense of its meaning. This example focuses on Earth Day:

> Rudy talked with the children in his class about the meaning of Earth Day and invited them to suggest actions they could take on that day. The children decided to "not waste food." They were already composting leftovers from lunch, but they decided to keep out "green things" to feed the chickens that one family kept. They also decided to make signs (dictated to the teacher and decorated by the children) to put up in the building reminding people to turn off lights when they left a room.

Community Celebrations

Find ways to include children and their families in community celebrations that demonstrate how everyone can work together to make the world better. For example, during National Book Month, one elementary school with a pre-K class decided to hold a small parade around the public library. The children made hats that represented a favorite book and invited family members to join them. The teachers prepared for the parade by talking about how people pay taxes and work together to support libraries and how librarians work to make books available. Later, when library funds were being cut, the children joined the local Friends of the Library group in a protest march on City Hall.

Visits from Local Activists

Invite people who are working to improve the quality of life in the children's communities. Make sure that you include a diverse group of people and that they visit several times with the children. Invitees might include activists who work to help people who are homeless, distribute food to families in need, or create community gardens. They might talk about something they thought was unfair, what they decided to do about it, and how they felt about it. Talk with potential local activist visitors about their participation in a social justice action before they come, so you can help them know what would be of interest to the children in your class and to prepare them for likely questions. If you have your own activism experiences, tell developmentally appropriate stories about them, too.

Remember that Culture Is Much Bigger than Holidays

Holiday curriculum can be one useful tool for exploring diversity (e.g., many people have many differing holidays, and even people who have the same holidays may celebrate them differently). But when holidays dominate early childhood curriculum, they obscure the realities and diversity of children's and families' everyday ways of being. Ongoing focus on holidays gets in the way of helping children understand that on every ordinary day there are many ways that families live, love, and work. Every family has a culture. Every child lives in a culture.

. . .

As an anti-bias educator, you want children to thrive in a diverse world and choose to stand up for themselves and others. This means you commit to helping them make sense of the confusing and often emotionally charged messages they receive about cultural diversity. It also calls on you to foster *all* children's positive cultural identities as well as their awareness of and ease with cultural differences. When you give children the words and encouragement to share their identities—and how they are the same and different—in an atmosphere of interest and delight, and you also give them tools to address the unfairness they will inevitably encounter, you help children to construct a strong foundation for the next phases of their lives.

Religious Literacy and Cultural Diversity

with Debbie LeeKeenan, early childhood consultant

At snack time, Paul looks at the teacher with a troubled expression and says, "Teacher, teacher, we didn't say grace yet!" The other children look up, some confused, some interested. Carlos, the teacher, replies, "You know, Paul, some families say grace before eating, and some families don't. Here at school we don't say grace as a group, but you may if you like." Paul puts his hands together and somberly says, "Dear God, please bless this meal."

This sets off a series of comments from the other children: "But he didn't say Gracie's name at all," "That's not how it goes. He said it wrong," "What's grace?," and "Can I say grace too?" Seeing how attentive the children are, Carlos takes a deep breath and respectfully asks the group, "What do you know about saying grace before a meal?" He listens carefully to the children's ideas, sums them up as best he can, and then says, "In some families it is very important to say 'thank you' for their food before they eat. That's called 'saying grace.' In some families they say their thank-you to their parents, in some families they say thank you to God. And people say their thank-you in lots of different ways. You get to say 'thank you' however your family likes to do it."

The children return to eating their snack. Carlos wonders if he said the right thing or not, and decides to pass the conversation on to the families of his snack group so they can follow through on the conversation if they wish.

Part of a child's cultural experiences and identity is the way her family identifies or doesn't identify with a particular religious faith and how the family practices that faith. Religious beliefs and practices are a central part of many families' home cultures. By 4 or 5 years old, many children make comments about their family's religious practices as well as about their family's attitudes toward other religious groups. They may also begin to ask questions about the concepts of God or spirituality. For example: Who is God? What happens when someone dies? Does Jesus love you? Who made the world? Who made the first person? What does heaven look like? Early childhood educators who have addressed issues of religious diversity with children find that children readily engage in and benefit from these learning experiences (Mardell & Abo-Zena 2010).

Unless a teacher works in a religious school with a mission to teach a particular religion, early childhood teachers tend to avoid conversations about religious beliefs. However, given a rise in religious intolerance and hate crimes in the United States, it is necessary to address the issues related to religious diversity and anti-bias education (Byrd 2018). (See further discussion in LeeKeenan & Nimmo 2016.)

The First Amendment of the Bill of Rights gives all Americans the right to believe in and practice any religion they choose. In a culturally diverse society where many religions coexist, it is not appropriate for a program to favor or impose any particular religion unless the school was explicitly created to do so. However, giving young children tools and language to figure out complex ideas about religions and to avoid developing negative attitudes about religious groups is an important step toward ending religious prejudice, discrimination, and hate crimes. This objective is pertinent for all early childhood programs, including faith-based programs.

Adding religious literacy to their work enables anti-bias educators to more effectively address religious diversity issues with young children. *Religious literacy,* a concept developed by Diane Moore of the Harvard Divinity School, is an approach to supporting families' specific beliefs as well as promoting children's awareness and respect for differences in beliefs and practices (Religious Literacy Project 2019). This approach is not the same as teaching religious beliefs. It contrasts with *religious illiteracy,* which denies the importance of religious beliefs and practices other than one's own, does not acknowledge any similarities among religions or with secular beliefs, creates stereotypes, and can lead to religious extremism and disrespect for religious diversity (Moore 2007).

Applying Anti-Bias Core Goals to Learning About Religious Diversity

The four anti-bias core goals provide a framework for promoting religious literacy with children (Nimmo, Abo-Zena, & LeeKeenan 2019). An anti-bias lens focuses on honoring diverse religious ideas and practices without advocating for a particular set of beliefs, which is the responsibility of a child's family. In faith-based programs, teaching respect for and honoring others' beliefs accompanies the teaching of a particular religious viewpoint.

Here are useful objectives, based on the ABE goals, for teachers to build children's understanding about religious diversity:

- Teachers recognize that religion or spiritual practices are a part of family culture and that children will talk about them. Teachers listen to children's comments and ideas without judgement. **(Goal 1)**

- Teachers help children understand and respect that different people have different religious and/or spiritual beliefs and practices. They help children appreciate that families who share a religious membership may have different ways of practicing it, and that people may share ideas *across* religious faiths. For example, almost all the world's religions have some version of what is known in Christianity as the Golden Rule: "Do to others as you would have them do to you." **(Goal 2)**

- Teachers develop children's ability to recognize untrue hurtful religious stereotypes and biases that they hear (e.g., all Christians have the same views about homosexuality,

the news and movies are controlled by Jews, all Muslims are terrorists). This includes biases *within* religious groups. **(Goal 3)**

- Teachers support children to speak up when others say untrue things or make fun of their families' religious or spiritual beliefs. Teachers create an atmosphere of inclusiveness that reinforces a matter-of-fact acceptance that different families believe different things. **(Goal 4)**

Support Diverse Family Beliefs

Anti-bias teachers model respect for religious literacy as they talk with children about their ideas. For example, religious ideas may come up when children are trying to understand issues of life and death.

> A 3-year-old asks her teacher if she can visit her grandfather in heaven. The teacher asks her what her mother says about that. The child replies she hasn't asked. "Let's ask her together when she gets here," the teacher says. This conversation inspires another child to announce, "If we all say our prayers before bedtime, we'll all go to heaven." The teacher replies, "Some families say prayers before bedtime, and some families don't. Here at school we don't pray all together as an activity. You can say a prayer before nap time if you want, or you don't have to." She then adds, "Every family has its own ideas about what heaven is or isn't; you can ask your family what they think."

Some children may bring family religious icons into school for cultural sharing activities or for specific personal reasons. Some families want their child to wear a cross or a Star of David or a head covering. These are legitimate statements of family culture as long as the school does not ask other children to wear them or treat some as acceptable and others as unacceptable. Here's an example about one publicly funded program's response to children bringing Bibles to their classroom:

> Maria and Bettina arrive at the center after a big fire destroyed their home, shaken both emotionally and literally. Each

child holds a white satin Bible that their mother has told them to keep with them at all times. But the school policy is that items from home stay in the cubbies.

It is clear to the teachers that the Bibles are a source of comfort and reassurance to the girls and to their mother. After some uncertainty about what to do, they decide to give the girls paper bags to hold the Bibles and keep them clean. They help the girls find clean places to put the bags near them during art and snack time. Over the weeks, as the family recovers, the teachers notice that the girls leave the Bibles in their cubbies for more of the day and eventually at home.

Intervene Immediately If a Child Makes Negative Statements About Another Child's Religion

Whether a child's comment reflects lack of knowledge or repeats disrespectful comments heard at home or in the media, it is important to intervene. As discussed in Chapter 4, silence in the face of negative comments about any aspect of a child's identity hurts the recipient and gives other children permission to say inaccurate, hurtful remarks without any consequences. Here's an example:

> After the December holidays, the teacher invites the children to talk about their family's celebrations. Most of the children tell stories about their Christmas holiday traditions. The single Jewish child in the class talks about Hanukkah. Later, the teacher overhears a few children wishing their classmate "Happy Jewish Christmas." The teacher, thinking this is cute, does not intervene.
>
> However, another teacher overhears and disagrees with the first teacher's silence. Raising the incident at the next staff meeting, the second teacher says that the comment was not cute, and she offers what she would have said instead of being silent. The teachers have

a rich discussion and come up with various ideas. One is that in the moment, the teacher could have said, "I like that you remember that Ben is Jewish, but his holiday is not a Jewish Christmas. His holiday is called Hanukkah, and you could wish him 'Happy Hanukkah.'"

The teacher also decides to follow up on the incident with the children. She uses a persona doll, Rebekah, to tell the story of Hanukkah and how Rebekah's family celebrates the holiday. In the story, Rebekah mentions that it hurts her feelings when someone says "Happy Jewish Christmas," and she wishes they would say "Happy Hanukkah!"

Stop & Think: Reflecting on Talking with Children About Religious Diversity

- Do you feel comfortable or uncomfortable, prepared or not yet prepared, reluctant or willing to discuss religious diversity issues with children? Why?

- What positive or negative feelings come up for you as you imagine yourself talking with children about religious diversity issues? How might you deal with these?

- What benefits do you see to including religious literacy learning in an early childhood program?

- What experiences have you had where your religious, spiritual, or moral beliefs have been ignored, trivialized, or attacked? What was this like for you? How do those experiences (or lack of experiences) influence your thinking about doing religious literacy learning with children?

Adding the subject of religious literacy to an anti-bias education program calls on teachers and program directors to talk openly with each other about their ideas and feelings on the topic. Teachers and program directors also need to share with families how they intend to support children's sense of their own families' beliefs and why religious literacy is important for children living in a diverse world.

CHAPTER 8

Learning About Racialized Identities and Fairness

"How do people get their color?"
asks 3½-year-old Thomas.

• • •

"I'm not Black. I'm African American,"
Ebonie says earnestly to her teacher.

• • •

Rosalie, a 5-year-old Puerto Rican, is reluctant
to move out of the shaded areas of the
play yard. She explains to her teacher, "If
I get sun on my skin it will get darker. My
family says I'm dark enough already."

As these comments illustrate, young children are
aware of and curious about physical features related
to what society calls *race*. Eye shape, skin color, and
hair fascinate children and are the first aspects of racial
identity that they notice. By age 4, children also begin
to pick up on social identity terms for their own and
other groups, which can be quite puzzling for them.

Biologically, there is no such things as race. All people
are members of one race, *Homo sapiens,* the human
race—even though everyone does not look the same.
However, in a society where systemic racism exists,
everyone has a racialized identity, an identity that
holds power in the life of each person. All children
grow up surrounded by and absorbing the socially
prevailing positive and negative messages about
themselves and others, which come from media; from
educational, religious, and legal institutions; and
from the behavior and beliefs of the important adults
in their lives.

Anti-Bias Education in Action: Preparing to Address Racialized Identity

From a teacher's journal: What do children need to
know? Notes for ongoing discussions.

● We all have skin. Skin keeps our insides in.

● We get our skin color from our birth
parents—sometimes a little lighter,
sometimes a little darker. There can be
different skin colors in one family.

● No one has skin that is black like licorice. No
one has skin that is white like a piece of paper.

● When people say they are Black, they mean that
they are part of a big, big family of people who
once lived in a place called Africa. Sometimes
they say they are African American.

● When people say they are White, they mean
they are part of a big, big family of people who
once lived in a place called Europe. Sometimes
they say they are European American.

● People come in lots of different skin colors, from
very dark brown to very light tan. All people are
members of a big, big family called human beings.

Applying Anti-Bias Goals to Racialized Identity

- Children will feel positive, but not superior or inferior, about their racialized identities. They will understand that their skin color or eye shape or hair texture does not determine their value as human beings. **(Goal 1)**

- Children will have accurate words and information about each other's different racialized identities. They will also appreciate their shared humanity and how they are similar to each other. **(Goal 2)**

- Children will develop beginning skills for identifying and questioning misinformation, stereotypical ideas and images, and hurtful behaviors directed at their own and others' racialized identities. They will know that it is not fair to treat people hurtfully because of who they are. **(Goal 3)**

- Children will demonstrate beginning skills for interrupting biased behaviors targeted at their own and others' racialized identities and for creating a fair classroom environment. **(Goal 4)**

The Big Picture: Race, Racism, and Racialized Identity

The concept of race is a socially and politically created, unscientific idea that divides people into racial groups ranked as superior and inferior, supported by misinformation and bias. It developed as a political, economic, and cultural tool, backed by the power and practice of a society's institutions, to justify one group of people's economic exploitation and cultural domination of other groups (Alexander 2012; Barndt 1991; Lane 2008; Rothstein 2017).

Racism and Racialized Identity Defined

Racism is the systemic, institutional policies, beliefs, and practices that create economic, social, educational, and cultural advantages or disadvantages for people depending on their membership in racial groups as defined by society.

Racialized identity refers to the way groups of people are defined by the society in which they live and how other people treat those groups because of those definitions. It is also about how people treat members of their own racial group. In this book, the term is used to indicate that racialized identity is imposed on people from forces outside, and also constructed internally by individuals. This process begins very early in a child's life.

The concept of race comes from a history of justifying European colonization of countries made up of dark-skinned people (Barndt 1991; Kendi 2016). The colonizers created a hierarchy of humans in which some people were considered genetically superior and destined to rule while others were viewed as genetically inferior and incapable of self-determination. European settlers brought this idea of race to what is now the Americas. They used it as a way to normalize and justify the enslavement of Africans and to steal indigenous people's lands and displace them onto reservations on inferior lands. The European definition of race made it possible for colonizers to think of certain groups of people as disposable and exploitable (Feagin 2000; Kendi 2016).

As part of setting up a system of slavery and racism in the United States, it was necessary to legally define racialized identities to make clear who could be "owned" by other human beings and who had the right to do the owning (Derman-Sparks & Ramsey 2011; Hannaford 1996; Kendi 2016). Skin color was made the primary marker that defined these racial identities, so white and black became central to the way people were categorized. And, just as distinctly different African peoples, with different languages, customs, and beliefs, were combined into one group called *Black,* so were Europeans of different languages, customs, and beliefs combined into one group called *White.* (See Derman-Sparks & Ramsey 2011 for a more detailed discussion of Whiteness.)

The ending of slavery did not end the power of the constructs of race and racialized identities. Rather, a system of legalized racism continued that ensured economic, political, educational, and cultural advantages to Whites as a group. Segregation, denial of voting rights, lack of economic and educational access, and the resulting inability to amass generational wealth all worked to keep White people in power. This system used misinformation, stereotyping, prejudices, biases, and violence toward people seen as "not White" in order to justify the inequality racism created (Gates 2019; Roediger 2005; Rothstein 2017; Wallis 2017).

Over time, changes occurred in legal definitions of who was White and who was not. One way of thinking about this is to see how terms in the US Census forms have changed over time. In 1790, there were only three choices: Free Whites, All Other Free Persons, and Slaves (Pew Research Center 2015). Native Americans were not even counted. The 2010 Census listed six racial choices: White; Black, African American or Negro; American Indian or Alaska Native; Asian; Native Hawaiian or Other Pacific Islander; or Some Other Race. In 1970, ethnic/racial categories were added, including Central or South American and Other Spanish/Latino/Hispanic.

As new groups immigrated to the United States, they too often experienced prejudice and exclusion based on their ethnicities and how they were placed into the system of racialized identity already in existence. Racism became a tool to utilize the labor of immigrants but keep them from having full citizenship and human rights (Kaye 2010). For example, this was the experience of people from China who were allowed into the country to build the railroads and for Filipinos and Mexicans who were allowed in to work in agriculture. The list of targets of racism came to include not only African Americans and Native Americans but also people who are Latinx, Asian American, East Indian, Pakistani, and Arab Americans (Marable 2016).

A major change in the dynamics of societal and interpersonal racism was the result of the massive Civil Rights movement of the 1960s and 1970s. The federal 1964 Civil Rights Act ended legal segregation and created additional policies to lessen the inequities experienced by people of color. Multicultural education became part of the curriculum at many schools; ethnic study courses were offered at many colleges and universities. The use of affirmative action policies brought many students of color to universities and colleges around the country with a subsequent growth of diversity within the professions.

However, structural, cultural, and interpersonal racism continued to exist and still do. While people of color might make a middle-class income and more easily choose to live in neighborhoods where White people were in the majority, the larger society continued to define them as not White, and they still experienced racial discrimination (Alexander 2012; Rothstein 2017). Similarly, some White individuals today might prefer not to be defined as White, might even deny that they think of themselves as White, but they still receive the advantages accorded to Whites by the society (DiAngelo 2018; Rothenberg 2016).

For many people, the US election of President Barack Obama in 2008 seemed to usher in a new era for the country. They believed the United States was entering into a post-racial society. To some, it meant that the constructs of race, racism, and racialized identity would end and racial equality would prevail. While President Obama's election was a significant step in the history of the United States—and certainly had a powerful positive influence on how African American and other children of color thought about themselves and how White children thought about people of color—structural and individual racism did not disappear.

Instead, at the time of this writing, the country is experiencing new federal policies and state laws that undermine key rights of people of color as well as those of other social identity groups. In 2018 there was also a 12 percent rise in violent hate crimes, with anti-black bias accounting for 27 percent of this increase. Hate crimes against Latinos rose nearly 14 percent (Beirich 2019a).

Racialized Identities and Choice

Just as the structural dynamics of racism continue, so too do the dynamics of racialized identities. No one has the individual choice to opt out of socially assigned racialized identities. *But each person has a choice about how to live with them.* People have the capacity for acquiring new knowledge and feelings about their individual identities as well as the identities of other individuals. Members of the White racial group can choose to believe in the myths of superiority that justify advantages and privileges to their group. Or they can reject those myths and work to end the system of racism that creates these dynamics. Members of groups targeted by racism can live as if the myths of inferiority are true descriptions of themselves. Or they can reject those damaging notions and work against the ideas and structures that create social disadvantage for them.

Some people think that if no one noticed and acknowledged differences in skin color, racialized social identities and racism would disappear. However, that isn't the answer. Pretending not to notice differences devalues the real-life experiences of people of color and ignores the reality of White advantages. ABE rests on the premise that, as long as racism continues to exist, everyone—children, families, teachers, community members—absorbs society's messages about racialized social identity groups. But—and this is a big but—*anti-bias educators can learn to clean their lenses to see with a more accurate eye and mind and a caring heart.*

Stop & Think: You and Your Racialized Identity

- In what ways has your racialized identity made life better or easier for you and your family? In what ways has it made life challenging?

- How did you know and feel about your racialized identity as a child, a teenager, and now?

- In what kinds of situations in your life today do issues of racial difference come up? What is that like? Are there things you wished you understood better so you could speak more clearly about them?

Recognizing Privilege

by Bryn Potter O'Shea, preschool teacher

I have a BA degree and all the benefits that come with it. I was taught that my good education was a right, deserved by and available to anyone. I went to public elementary school in a largely middle-class White neighborhood, with enough funding to offer a very good education.

My high school offered gifted and talented education and Advanced Placement courses for those who were on track for college. This offered all kinds of advantages. My senior year, we wrote our college entrance essays in English class, and I completed my college applications in government class. I took all of this for granted as my high school's responsibility, when in fact I now know that many high schools do little to help students with college plans.

If I had been asked how I ended up on the college track at my school, I think I would have answered that I worked hard and that my family valued education. These statements are both true, but they evidence the blinders of internalized privilege that prevented me from seeing the advantages afforded by my economic class and racialized identity. The experience of people without a degree or the means to get one was invisible to me. If someone didn't go to college, I assumed that they didn't want to (which is funny, because I never asked myself whether I wanted to go, or what I'd be willing to do to get there).

Intersectionality of Race and Class

Systemic racism continues to powerfully affect the lives of children and their families. According to the National Center for Children in Poverty (NCCP), children of color are still more likely to experience societal adverse conditions than White children. "Poverty is the single biggest threat to children's well-being" (NCCP 2019, 1). NCCP's analysis of 2016 statistics illustrate how the relationship between

families living with low income (below 200 percent of the federal poverty threshold) or in poverty (below 100 percent of the federal poverty threshold) varies by race and ethnicity. While some young children of *all* racial backgrounds live in low-income, poor, or deep poverty (less than 50 percent of the federal poverty threshold) families, the data reveal the impact of institutional racism on economics (Koball & Jiang 2018). (See Chapter 10 for more on economic class.)

In 2016, 13 percent of White children lived in poor families and 6 percent lived in deep poverty (Koball & Jiang 2018). Thirty-seven percent of African American children's families were in the poor category, and 19 percent in deep poverty. In addition, 30 percent of Latinx young children's families lived in poverty, and 13 percent in deep poverty. Among Native American children's families, 39 percent were living in poverty and 19 percent in deep poverty. These systemic economic facts tell us that White children and families are still more likely to have access to resources that support healthy development and future success than are children and families of color. Risks are greatest for children who experience poverty when they are young or experience deep, persistent poverty (Smith, Granja, & Nguyen 2017).

Incarceration of a family member is another developmental stressor that reflects the systemic racism in the lives of children of color. The Annie E. Casey Foundation looked more closely at the 5 million children with a parent in jail or prison at some point in their lives. African American and Latinx children are over seven times more likely than their White peers to have a parent who is incarcerated. This

situation exists for several reasons, including racial profiling, lack of money for bail, and longer prison sentences. "More than 15 percent of children with parents in federal prison—and more than 20 percent with parents in state prison—are age 4 or younger" (Annie E. Casey Foundation 2016). The incarceration of a parent has a great impact on a child's well-being.

Early Childhood Programs Can Make a Difference

There is research evidence that high-quality early childhood education programs can play a valuable role in countering the traumatic effects of poverty and racism. One world-renowned longitudinal study explored the outcomes of the Ypsilanti Perry Preschool Project (1962–1967), an experimental high-quality preschool program for African American children living in poverty in a small Michigan city. The HighScope Educational Research Foundation documented the lives of the children attending the preschool program and followed them until midlife (Schweinhart et al. 1993, 2004; Weikart 1993). A control group of children with similar demographics but no preschool experience was also followed. The Center for the Economics of Human Development, at the University of Chicago, then carried out further assessments when the children were in their mid-50s (Heckman & Karapakula 2019).

These studies found that children participating in in the Perry Preschool Project had important lifelong gains in education (completing high school and, for a few, college), in employment, and in personal life outcomes. All of these outcomes were significantly better than those of the children in the control group. Of equal importance, the next generation, the children of the Perry Preschool participants, also showed significant gains in education, health, employment, and civic life.

Young Children Construct Ideas and Attitudes About Racialized Identities

From infancy on, children absorb messages about the construct of race from a range of sources—family, teachers, media, peers, books, and social, political, and religious institutions. From these messages they gradually form an internalized racialized identity. Thus, everyone's racialized identity is imposed from the outside and constructed from the inside.

This process is based on three dynamics. One is how the society into which children are born defines racial groups and assigns racialized identities. These definitions are often codified in law and then disseminated through a range of sources. A second dynamic is a child's life experiences, particularly how a child is valued and treated by the significant people in his life, such as family and teachers. The third dynamic is how each child comes to think and feel about who he is, a process that continues throughout life.

Research studies exploring young children's awareness and attitudes about racialized identities seriously began in the 1950s (Clark 1963; Goodman 1952; Trager & Yarrow 1952). This body of research contradicts the mistaken belief that young children do not notice or show interest in features connected to racial group membership, particularly skin color. Even infants and toddlers begin to notice and show curiosity about differences in skin color (Bronson & Merryman 2009). By the time children are 3 and 4 years old, they become aware of value judgments and feelings related to various racialized identities and begin to act on negative feelings about others that they absorb (Lane 2008).

Diversity does not cause prejudice, nor does children noticing and talking about differences, as some adults fear. Children learn prejudice from messages and images of prejudice. They also learn from the silence or discomfort of adults when children ask or comment about the human differences they see around them.

In contrast, when you pay attention to children's developing ideas and feelings about racial identity, you can foster their ability to gain accurate knowledge and develop self-esteem. Interacting with children about their developing ideas and feelings also counters misinformation, unease, or hurtful ideas about members of various racialized groups. By not staying silent, you and the children's families can nurture their accurate knowledge, empathy, enjoyment, and anti-bias relationships with racially diverse people.

Infants and Toddlers Are Aware of Skin Color

Infants pay attention to the human face. Newborns gaze and stare at faces, learning to recognize who is familiar and who is new. One attribute they pay attention to is shades of darkness and lightness in skin tone. When shown a series of photographs of faces, infants less than a year old showed less and less interest as similar faces continued to appear. However, when a photograph showed a face with a different skin color, the infants' interest picked up, indicating that they were clearly aware of and interested in the color difference (Bronson & Merryman 2009; Katz & Kofkin 1997).

Young Children Notice Features Connected to Racialized Identities

Children's comments and questions about the color of people's skin, as well as hair color, hair texture, and eye shape, reflect their curiosity and efforts to understand human differences, as shown in the following examples.

Four-year-old Rudy tells his teacher, "I want my skin to be as dark as Paolo's. He's my best friend." His teacher responds, "It's great that you and Paolo are best friends. I know you have a lot of fun playing together at school and at home. You don't have to be just the same to be best friends."

• • •

Grayson comes into the classroom late one morning, looks around, and asks where Kim is. His teacher, an African American woman, is named Kim, and his best friend, who is White, is also named Kim. Another teacher asks him which Kim he means, assuming he will say "friend" or "teacher." Instead, he stops to think about the question and then says, "The peach one."

• • •

Two 4-year-old friends, one Black and one White, are chatting.

Roger: I'm going to get new pants.

Reese: What color?

Roger: Blue.

Reese: What about brown?

Roger: I don't like brown.

Reese: Oh, then you don't like me.

Roger: (*Looks surprised.*) Yes, I do.

Teacher: There's something important I want to help the two of you figure out. Reese, why do you think Roger doesn't like you?

Reese: I'm brown; he said he didn't like brown.

Teacher: Roger, Reese thought when you said you didn't like brown, you meant you didn't like his brown skin either. Is that how you feel?

Roger: No, I don't like brown pants; I like brown Reese.

Teacher: Reese, is that okay?

Reese: (*Nods his head and the two boys go off together.*)

Children Want to Know Why Physical Features Differ

Children's questions reveal their powers of observation, their interest, and their efforts to make sense of what they see. In the process of sense making, they create their own unique explanations about the physical features of racial identity based on their experiences and according to the cognitive tools they possess.

"Why are people different colors?" asks 3½-year-old Candra. "What are some of your ideas?" her teacher responds. Candra, who likes to color her hands and arms with different colors, explains, "Well, I was wondering about colored pens." "I'm glad you are trying to figure things out," her teacher tells her, "but that's not how people get their skin color. We get our skin color from our birth parents."

• • •

"What color blood do we all have?" a teacher casually asks a group of 3-year-olds. "I have light red," says Meredith, who is White, "but

I think Janine (who is Somalian) has dark red." As the children have certainly seen each other's blood from the times they have scraped or cut themselves, their surprised teacher asks if anyone else thinks, like Meredith, that people with different skin colors have different colored blood. Most say yes; a few say no. She then explains, "I can see why some of you might think that if people have different skin color, their blood might also be a different color. But everyone has the same color blood, no matter what the color of their skin is."

• • •

Vivian, an African American girl, lived with Anna, a White woman, for a while. Her closest friend at school asked Vivian if she would become White if she lived with Anna long enough.

Children Try to Understand the Names of and Criteria for Racial Categories

Young children find the connections between racial group names and the actual color of a person's skin confusing. They wonder why two people with different skin tones are in the same group, trying to make sense of society's invented racial groupings.

"Why am I called Black? My skin is brown."

"I'm not yellow; I'm tan."

"My skin isn't white; it's pink."

"This side of my hand is my Black me," explains Douglass, "and this side is my White me!"

Young children also confuse the relationship between color terms and names of different ethnic groups.

"Is Mexican my color?"

• • •

"Am I red?" Leroy, a 4-year-old Navajo child, asks in a puzzled tone. "Taft (a 4-year-old White child) said I'm a 'Red Indian,' but I don't see any red on me." His teacher responds, "You're right, Leroy, there is no such thing as a 'Red Indian.' You are Navajo, and your skin is brown, not red. Let's go talk with Taft and explain to him so he won't make the same mistake again."

. . .

"You're not Black, you're White," says 4-year-old Leticia, an African American child with dark brown skin, to 4-year-old Chandelle, a light-skinned African American child. Chandelle looks confused. The teacher intervenes, saying, "Leticia, Chandelle is African American just like you even though the shades of your skin are different. You are both Black because you are part of a big family called Black people, or African Americans. At group time I'll read a book about the different skin shades of African Americans. It's called *Shades of Black: A Celebration of Our Children* (by Sandra L. Pinkney)."

Racialized Identity and Biracial and Multiracial Children

with Tarah Fleming, educator, speaker, and facilitator

Biracial and multiracial children, with at least one parent of color, are a growing population in the United States (Livingston 2017). Their identities reflect a wide range of racial and ethnic combinations.

Knowing who they are, and having a name for their identities, is essential for children's positive identity development. Families tend to choose one of several ways to name their child's biracial or multiracial identity:

- The child's identity is named as that of the parent of color.

- The child's identity is named biracial or multiracial or mixed, and each parent's heritage is considered equally important.

- The child's identity can be either White or a person of color depending on the child's appearance and choice.

- The family feels confused about how to deal with the child's racialized identity and uses no identity name.

- The family feels that the child's racialized identity is not important and uses no identity name.

According to research studies (Nayani 2017) and the personal stories of many young adults of multiracial, multiethnic, backgrounds, the first two approaches are most likely to foster a healthy sense of self and social identity development. The other three approaches may leave children to figure out who they are by themselves and potentially develop poor skills for dealing with the realities of racism. As children reach adolescence, they may choose a different identity term for themselves than the one their family chose.

In many ways, issues of identity development are similar for children in families that are biracial or multiracial by marriage or partnership and children adopted by parents of a different racial identity (transracial adoption). Children with at least one birth parent of color experience explicit and implicit racial bias and need guidance in developing resilience and skills to counter them. For children of color adopted by White families, identity development can be complicated by parents not looking like the children and by the families' lack of experiences, knowledge, or skills needed to prepare their child to negotiate a race-conscious society. When needed, help families connect with resources and community support.

Every family with biracial or multiracial children experiences racism in some form, although people feel the impacts differently depending on the family's backgrounds, identities, and strategies for addressing stereotypes, bias, and racism. Early childhood educators play a critical role in supporting these families as they deal with issues of identity, culture, and racism (see "What Would You Do?" on page 114). Ask what terms a family uses to describe their identity as well as their child's. Look for ways to consciously help multiracial children embrace how they and others look. Listen for and be responsive to children's questions, and help them sort out their ideas and feelings in ways that fit with their developmental levels.

White Children Also Develop a Racialized Identity

Contrary to what some people assume, White children also develop a racialized identity. White children continually receive messages from families, communities, and media about White normalcy, superiority, and entitlement and construct their ideas about being White in the context of systemic, cultural, and individual racism (Derman-Sparks &

by Tarah Fleming

Scenario 1. Nala, 4 years old, has been adopted by African American parents. Her case file says her birth mother is African American and her birth father is Latino. However, the file identifies her only as Black/African American. Nala's friends in preschool are Latinx, and she tells them that she is too, and she pretends to speak Spanish. Her adoptive parents want to support her in the best way possible but are not sure how. They want to talk with Nala about this issue, which has come up a number of times at home and at school. They ask you to give them ideas on how to handle this important issue.

What ideas would you share with Nala's parents?

Scenario 2. Sam, whose mother is White and father is Black, and Jilly, whose parents are White, are playing on the outdoor climbing structure. Jilly says, "Sammy, who is your mommy?" Sam looks upset because he has been asked this question many times before. He says, "You know my mommy. She brought the muffins yesterday."

Jilly replies, "She can't be your mommy; she's White, and you're brown." Sam starts to cry. One of the teachers overhears the conversation and comes quickly over. She squats down at Sam's eye level, puts her arm around him, and pats him a couple of times. He stops crying. "Look," she says enthusiastically, "Miss Diane is setting up a new activity in the yard. Let's all go try it out."

How would you have handled this situation? Why?

Scenario 3. Max and Tina, a White couple, adopted a 2½-year-old girl from China, whom they named Ali. One day Ali is still finishing snack when her parents come to pick her up. You have a few minutes to chat with them and mention that they now have a multiracial family. They are quick to respond: "There aren't any differences—she's American now, like us." "Ali doesn't see race; and we see everyone as equals, so we're not making it an issue."

What more would you like to know about what Max and Tina think? What ideas about identity and child development might you share in a conversation with them?

Ramsey 2011). Very early, White children come to value their Whiteness, presume it is the definition of normal, and believe that therefore all other skin colors are strange and less-than (Derman-Sparks & Ramsey 2011). While early childhood teachers want all children to like who they are, the challenge for an anti-bias educator is to enable White children to like who they are without developing a sense of White superiority. For example, consider these examples of young White children's early ideas about the importance of being White:

"I like playing with Sophie and Ava better than Deja," says 4-year-old Emily. "They have nicer hair." Emily, Sophie, and Ava are White. Deja is African American.

• • •

A White 4-year-old explains to her teacher that all people who look like her got their skin from God, but she does not know where brown people got their skin (Baker 2010).

• • •

A 4-year-old White child, noticing that she is darker than her two White companions, worriedly asks her teacher, "Does that mean that I'm not White anymore?" During the day, she repeatedly asks for reassurance that she is still White (Van Ausdale & Feagin 2001, 48).

• • •

Three preschoolers, one Asian and two White, are playing with a wagon. One White child is pulling the others. When she gets tired and stops, the Asian child jumps from the wagon and starts to pull it. The first wagon puller declares, "No, no. You can't pull this wagon. Only White Americans can pull it" (Van Ausdale & Feagin 2001, 103).

One of the pioneers in the study of how young children develop identity and prejudice, Dr. Kenneth Clark, noted many years ago the ways racism also harms White children's development (1963). He describes how growing up with the societal contradiction between the professed goals of equality and democracy and the pressures to violate them by acting on racial prejudice can create moral conflicts and guilt for White children. He also warned that White children "are being given a distorted perception of reality and of themselves, and are being taught to gain personal status in unrealistic ways" (81).

Derman-Sparks and Ramsey (2011) suggest strategies for fostering White children's growth in the four ABE core goals. One is to help White children develop a racialized social identity based on personal abilities and interests, family history, and culture that includes anti-bias principles. The second is to also help children form a White identity that does not include the idea of Whiteness as the norm or superior. A third is to support children to be aware of the similarities they have with people of color and also value the diversity of physical characteristics, interests, and abilities among White people.

Children Need Help Resisting Harmful Messages

Children absorb socially prevailing messages about what is normal and right or not right in regard to physical features connected to racialized identities. Thinking that how they look is not right undermines young children's evolving self-concept and confidence (Lane 2008; Ramsey 2015; Tatum 2017). As their teacher, you can provide immediate and follow-up strategies for interrupting and handling these messages.

> Kim Lee keeps insisting that his black hair is yellow and that his skin is pink like his mother's. He always colors his mother and himself with the same hair and skin colors, although he colors his father with dark hair and eyes. The teacher decides to talk with Kim Lee's family about ways they can help him eventually understand that his mom is his mom even though they don't look the same and that she and his father love him just as he is.

. . .

> "I'm going to make my eyes straight and blue," 4-year-old Tomoko tells her teacher. "Why do you want to change your lovely eyes?" Natalya, her teacher, wonders. "It's prettier," Tomoko says. Natalya replies thoughtfully, "Tomoko, I don't think straight eyes are prettier than yours are. Your mommy, grandma, and grandpa don't think so either. We like you just the way you are with your beautiful, dark brown eyes shaped just as they are. Why do you think straight, blue eyes are prettier?" Tomoko answers, "Charlotte said I had ugly eyes. She likes Abigail's better." Natalya tells Tomoko that Charlotte was wrong to say that, adding, "It is not true that you have ugly eyes, and it is unfair to say that. Let's go talk with her about it."

. . .

> Daisy, a White 3-year-old, is washing her hands for snack next to Xavier, who is African American. She looks over and says to him and says, "Why don't your hands get clean?" Xavier replies with annoyance, "They are clean! I just washed them." Their teacher steps in and

says, "Soap and water make our skin clean no matter what color our skin is. Our skin color is part of us, and it doesn't wash off."

Stop & Think: Talking About Racial Issues with Children

- As a child, were you ever the target of racial teasing or slurs? Did you ever observe someone else being the target of such attacks? What was that like for you? Did anyone talk to you about what to do in this kind of situation?

- Do you have any memory of a time when an adult helped you sort out confusing or frightening experiences or ideas about race? Can you remember a time when you *wished* an adult would help you sort out these experiences but didn't? What was each experience like for you?

- What is it like for you when you hear or observe a child demonstrating ideas about racial identity? How comfortable are you talking about this topic with children? What might make you uncomfortable? What could help you to respond with ease?

- As an adult, what, if anything, do you do when you see or hear racial prejudice, including a racist joke? What would you like to do instead of what you did or didn't do?

- What would you feel or do if someone said that you spoke or behaved in a racially prejudiced way?

Strategies and Activities About Racialized Identities and Fairness

Anti-bias educators intentionally and proactively integrate the message into the daily life of their classroom that people of every racialized identity are valuable and deserve caring and fairness.

Use Your School Philosophy, Handbook, and Admissions Materials to Welcome All People

It is not enough to say you are a program that does not discriminate. Throughout the setting and in materials provided to families, include images of peoples of many racial groups. Ask *all* families questions about what terms they use to describe their racial and ethnic identities so you can respect their choices. You may also learn that some families aren't sure how to name their children's racialized identities or prefer not to give them a racialized identity at all. As all children are exposed to language about skin color, it becomes important that they have words to describe themselves and others. This is likely to be an ongoing conversation with families (see Chapter 5).

Make Racial Diversity Visible in Your Learning Environment

Children learn what is important to adults in the program by observing what is and isn't in the learning environment. Here are a few examples (see also Chapter 3).

- Make racial diversity visible in the books, posters, dolls, puzzles, and art materials (crayons, felt pens, paints, and paper in different skin tones). Be sure to include accurate images of children and families with biracial and multiracial identities. Some teachers mix up all the people figures in one box so children can form whatever variation of a family they wish.

- Go through your classroom library and assess your collection. How many books do you have in which the main characters are White? In how many are people of color the main character of the story? What stereotypes of people of color do your books perpetuate? Make a list of books you would like to have in the classroom and outline a plan for how you will acquire new books. Add to your collection with books from your local public library.

A Mother Speaks About Her Black Sons

by Dana Brightful, an African American mother of two young boys

What follows was written in response to a questionnaire sent by Anna Hindley, the director of early childhood education programs at the Smithsonian National Museum of African American History and Culture. The question Dana answered is "What do you wish your child's teacher knew about your child's identity?"

As a parent of two children (3 and 8), [I want to raise them] to excel in education, care for all people, and become respectful global citizens of the world. My desires and concerns for them vary . . . but they both are young Black boys that stand to face tremendous adversity from the world.

For my younger son, I wish his teachers knew how important it is to us that he sees and hears stories about positive and innovative Black men and women on a consistent basis. In our home, we try hard to have books, toys, and videos of people who look like him. We always want him to know and feel that he, his brother, and his entire family are capable of doing anything.

We . . . make a point to always have art materials that he and his brother can use that resemble the skin of the people in our family. His teachers do a good job of creating a safe and loving place for all of the children, but I wish they knew how much it would mean to us and our values if his teachers used many opportunities to share stories of Black men and women. Just something as small as having more books on their shelves where Black men/women or boys/girls were the main characters would change our lives and his too.

For both of my sons, I wish their teachers knew that words matter. Black men and women are often labeled as the aggressor in situations when that may not be the case. I wish their teachers knew that they really have to be careful not to handle the situations [of conflicts between children] like the rest of society [does]. I wish they knew how important it is to allow both persons involved to speak, then interpret each person's truth, come to a resolution, and allow the children to go about their activities without making one child feel invalidated. I've witnessed far too many times, without teachers realizing that I was watching, teachers inadvertently invalidate my children or other children of color and inaccurately make them out to be the child who was wrong in the situation.

Use Teachable Moments

The examples of children's questions and comments throughout this book are all potential teachable moments. What may seem like a little thing by itself can be a big thing to a child. If you can't think what to say or become uncomfortable responding directly and matter-of-factly to an incident, or later feel you didn't handle your initial response well, talk to someone you trust to explore your feelings and possible alternative responses. Then, *always* go back to the children with your new response. (See Chapter 4 for more on conversations during teachable moments.)

During story time, Hector (White, age 4) leans over and touches Jamal's hair. Jamal (African American, age 4) pushes his hand away. Their teacher observes the interaction and steps in.

Teacher: What's happening?

Jamal: Don't like him touching my hair. He didn't ask me if it's okay.

Teacher: How come you touched his hair, Hector?

Hector: Wanna know what it feels like.

Teacher: Jamal, would it be okay if Hector asked first?

Jamal: Yes. (*He turns to Hector.*) Ask me and then you can touch it. Then I want to touch your hair.

Because Jamal has given his permission, the teacher says, "Yes, it's interesting to touch and learn about each other's hair as long as we ask first. Did Jamal's hair feel the same as or different from your hair?" (If Jamal had said it was not all right for Hector to touch his hair, then the teacher might have said, "We need to respect what Jamal says. There are other ways to learn about each other's hair.") The teacher decided to plan a series of activities for children to learn about and appreciate different kinds of hair.

In this next example, the teacher also chooses to use a teachable moment as the starting point for a series of activities:

A predominantly White kindergarten class regularly walks with their teacher to a nearby park where someone has written on a playground wall. The children want to know what the writing says. The teacher explains, "This writing makes me very angry. These are very hurtful words about Mexican American people." He asks the children what they think they can do about the words being on the playground wall where they could hurt people who see them. After some discussion, the children decide to paint over the words. They go back to the school, get some paint, and go back to the playground to cover the wall with paint.

The next day, at circle time, the teacher raises the idea of the children dictating a letter to the people at the parks department, who take care of the nearby parks. The children could tell them what they did to the wall and why. The children like this idea.

As follow-up, bringing the issue of name calling closer to home, the teacher leads a discussion with the children about what to do if a friend says something hurtful to them or if another person makes fun about their looks or who they are. The children make several suggestions, which the teacher writes down on easel paper. They then discuss which ideas might work or not, with the teacher also giving input. The teacher creates a final version of the chart and hangs it up in a place easily seen by the children and their family members. He also sends a note home to all the families with the chart description and explanation of why they made it.

Explore How Physical Features Are Both Alike and Different

Make a life-size cutout of each child from butcher paper. Use mirrors to help each child observe and paint their skin, eyes, and hair color. Be sure you have crayons, paints, and yarn in all the shades you need.

Ask children for their ideas about what skin, hair, and eyes do for them. Talk about how skin, hair, and eyes do the same work for all people, regardless of their color.

Explore the range of ways that children and staff look. (Even in a classroom of all White children, there will be differences in skin color and features like freckles, skin tone, eye color, and length of hair).

Make a bulletin board of color photographs of each child and the members of each child's family. You can take photographs of the family members yourself or invite them to provide their own. Talk about ways in which each child looks and does not look like her or his family members. Focus on the fact that everyone gets their looks from their birth parents, but they never look exactly the same as their birth parents. Also, make clear that children who are adopted get their skin color, eye shape, and so on from their birth parents, and these attributes may or may not be like those of their adoptive parents. Place the bulletin board at the children's viewing height.

Explore how children who look different from one another still often like to do the same things. Take photographs of the children doing various activities and make a book featuring children who look different doing the same activity (e.g., "Pedro and Amani like to create new songs and dances" or "Heather and Kia like to write messages on the drawing tablet").

Read books about the beauty of the different ways we look, such as *Shades of People*, by Shelley Ratner and Sheila Kelly; *All the Colors We Are/Todos los colores de nuestra piel*, by Katie Kissinger; and *I Am Latino: The Beauty in Me*, by Sandra Pinkney. All of these have simple language and beautiful images.

Pay Attention to Indicators of Confusion or Self-Rejection

When children make self-portraits or family drawings, sometimes a child chooses colors that do not correspond to his actual skin, eye, or hair coloring. It is important to ask the child about these choices. Sometimes they indicate discomfort or shame about the child's actual coloring. It is useful, in a conversational tone, to ask the child to talk to you about the portrait. If the coloring is playful (some children paint themselves with rainbow colors or bright green) and the child seems relaxed, you need not take further action. If the child seems uncomfortable describing the colors in the portrait, it is useful to watch for additional indicators of confusion or self-rejection.

If you are concerned, observe the child and make a plan for what you can do to strengthen the child's identity. Check in with other staff about what they have observed and speak with the child's family about what they want their child to know about his racial identity and how you can support the child's positive sense of self in the classroom.

Expand What Children Know About People of All Racial Backgrounds

Introduce children to people in their wider community in ways that are respectful, interest the children, and counter prevailing stereotypes. Many areas of the United States are racially and ethnically diverse, and young children see increasingly diverse images of people on television and videos (although some of these may be misleading or stereotypical). Here are some strategies to consider.

- Look for racial diversity throughout your community. Depending on where you live, you may find individuals of many different racial identities working as the cashier at the neighborhood store, serving as a waiter at the local café, serving customers at the bank, filling prescriptions at the drugstore, helping patrons at the library, building or repairing homes, trimming trees, selling produce at a farmer's market, and so on. Discuss what these people do to help the community. Have the children dictate thank-you notes to them, and deliver the notes with children's drawings.

- Read books about children from different racial backgrounds who do activities familiar to children in your program, such as going to a birthday party, visiting the doctor, and welcoming a new sibling. Help children identify similarities and differences between the child in the story and themselves. Ask: What did you like about the story? What is the child doing that you like to do? What is different from what you do? How is the child's family, home, etc., the same or different from yours? Do the children have the same color skin, hair, and eyes as you do? This is another place where "We are all the same, we are all different" makes a lot of sense to children. Keep track of misinformation or stereotypical or pre-prejudice comments from the children and plan activities to counter children's specific mistaken ideas and teach them accurate information.

- Invite artists, musicians, and crafts people from the children's wider communities to share what they do with the children. If possible, arrange several visits over time. Make sure you invite a racially diverse group of people.

- Plan special developmentally appropriate circle times honoring people of color who have faced adversity and worked to make the world a better place, such as Frederick Douglass, Mahatma Gandhi, Dolores Huerta, and Maya Lin. Include popular sports figures or musicians who have created scholarship programs or led other philanthropic efforts, such as Lebron

James, Colin Kaepernick, Carlos Santana, and Kristi Yamaguchi. Show the children pictures of the people when you talk about them.

Foster Critical Thinking and Acting with Fairness

Cultivate children's empathy and teach them ways to deal with the hurt of stereotyping:

- Use persona dolls, puppets, or felt figures to tell stories about a discriminatory incident between dolls, such as one doll saying to another that her skin is dirty because it is dark. Engage the children's empathy and problem-solving skills as described in this chapter.

- Intentionally plan activities to counter misinformation or stereotypes about groups of people in the children's community. Here's an example:

   A harvest curriculum is being planned for late October. Living in an agricultural area where many of the farm workers are Mexican or Central American, the program staff worries that some of the children might believe that only people with brown skin harvest food and that only White people sell food. They decide to invite some farm workers to school, making sure that it is a multiracial group. They read books such *Gathering the Sun,* by Alma Flor Ada, which celebrates Mexican farm workers, and *Apple Picking Time,* by Michele Benoit Slawson, which shows a family of pickers who are White.

- Support children as they demonstrate awareness of stereotyping.

   Noah is playing with LEGOs, one of his favorite toys. Suddenly he looks at his teacher and announces, "You know, all of the people in this set are White!" His teacher responds, "Hey, you're right. There should be Black and Asian and Latinx figures, too. Maybe in the country where people make LEGO, in Denmark, most people are White. I'm proud of you for noticing because it is important to notice when things are unfair like that."

Engage Children in Group Action

It is empowering when you help children take action to turn something unfair into something fair. Sometimes this involves addressing personal conflicts, such as helping a child speak up to another child. But it is particularly powerful when a group of children act together. The following example illustrates how an early childhood teacher worked with children to respond to specific issues of racial bias in their programs.

   Nancy Spangler's class of 3- and 4-year-olds is a multiracial group, and she works hard to make sure her classroom reflects every child. One day she looks at a box of game cards that matches people in work outfits with the tools they use. The cards are wonderfully gender neutral, but Nancy notices that all the people are White. She calls the children together and asks, "Do the people on these cards look like all the people you know?" The children say no, identifying skin color, age, and even pregnancy status as missing. "Is it fair to have cards that exclude so many people?" Nancy asks. The children agree that it is not. With Nancy's help, the children write a letter to the manufacturer explaining what is wrong. Then she gets out the skin-tone pens and the children re-color the cards so they will "look real."

The social-political and psychological dimensions of race remain a contentious and painful issue in society. If early childhood educators want children to thrive in a diverse world, they must commit to helping them make sense of the confusing and often emotionally charged messages they receive about people's racialized identities. Give children language to discuss their identities, and answer their questions in an atmosphere of interest, delight, and respect. Plant seeds of openness and connection. Teach them tools for addressing the unfairness they will inevitably encounter, and encourage them to stand up for themselves and others. You can help children construct a strong foundation for thriving in a diverse world now and into the future.

CHAPTER 9

Learning About Gender Diversity and Fairness

Annie, who is 4 years old, loves running outside. In the classroom, she speaks up in a loud voice and rarely sits still. At circle time, the class is talking about a book we have just read together and the gendered stereotypes we see in it. Annie says, "But, Julie, I don't like girls." I am surprised. "Why not, Annie?" I ask. "'Cause girls can't run and shout and have a good time," she says sadly. "But Annie, you say you're a girl. And you love to run and shout and have a good time." "No," she replies, "I'm a pretend girl."

Like all social identities, gender identity is imposed externally by society and internally constructed by the child. The first question asked about a new or expected baby is almost always "Is it a boy or a girl?" The answer to that question will affect multiple aspects of the child's experiences and development for the rest of the child's life.

Gender is the first core identity that attracts young children's attention. By age 2, most toddlers call themselves a girl or boy. They don't yet have understanding of the two words, but they know they are important. By 4, most children clearly state that they are either a girl or boy and have absorbed dominant culture ideas about what boys and girls are supposed to do and how they are supposed to look. They frequently insist that the stereotypical behaviors are right even when those contradict their own experiences or desires (e.g., insisting that boys don't cry).

Anti-Bias Education in Action: Gender Role Expectations Start Young

Katie and Max attend a program for 2-year-olds. Katie is small with big brown eyes and brown curls. She comes to the toddler room each day dressed in pastel-colored dresses, socks, and barrettes. People often comment with delight that she looks like a "living doll." Max is affectionately nicknamed "Mack Truck." He is sturdy, strong, and big for his age. Katie fascinates Max. Every day he waits for her to arrive, runs across the room to her while shouting her name—and pushes her down. Katie usually bursts into tears and the adults gather her up into their arms, comfort her, and take her to another part of the room. Max is sternly told to use his words and not to push and is sometimes shepherded out into the yard to "run off some of his energy."

After several weeks, the center director steps in. "What do you think Katie is learning from the way you are handling this?" she asks the teachers. "What do you think Max is learning? Can you find a way to help Katie not be a victim? Can you help Max not be the aggressive 'bad boy'? Let's figure out how you can support these two children."

The next day, one of the teachers takes Katie over to the mirror in the playhouse and asks her to copy her as she plants her feet firmly and widely on the ground (stomp, stomp), pushes her hands out in front of her, and says in a clear, firm voice, "Stop it! Don't push. Stop it! Don't push!" Katie looks amazed and a little puzzled, but the teacher repeats what she did, encouraging Katie to join in. As several other children come over and imitate the teacher, Katie, tentatively at first, begins to join in. Throughout the day the children play at planting their feet and watching themselves in the mirror as they chant, "Stop it! Don't push!" Katie becomes more and more animated each time she practices this response.

At home, Katie's mom continues the "game" with Katie, who on her own adds Max's name. Two days later, Katie arrives at the center. Racing across the room, Max is greeted by Katie standing firmly on both feet, punching her hands up in front of her body and saying the powerful words loudly, "Stop it, Max! Stop it. Don't push!" Max is stunned. He collapses on the ground in tears, while Katie triumphantly steps around him and walks over to the art table and sits down.

This time the teachers' focus is on Max. He is comforted and given words he might use: "Katie, come play," "Hello, Katie," or "Here's a toy we can share." And over the next weeks the staff works thoughtfully with him, telling him what a friendly, caring child he is, helping him find children to play with, supporting his need for both big motor and companion play. He and Katie never become good friends, but both children have their sense of themselves widened and enriched. And the staff become much more aware of how their language and implicit assumptions had cheated both children out of developing new skills.

Applying Anti-Bias Education Goals to Gender Identity

- Children will express their ideas and positive feelings about their gender identity and be comfortable with their own way of expressing gender. **(Goal 1)**

- Children, regardless of gender identity, will participate in a wide range of activities necessary for their full cognitive, social, emotional, and physical development. **(Goal 1)**

- Children will have vocabulary for, and ease in talking about, the great diversity in appearance, emotional expressiveness, and behavior of children across the spectrum of gender expression and identities. **(Goal 2)**

- Children will recognize stereotypical ideas and images and hurtful behaviors directed at their own and others' gendered identities. They will know that it is not fair to treat people hurtfully because of who they are. **(Goal 3)**

- Children will recognize and respect the power each person has, including themselves, to determine their own gender identity and say who they are, regardless of adult interpretations of their bodies. **(Goal 4)**

- Children will practice skills for supporting gender diversity in their interactions with peers and adults. **(Goal 4)**

The Big Picture: From a Binary to a Multifaceted Understanding of Gender

Historically and currently, a binary perspective—meaning only two options—on being female or male has prevailed in the United States and many other societies, with proscribed sets of rules of behavior, dress, and roles for males and females. These binary, gendered expectations of people influence children's socialization and early childhood educators' interactions with children (Butler-Wall et al. 2016; Jaboneta & Curtis 2019). Current thinking reveals a more complex and nuanced understanding of gender development that goes beyond a binary approach and casts greater light on how expectations of traditional femininity and masculinity limit children's development (Bian, Leslie, & Cimpian 2017; Brown & Stone 2016; Pastel et al. 2019).

The Binary Model of Gender Identity

The prevailing model of gender rests on binary opposites of expected behaviors, attitudes, skills, feelings, appearance, and life outcomes. A range of societal policies, rules, and actions—some built into the law, others part of traditional thinking—spell out these assumptions about gender (Butler-Wall et al. 2016; Rajunov & Duane 2019).

Critically considering common stereotypes about men and women is one way to become more aware of the expectations of a binary gender model. As you read this list, think about where you have seen or experienced these assumptions about people based on their gender:

Men are	Women are
Physically strong	Physically weak
Decision makers	Peacemakers
Key wage earners (may "help out" at home)	Homemakers (may "help" support the family)
Disciplinarians	Nurturers, healers
Driven by desire for achievement	Driven by the desire to be loved
Admired for economic success	Admired for appearance
Potentially violent, dangerous	Potentially victims, in danger
Good at math and science	Good at reading and psychology
Bad at close relationships	Bad at physical relationships
Logical	Emotional
Honorable	Sweet
Energetic	Sentimental
Predatory	Fearful

Of course, it is unlikely that anyone ever acts out *all* the binary gender expectations listed here. And, many people's lives reflect specific behaviors from both sides of the list. Moreover, the components of a gender binary way of being are not necessarily the ideals for being male and female in all cultural groups in the United States or in all parts of the world. Yet, to one degree or another, everyone experiences the power of binary gender messages about how women and men are supposed to be. Most people have been rewarded or injured by living out or not living out those stereotypical gender characteristics.

Stop & Think: What Did You Learn About Gender Binary Expectations?

- What were your earliest lessons about your gender? What were major messages about behaviors and feelings that were okay for boys but not for girls? Okay for girls but not for boys?

- As a child, what did you like about being the gender you learned to call yourself? Did you feel any conflict between what you liked to do or wanted to do and what you were supposed to do?

- How did the adults in your family divide work and responsibilities by gender? In what ways did your teachers make distinctions based on the gender binary model of being a girl or a boy? Were the lessons about gender you learned at home the same or different from those you were learning at school and other places?

- Do you remember knowing or learning about people who did not conform to binary gender roles? What messages did you receive about these people? How did you feel about them?

A Multifaceted Understanding of Gender

As an early childhood educator, you teach young children who are in the foundational period of developing their gender identities. One necessary step to positively support this development is understanding distinct yet interrelated aspects of gender: **assigned sex, gender role, gender identity, gender expression, and sexuality.**

These concepts support a deeper understanding of the young child's internal construction of gender identity and offer a more complete way to guide children's individualized paths in their gender development journey.

Assigned Sex at Birth

Assigned sex at birth refers to the naming of an infant as a boy or a girl based on the first sight of the infant's genitals. Assigning a newborn's sex used to take place only at birth; now it often happens using sonograms toward the end of the fourth month of pregnancy. The assigned sex designation has profound legal implications for the rest of a child's life. However, gender binary assigning of sex does not take into account the many genetic variations beyond XX and XY chromosomes or the many hormonal patterns that impact children prenatally. In addition, some children are born with ambiguous genitals or genetic or hormonal variations and are termed *intersex*. Early childhood educators serve all these children and need to know how to best support children and families as children work to construct their gender identity.

Gender Role

Gender *role* is the way society and families think about, interact with, and treat people based on their assigned sex. A society's expectations of gender roles influences what early childhood educators and families do with and for children (Butler-Wall et al. 2016; Jaboneta & Curtis 2019). This starts during infancy and becomes more evident in the preschool years.

It is necessary to uncover and identify both explicit and implicit assumptions about gender role in order to create learning environments for children based on anti-bias education goals. This means providing an environment that supports *all* children to be physically strong and competent *and* emotionally open and resilient; successful in family life *and* work life; and able to grow their gifts and interests to their full potential. It also means encouraging children to explore a wide range of activities and not be limited to interests, skills, and experience typically considered to be acceptable for only boys or only girls.

Gender Identity

Gender *identity* is one's internal experience of one's gender. It is how one thinks of and comes to name oneself. A person's gender identity may or may not conform to one's assigned sex and may change throughout one's lifetime. Some of the terms that describe gender identity include *cisgender, agender, transgender, nonbinary,* and *gender fluid* (see the glossary for definitions). Terms evolve and vary from one locale to another. Adults and children may also change the pronouns used to describe themselves. Anti-bias education calls on teachers to learn and treat respectfully the gender identity terms families and children use.

Gender Expression

Gender *expression* is the way people present themselves to the world. It includes how they dress, speak, play, and behave. Some children are mainly *gender conforming*, appearing and behaving in ways that mostly match binary expectations. Other children may be *gender creative* or *gender expansive*, dressing, playing, and expressing themselves in ways that push the boundaries of binary expectations. Gender expression may or may not indicate the child's eventual gender identity or sexual orientation. An anti-bias educator acknowledges and supports each child's current gender expression as an important part of the child's developmental journey.

To fully understand gender development in the early years, it is also necessary to distinguish the concepts of *sexuality, sexual orientation,* and *sexual behavior* (which come into play more fully as children grow) from the other components of young children's developmental paths. (See the glossary for definitions of these terms). Anxiety about a child's sexuality often underlies a parent's concern that a child playing or dressing contrary to gender binary expectations will set the child up for shaming or bullying and that such play can shape the child's eventual sexual behavior.

> During the many years I (Julie) worked directly with children, it was pretty common for some parents to become upset when seeing their child, usually a boy, playing with "the wrong toys" for their gender. The fear that the child would grow up to be gay because of their

play was almost always behind these parents' concerns. I always listened carefully and then reassured the parent that a child's eventual sexuality could not be changed, one way or the other, by the toys they played with or the clothing they liked best. Sometimes my assurances helped. Sometimes they didn't. But at one point, one of my colleagues, who was gay, stopped me and said, "What you didn't say is that if their child *is* gay, he is still their child." With a shock I realized I was unconsciously playing into the biased message that there was something awful about not being heterosexual.

My new message still included the information that toys and clothes neither create nor shift anyone's sexual orientation. But now I also added, "And if it were to become true that your child is gay, he will still be your beautiful, wonderful child. And it will always be your job to love and protect him." Somehow, these words always deepened and changed the conversation and led to more conversations—and to parents being more open to the ways their child was exploring the world.

What's in a Name? Gendered Terms and Pronouns

Many young children, like Annie in the opening vignette, create names beyond the binary terms of girl and boy to describe how they think of own gender identity and how they perceive other people's gender identity. They may use descriptive names such as *inbetweener*, *boy-girl* or *girl-boy*, or *Casey is a she/he*. They may shift pronouns to try to describe nonconforming behavior, such as "Marcus is a boy, but she has long hair and likes to wear barrettes." Pay attention to these terms because they are one indicator of how a child is thinking about gender.

The use of pronouns is one important declaration of how some people identify their gender. For example, instead of using the pronouns *she/her/hers* or *he/him/his,* a person might prefer *they/them/theirs* as more accurate singular pronouns. Others may create new pronouns that do not connect them to a binary gender identity.

Understanding the multifaceted aspects of gender development focuses educators' and families' attention on the young child's internal construction of identity as well as the external influence of societal and family gender expectations. Anti-bias early childhood programs create a supportive environment in which all children's feelings and explorations about their gender are taken seriously and listened to compassionately and where each child is helped to flourish beyond hurtful stereotypical gender expectations.

Stop & Think: You and New Understandings About Gender Development

- Think about some specific ways in which you do *not* conform to binary gender expectations about how men or women are supposed to be. What is that like for you? What parts feel good? What parts get hard?

- Are there people you know, or know of, whom you admire because they live in ways that are not limited by stereotypical gender assumptions? Why do you admire them?

- What are your current thoughts about this multifaceted model of gender development? Which concepts are most helpful and important to you in relation to yourself? In relation to being an early childhood educator?

Young Children Construct Ideas and Attitudes About Gender

Observing children's behavior and listening to what they have to say is the best way to pay attention to how they are making sense of complicated ideas such as gender.

"She can't be Toby. That's a boy name."

"Boys don't cry," says Carlos fiercely as he watches his friend Tyrone crying about his skinned knee.

"William has long hair and is so pretty! Is he a girl?"

"Rose plays train and trucks all the time. Is she a boy-girl?"

The Gender Journey

Children's development of gender identity begins early—and visibly influences their behavior and their perceptions of others. For example, while 2-year-olds, regardless of gender, still play with dolls and soft stuffed toys, by the end of the third year, doll play tends to become a girl's activity. At 3 and 4 years of age, children also tend to use clues from stereotypical expectations of dress and appearance to decide who is a girl and who a boy.

> Alfonso, a teacher in the 3-year-old room, wears an earring. At snack time, the children at his table ask him whether he is a man or a woman. He asks, "What do you think?" They cannot agree—some insist he must be a woman because "only women wear earrings." Others say, "But he said he was a daddy!"

By age 4, children often insist on stereotypical gendered behavior for others as well as themselves, even when their life experiences show them more expansive behaviors.

> Four-year-old Myles and the teacher are looking at a picture book about various kinds of transportation. When they reach the page about cars and trucks, the teacher stops: "Myles, this book is showing only men as the drivers, and that is not true. Women drive cars, trucks, and buses too." But Myles shakes his head. "Uh-uh, ladies don't drive trucks," he declares. "But, Myles, how did you get to school today"? asks the teacher. "My mother brought me," he replies. "In what?" asks the teacher, already knowing the answer. "In our red pickup truck," say Myles. "And your mother is a woman, isn't she?" asks the teacher. There is a long pause, then Myles replies, "Yeah—but the truck really belongs to my uncle."

Children Are Curious About Anatomy

Young children figure out quickly that people have different kinds of bodies—including genitals. They are curious about the differences they see. Their families may or may not have given them names for genitals (sometimes, the names are unique to the family). By age 3 or 4, children have often absorbed embarrassment about genital anatomy, which generally manifests itself in giggling and teasing.

Young children eventually realize that genitals have something to do with why people are called male or female. This connection between gender and genitals adds to children's confusion and tension about both topics.

> Milo has had a toileting accident and wet his pants. It is the end of the week and the center's drawer of extra underwear is almost empty. The only pair of underwear that fits Milo is patterned with flowers. "I can't put that on," he wails. "My peepee will fall off!"

At this moment, Milo needs simple reassurance, such as "No piece of clothing changes our bodies." His teacher could then help him find a costume or dress-up items he could wear home without underwear. But his concern motivates the teacher to begin an exploration of clothing and the idea that putting on costumes (cat ears, pirate hats, butterfly wings), changing shirts from blue to pink, or putting on masks does not change children's bodies or who they are.

Children Pay Attention to Social Expectations About Gender Roles

Because children are so skilled at absorbing societal messages, they often self-limit their behaviors. Although some children are particularly resilient about their gender expression, others experience emotional conflict when they engage in activities that contradict the stereotypical expectations.

> Some of the favorite dress-up clothes in the center are made from adults' skirts. Small slits cut under the waistband for the children's arms let the skirts become superhero capes, princess gowns, doctor's uniforms—anything the children want them to be. One morning the teacher put out some of the costume skirts. Brad puts on the red one, but Victor hesitates. He reaches for the bright turquoise satiny one. "Is this a boy's costume?" he asks. "This is a costume for everyone. Do you call yourself a boy?" the teacher responds. "Yes," he replies soberly. "Then if you wear it, it's a boy's costume," she says. Victor's face

brightens and he puts it on and with arms outstretched swirls around with delight.

A few minutes later Giovanna comes over and stares at Victor. "That's a girl's dress," she says emphatically. Victor's face clouds. His arms come down. He pulls the skirt off and kicks it, saying, "You're ugly," and leaves it on the ground. That is the last time he plays in one of the bright, shiny costumes.

It is experiences like this that call on teachers to interrupt attacks on children's gender expression and develop curriculum that supports children's free play and exploration.

Socializing Children into Binary Gender Roles

Preparations for a new baby are typically heavily based on gender binary assumptions. Before families know anything about what the child will be like—energy level, style of interacting, personality, temperament, and so on—assumptions about gendered behavior and appearance begin to influence families' interactions with the child. For example, the way people hold babies and how much they hold them; whether they encourage or discourage infants' movement; and how they respond to infants' distress are all heavily influenced by gender assumptions. As the infant grows, explicit and

Transgender Children

Transgender is a term for people whose gender identity differs from the sex they were assigned at birth. These children *know* they are not a boy or a girl as they have been told. They are often deeply troubled that the world does not acknowledge what they know to be true about themselves. Psychologist Diane Ehrensaft (2016) describes these children's knowledge of their transgender identity as being *"persistent, insistent, and consistent"* (author's emphasis).

While many young children experience confusion about the supposed permanence of assigned sex (for example, thinking they can change from boy to girl by changing clothes), and while some children call themselves by their assigned sex but resist gendered limits on their behavior (their gender expression), there are some young children who insist that their assigned sex doesn't fit their gender identity. For these children, clarity about their gender identity may come in adolescence or adulthood. But for some, there is clarity as young as the preschool years, and they strenuously object to being called by, and treated as if, their assigned sex truly represents them. These children are actively unhappy with clothing, toys, and behaviors that are stereotypically associated with their assigned sex. They make it clear that their body is the wrong body for who they really are. Other children who experience dissonance between

their feelings and assigned gender may internalize a sense of shame, retreat inward, and not make their feelings clear with persistence, insistence, and consistency. That is one major reason teachers must work hard to create a supportive environment for gender diversity where children feel empowered to communicate their individual truths.

Ehrensaft (2016) believes when children are clear and persistent about believing that their identity does not match their body, it is time for a social transition. This consists of using the pronouns the child prefers, allowing the child to dress according to the gender the child claims, and usually changing the child's name. In some parts of the country it may include changing the child's birth certificate (Nutt 2015). These social transitions precede for many years the potential use of puberty blockers or hormone therapy and surgical options (Letzter 2018).

Some families of transgender children may be fully supportive, ready to be advocates, and have access to helpful resources. Other families may be confused or frightened or angry. In either case, it is your responsibility as the child's early childhood teacher to listen thoughtfully, to share developmental information, to assure the family that their child is fully accepted and supported at school, and to help the family find community resources for what may be a long-term journey.

implicit gender conditioning is so pervasive that it often looks as if children are freely choosing to "just be who they naturally are!" (Brown & Stone 2016; Ehrensaft 2016).

> Cassandra's 4-year-old nephew, Stephen, loves trucks and buses. He shrieks with delight when he sees one. When the sanitation workers come to collect the bins, he demands that a family member follow the truck down the block so he can continue to watch the machinery.

> One day, as Cassandra is helping to pack up her nephew's baby clothes and toys for a friend's new baby, she notices that all the infant clothing has pictures of trucks, cars, fire engines, and balls. She then checks the bag of baby toys and finds that even the soft, stuffed toys are either balls or cars (except for two teddy bears). For the first time, she begins to wonder when the family began pointing out trucks to Stephen. She also wonders if she ever pointed out trucks to her daughter Jacqueline. That starts the memories of how often she pointed out other babies to Jacqueline. Maybe, she thinks, the family taught her nephew, at least to some extent, to love trucks and cars.

Early childhood educators' interactions with children, whether intentionally or unintentionally, frequently reflect binary expectations of gender roles that narrow children's opportunities for their fullest development. For example, teachers may line children up by gender or may unconsciously ask boys to help with physical activities (moving the chairs, getting the nap mats out) and ask girls to help with nurturing activities (getting an ice pack out of the freezer, helping the new child find her cubby). Teachers may not recognize the implicit bias in these interactions and may not even believe in the messages they are conveying.

> When I (Julie) was working at a university preschool, we were videotaped so student teachers could see what good practice looked like. My video showed me greeting children as they arrived, down at their eye level, speaking to each child individually, like the good master teacher I was.

> Suddenly, I had a shocking moment of self-realization: I greeted every girl with a comment about her appearance: "Hello, Laurie! What a pretty blue blouse you're wearing." "Hi, Noli! You have two bouncy ponytails today." And I greeted every boy with a comment about action: "Hey there, Anil, I put the blocks out for you." "Good morning, Isaac! Your friend Karl is here already, waiting to play with you." On the tape, one little boy stood in front of me, stamping his feet. The power of unconscious stereotyping was evident, as not until he stuck his foot in my face did I notice what he was saying: "Look, Teacher! I got new boots."

Stereotypical Binary Gender Roles Have Long-Lasting Effects

Psychologist Carol Gilligan (1993) has explored the ways societal ideas of a gender binary teaches people to perceive and understand the world in two distinctly different ways: as boys and girls and later, women and men. She argues that boys learn to see the world as a place of individualism and competition, where men endeavor to get higher and higher in a power hierarchy (Chu 2014). In such a world, the higher you climb, the better you are. In a "ladder" world, the best place to be is on top with as much space as possible between you and anyone else. Girls learn to see the world as a web where everyone is connected and interrelated. In such a world, the most important place to be is in the center, holding all the pieces together. In a "web" world, anyone making space, or moving away, threatens the integrity of the whole web. Each of these ways of

Anti-Bias Education for Young Children and Ourselves

being and knowing has strengths and weaknesses, and each, by itself, limits a person's development to only part of what human beings can be. Similarly, Belenky et al. (1997) explored different ways of knowing that appeared to be learned gender-based approaches. Women tended to rely on connected knowledge, attempting to build on each other's ideas. Men tended to rely on independent, competitive knowledge, where each individual defends his way of understanding. It is interesting to consider what kinds of gender socialization promotes one or the other kind of knowing.

These gender observations can become stereotypes that may be used as justifications for institutionally unequal treatment of women and men. Some examples are that it is okay to pay men more than women for doing the same job because men have to take care of a family; men aren't patient and nurturing enough to work with young children; women are not suited to being president of the United States because they are too emotional; women who get raped are responsible for it because of how they dressed or acted; and sexual harassment is no big deal because boys will be boys. One view that is especially relevant to early childhood educators is the justification of inadequate wages with the reasoning that taking care of children is natural for women and takes no special skill.

Strategies and Activities About Gender and Fairness

As with all social identities, anti-bias teachers ground curriculum planning in their knowledge about gender development in general and specifically on observations of the children with whom they work. Observing children's play during choice time is one useful way to learn about children's thinking regarding gender and how gender is affecting their lives. It's important to note in which ways children's choices divide along gender lines. Who plays in the housekeeping area and uses "quiet" materials like puzzles, books, or art supplies? Who plays in the block area and uses "action" materials like cars and trucks, tools, balls, and climbing structures? During dramatic play, which children are the doctors, superheroes, or firefighters most of the time and which are the nurses, babies and mamas, or cashiers? Do only some children join in on dancing? Do

children tell classmates that they cannot play in a specific area because they are a particular gender? Which children are more gender conforming and which are more gender expansive?

Remember that while you want to support choice, children's choices are not completely their own; they are influenced by socially explicit messages and, all too often, by unconscious practices in their early childhood programs. Ensure that all children engage in a wide range of activities valuable for their cognitive, social, emotional, and physical development. Use your observational data to plan ways for children to engage in their activities of choice *and* in activities they typically do not choose. Create a learning environment that supports development beyond gendered expectations. To build your skills to support children to be fully who they can be, reflect on your own experiences and feelings about how gendered expectations shape *your* life.

Establish Nongendered Routines and Experiences

Children are excellent observers and learn a great deal from how adults organize their lives. The covert messages children acquire (when Mommy and Daddy are together, only Daddy drives the car) are stronger than the overt messages (you can be or do anything you want to be). They absorb the covert messages when someone says, "How about you boys go outside and run some energy off," or when the only male teacher on the staff is the one who always supervises outdoor active play. Regularly assess what gendered messages are sent to children by your routines and consider the strategies you can use to expand children's experiences.

- Insist that all children take equal responsibility in carrying out the jobs necessary for maintaining the classroom or center. Create diverse teams that rotate responsibility for each task. At group times, show your appreciation for the work that the teams do.

- If you use lining up as a method for organizing children's group movement, invite children to make a list of all the ways they can line up other than "boys here, girls there." Then use their ideas! One of our favorites was a group of 3-year-olds who came up with "If you like cake better than ice cream, line up here. If you like ice cream better than cake, line up here." Think of other ways: "If you are wearing blue, line up here. If you are wearing red, line up here! If you are wearing both, you can choose which line." "All children with baby sisters or brothers line up here. All children who are the youngest or are the only, line up here!"

- Ensure that all the children get equal opportunities to speak at group times and snack times and in learning centers. Be conscious of the stereotype around girls learning to talk about feelings and friends and boys learning to talk about ideas. Encourage *all* the children to talk and listen broadly.

- Give all children, regardless of gender identity, support in figuring out solutions to problems rather than going to their rescue (most commonly done for girls) or judging behavior as negative (most commonly done with boys).

- Have a classroom motto such as "Everyone is safe here. Everyone gets to be different in their own way." Repeat it frequently and never allow teasing, exclusion, or bullying of gender fluid and gender creative children (or any child).

Use Teachable Moments to Have Clarifying Conversations

Here are some examples of using children's comments to help them explore gender identity:

Wesley has been watching Raj play with the baby dolls and rock them to sleep. "Teacher, is he a girl?" Wesley asks. "Why do you think he is a girl?" questions the teacher. "Well, he's playing like a girl, but he's a boy!" Wesley says, sounding puzzled. "You're right, Raj has a body people call 'boy,' and he likes to play that he's a daddy. But dolls are for everyone, so that doesn't tell you if Raj is a girl. Only Raj can tell us that. Shall we ask?"

• • •

Harper, a 4-year-old, asks her teacher, "How do you think I look today?" Her teacher responds, "I think you look fine. Why?" Harper replies, "Sometimes I think I look ugly." Her teacher pursues this: "But why?" "Grandma says I look pretty when I put on a dress for church." "You know," says her teacher, "you

also look wonderful in jeans and a T-shirt, and sometimes it's easier to play in them because they don't tear as easily. You look like Harper no matter what you wear. People look wonderful in all kinds of clothing!"

• • •

Jamir and Luis have put on capes and are running through the yard being superheroes, and "zapping bad guys" with their imaginary guns. After watching for a few minutes, Claire begins to run alongside them, shouting "Out of the way, bad guys!" Jamir stops and says sternly, "You can't be a superhero! Only boys can!" Claire stops, and looks at the teacher, and asks, "Girls can be superheroes, too, can't they?" The teacher responds by asking Jamir, "What makes a superhero?" After a short discussion, the three children decide that superheroes must be smart and strong and fast and want to help people. "I think that means that all people can be superheroes," says the teacher, and the game starts again with all three children playing.

• • •

"He's fat!" comments Vincent about Devin, a new child in the program. "You're noticing that Devin's body is bigger than yours," the teacher replies. "*Fat* is a word that is hurtful. Let's go see what kinds of things Devin likes to do so you can get to know him better."

Go Beyond the Teachable Moment

Using teachable moments is a valuable part of ABE, but it is not enough. It's essential to expand on the ideas, information, and feelings that teachable moments bring forth. For example, you can use persona doll stories that explore children's ideas about gender as well as provide accurate information and opportunities for problem solving. Read books that depict girls and boys in activities that go beyond traditional gender roles, such as *Carmela Full of Wishes*, by Matt de la Peña, or *I'm Jay, Let's Play,* by Beth Reichmuth. Invite adults whose work counters stereotypical ideas of gender to talk with the children about who they are and what they do.

Here is an example of going beyond a teachable moment with planned activities. It focuses on the issue of body shaming—humiliating someone by making mocking or critical comments about their body shape or size. While standards of body appearance vary in different cultural and racial groups, the anxiety about not living up to unrealistic body appearance standards can and does have long-term negative outcomes.

> A new teacher, whose body is an ample size, has been hired to work in the preschool program. With her permission, the teacher currently in the room decides to proactively discuss body size with the children and sets up an activity in which the children trace their bodies on butcher paper, decorate the forms, and hang them around the room. As the children admire their work, the teacher starts a conversation about how interesting it is that some children are taller, some shorter, some rounder, some thinner. One of the 4-year-olds adds, "I used to be little but now I'm big," and uses her arms to indicate the difference in height. Delighted, the teacher agrees and reminds the children that bodies change but people are still the same people. "Isn't it wonderful that we have such different bodies," she says. "Otherwise we would all look alike!"
>
> The next day the teacher tells a persona doll story about a child not wanting to play with a classmate because he is fat. "What do you think about that?" the teacher asks. The children are staunch in their statements that it isn't fair, but they wonder how to describe someone who is, "you know, big and round." "Well," replies the teacher, "*big and round* sounds okay to me. What other words could you use?" The children come up with words like *snuggly, squishy, just a different body*. "Can you tell what kind of friend someone will be by the shape of their body?" the teacher asks. The children make clear that wouldn't work.
>
> When the new teacher comes, several of the children mention with interest that she is a "round kind of person." She agrees, adding "I'm also very strong and I love to run!"

Encourage active play for all children. Focus on children's personal strengths instead of appearances. Initiate conversations about the naturalness of people having many types of bodies. Body shape and size is another arena where the key anti-bias idea "We are all the same. We all have bodies. We are all different.

Our bodies are different shapes and sizes. Isn't that wonderful!" can be very useful to help children avoid the harm of body shaming.

Create Curriculum that Encourages Children to Try New Learning Centers

Based on your observations of the children's interactions with each other and the materials in the classroom, resupply and reorganize areas in the classroom to encourage choices that are more diverse and less gender limited. For example, expand the dramatic play area beyond housekeeping props. Add tool belts and tools for making home repairs, put writing and reading materials (paper, pencils, brochures, computer keyboards) on a table with a chair (children may name it the study or the office).

> After a field trip to the zoo, Miss Zela decides to move the dramatic play area next to the blocks. She places stuffed animals in both areas. For several days the girls play with the animals, putting them to bed and feeding them while the boys build enclosures in which they place the hard-plastic animals that had always been with the blocks. Concerned about the gendered play, at group time the teacher leads a conversation about what kinds of places the different animals need to play and sleep, and how it is the zookeeper's job to take good care of them. She passes around various cuddly animals while they talk. "Do you think you could play zookeeper and take care of the pandas and build them a safe home?" she asks. The children consider the question, and both boys and girls begin to build spaces for the animals and also play at feeding and caring for them.

While rearranging the environment encourages most children to try new activities, some children need extra support. You can invite children who are reluctant to work in a particular learning area to try new materials and activities *with* you until they initiate such activities themselves.

If you notice boys avoiding dancing and rapidly turning any dance into raucous jumping, invite a man who likes to dance to demonstrate with the children.

Follow up with reading a book that shows males dancing, such as the gorgeous photo book about Bill T. Jones (*Dance!* by Bill T. Jones and Susan Kuklin).

Have an "Everybody Plays Blocks" day and an "Everybody Does Art" day once a week for a month until all the children freely choose block play and art activities. (This method may require extra blocks: Team with another teacher to use her blocks on your block day and then switch.) Work with individual children who are hesitant or resistant.

Here's an example:

> Nancy is concerned about the 4-year-old girls in her class who usually avoid the block corner, which is almost always dominated by the boys. She makes a list of the children who avoid the blocks and creates "work teams," whom she invites to help her build something special in the block area. She assures the other children that they will all have turns later. It only takes about a week before the "nonblock" kids feel at home with the blocks, and when the area is again open to all, they continue to play there.

Acknowledge Children's Nonstereotypical Gender Expression

Providing support when children choose nonstereotypical gendered behaviors is a significant way to make child choice an acceptable way of being. Often, this simply requires a brief comment.

> Sofia is playing firefighter, wearing a real fire hat and jacket. Mateo wants them for himself. "Girls can't be firemen," he tells Sofia, trying to take off her hat. "Yes, they can," Sofia insists, pushing his hand away from her hat and continuing to play. Mateo shakes his head but walks off. Their teacher, seeing their interaction, comments to Sofia, "I'm glad you spoke up for yourself when Mateo said girls can't fight fires. They can."

• • •

> Chun has put on the blue sparkly cape and announces to the other children that he is Princess Elsa. "You can't be a princess," replies Olivia. "You're a boy!" Chun laughs and says "No, no, no. I'm a girl-boy and a princess boy and girl princess," and races over to the big mirror to dance. The teacher turns to Olivia and says, "You heard Chun. She/he is a princess!"

At other times it is useful to initiate follow-up activities with the whole group, as this teacher did:

> Casper loves playing with the dolls in the dramatic play center. His dad takes care of him and his siblings while his mom works at a factory. One day his teacher sees Derek playing with the blocks, which are next to the dramatic play center. She overhears Derek tell Casper, "Boys don't play with dolls." "Yes, they do," insists Casper. The teacher decides to step in, "Derek, many boys play with dolls. Do you know that men take care of children, like Casper's dad takes care of him, his brother, and his sister!" Derek looks dubious and goes back to play with the blocks. The teacher decides to do several activities with all the children about men who take care of children as daddies, uncles, and teachers.

Model Behaviors that Transcend Traditional Gender Stereotypes

Children pay more attention to what you do than what you say. As an early childhood teacher, examine the ways you do or don't fall into stereotyped behavior. Model a commitment to treat everyone with equal respect regardless of their gender identities.

● Actively contradict staffing stereotypes by having female staff do carpentry, male staff take care of snack preparation, everyone take turns leading group times, and so on.

Anti-Bias Education for Young Children and Ourselves

- Look for staff behaviors that subtly reflect stereotypical gender roles. For example, which teachers ask questions and which explain things? Who takes care of small injuries and who is responsible for fire drills or emergency drills?

- Model genuine, caring, respectful, cross-gender friendships.

- If your program has not yet hired men and gender expansive or gender fluid people, invite family members, staff friends, or community members who represent a variety of gender identities into the classroom as often as possible. However, avoid using one person as a representative of a single group (such as one person who comes often and is the only transgender man seen in the program).

Include Men in Early Childhood Education

adapted from Bryan Nelson
(Derman-Sparks & Edwards 2010, 100)

There is a long history of men caring for children as fathers, uncles, brothers, and grandfathers. How they did this varied by culture and throughout history—so too has the way women care for children varied. Positive male figures are particularly important for children in the context of social changes that have made them absent from, or marginal, in many children's lives. Critical research studies show that

having more male educators in early childhood education could benefit all children by providing opportunities for them to observe and interact with men in a nontraditional role. Many researchers agree that if there are more men in early childhood settings demonstrating caring behaviors, this could help to counter children's sex-stereotyped views of gender roles, reduce sexism, and generally advance gender equality (Yang 2013). Male teachers may also make early childhood programs feel more welcoming for fathers and grandfathers.

> As they grow, all children need to see and be part of relationships in which male children and adults are allowed to be emotionally expressive and deeply connected. This is especially true for children who identify as male, since our culture often discourages them from such expression. Improving the gender balance of the early childhood workforce would provide all children with a richer variety of role models at this critical time in their gender identity development. (Cole et al. 2019, 40)

Keeping children safe is always a priority in early childhood programs. But fear that men will molest children has resulted in some programs instituting no-touch policies for male teachers or refusing to hire them at all. Neither of these solutions, based on misinformation and biases, keeps children safe. Actions that *do* work include careful screening, recruiting, and supervising of *all* staff and volunteers; providing staff training on preventing and recognizing child abuse; and building close partnerships with families.

Support Development of Children's Critical Thinking About Gender Injustice and Gender Fairness

Young children are very sensitive to behaviors that feel unfair to them and are eager to be part of changing unfair to fair. Ellen Wolpert, a longtime center director and anti-bias educator, describes a useful critical thinking tool to counter children's absorption of stereotypes, which she calls the Fact or Stereotype game. This is great game to help children investigate their own world and test out information themselves. It is very empowering, and the children love the big word *ster-e-o-type!*

> Introduce the word *fact* as "something we all agree is true" and then the word *stereotype* as "something that isn't always true but that some people believe is true about a group." Then suggest that the children test out some possible stereotypes—for example, "Some people say that only mommies cook. Fact or stereotype? Let's find out." Then have the children go around the room asking, "Do men ever cook food?" When the children find out that in some families daddies or uncles or big brothers cook, their "research" has shown them . . . it's a stereotype!

Support children's critical thinking by setting up activities that help children develop a vocabulary for gender justice and injustice:

- Make a chart about what girls and women can do and what boys and men can do. Write down what the children say. Save the chart to use after you have done several planned critical thinking activities with the children. Then, pull out the children's original comments about what people can and can't do. Invite them to add to the list based on what they have learned. Point out what the children used to think and contrast that with what they know now.

> Daniel, troubled by the exclusion of girls in firefighter play in his classroom, invites a local female firefighter to visit the classroom. At group time she talks about what her work is like and answers the children's questions about her work ("Do you go down a pole?") and her life ("But who takes care of your babies?"). Daniel takes pictures of the visitor showing her tool belt to the children. After she leaves, he asks the children what they learned. When one of them says, with some awe in her voice, "I didn't know girls could ride fire trucks," Daniel replies, "We all keep learning new ways to think, don't we?"

Here are more examples of critical thinking activities:

- Create a class book or a display of pictures of adults of all genders doing the same home or work task—for example, participating in a meeting, walking the dog, cooking, carrying a child, and so on. Talk about the many kinds of tasks the children's family member do and about what kinds of tasks the children do now at home and would like to do when they grow up.

- Collect pictures and books that show people of all genders expressing a wide range of emotions. Tell persona doll stories that reveal and then contradict stereotypes about gendered behavior. Invite the children to figure out strategies for responding to negative comments or exclusion based on gendered behavior.

- Invite visits from adults who will broaden the children's ideas about gender roles and challenge gender stereotypes (a male nurse, a female firefighter, a female auto mechanic, a stay-at-home father, a female farmer, a mother who does construction work, etc.). Ask the adults to talk about their work and invite questions from the children. If possible, take field trips to see the adults at work. Have the children dictate stories about what they learned.

Acting to Change Unfair to Fair

As children learn to recognize unfairness in gender stereotyping, teasing, and rejection (or any other kind of hurtful attitudes related to social identities), they may be left feeling angry and helpless unless their learning is coupled with ways of changing unfair to fair. When you encourage children to take responsibility for making life better for themselves and others, they gain confidence in their ability to work with others to create positive change (Kissinger 2017; Murray & Urban 2017).

- Engage the children in discussing ways to handle hurtful or discriminatory behaviors. Here's a list compiled during group time with 3- and 4-year-olds.

Anti-Bias Education for Young Children and Ourselves

"You can say, 'Stop that!'"

"You can ask another kid to help."

"You can just do what you want anyhow."

"You can say, 'We got a rule: we all get to be different!'"

Use persona dolls to help children practice their good ideas. Post the list of strategies that the children develop.

- Acknowledge and honor children when they stand up for themselves or for others. For example:

  Several of the children are building a train out of big cardboard boxes and small chairs. When Chloe announces she is going to be the engineer, Malik and Cruz shout back, "No, no! Girls can't be engineers. You can ride *in* the train. You can't be the engineer." Chloe begins to back away, but Diego puts his hands on his hips and says loudly, "She can too! Girls can be engineers! And it was Chloe's idea to make a train." The teacher had been coming over to help Chloe, but now she smiles at the children and says, "I'm going to take pictures of this wonderful train you have all built. Thank you, Diego, for reminding us that anyone can be an engineer, and that it was Chloe's idea in the first place."

- With kindergarten or school-age children, pay attention to how they might use terms of gender or sexual orientation as put-downs. Such slurs often reflect bias against people who are LGBTQ; however, even teasing another child as being "girly" or "acting like a boy" are hurtful. Young children may not understand the full significance of the words, but they do know they are put-downs.

- Celebrate International Women's Day in March by honoring important women in the lives of the program's children and staff as well as women who have made and are making important contributions in the larger society. These women do not have to be famous, just important to the children. When telling stories about brave women, include the struggles they have had to overcome. This activity helps to broaden children's ideas about the role of women as heroic since most media heroes are men.

. . .

Narrow expectations for gender expression, gender roles, and gender identity hurt children in every area of their development—cognitive, emotional, physical, and social. People engaged in social justice movements all over the world continue to support everyone's rights to develop to their full human potential. When human characteristics such as empathy *and* self-care, connection *and* assertiveness, and emotional *and* cognitive intelligence are seen as essential for each person to successfully function in the world, everyone benefits.

CHAPTER 10

Learning About Economic Class and Fairness

"Mommy, can I go play at Isobel's house? She's my bestest friend! She's got a big, big house and she lets me try on her clothes. I wish you would buy me clothes like she has."

• • •

A 4-year-old says, "Jorge's mama smells funny. I don't like her" about a mother who arrives from picking lettuce in a field where insecticide was sprayed that day.

Inequitable opportunities, privileges, and life experiences based on economic class deeply affect young children's lives. Although a family's economic resources do not determine how much they love their child or how skilled they are at parenting, a lack of those resources can make the fundamental necessities for their children's healthy growth and development—safe housing, nutritious food, and regular health care—very difficult or impossible to acquire.

Anti-Bias Education in Action: Food Is for Eating!

Like many teachers, Marina plans activities for children that include stringing pasta to make necklaces, creating collages with beans, or exploring the texture of cornmeal at a sensory table. One day three parents ask to meet with her. Nervously, but firmly, the parents inform Marina that they do not want their children

playing with food. "Food is for eating," one explains, "not for wasting." Chagrined, Marina thanks the parents for talking to her and agrees in the importance of not wasting food. She then rethinks what she has been doing and decides to stop using food for curriculum projects and to address the amount of wasted food at snack and lunchtime.

After a discussion among the staff at the child care center where Marina works—including the cook and the custodian—everyone decides to limit food waste and to help the children realize what a precious resource food is. They start serving lunch family style so that children can control the amount of food they put on their plates. They make a worm compost box in the play yard and encourage the children to scrape their leftovers into the compost. With the help of the children's families, they build a series of planter boxes to create a vegetable garden and use the compost in the garden. The children find the project fascinating. Watching food scraps turn to dirt is as interesting to them as watching the seeds sprout. The children can hardly wait until the lettuce and carrots grow (Adapted from Derman-Sparks & Ramsey 2011, 162).

The Big Picture: Economic Class Is Real

Classism, the system of economic inequity and bias against working class or poor people, is very real in the United States but is often not well understood. Millions of children face challenges due to the multiple consequences of poverty. Statistics contradict the myth that in the United States there are a few very rich people and some truly poor people and that most are middle class. The data indicate the magnitude of children in poverty in the United States (Christensen & Gast 2015).

- Fifteen million children live in poverty. Of children younger than 18 years in the United States, 41 percent live in households with low income (less than 200 percent of the federal poverty threshold—a term that describes the minimum household income the federal government believes a family must have to meet their most basic needs) and 19 percent are poor (below 100 percent of the federal poverty threshold). There are many more families with young children whose incomes are just above the poverty threshold. All areas of the country include families that experience intense poverty (Koball & Jiang 2018).

- The inequities of poverty are not the same across racialized identity groups. Approximately 33 percent of African American and Native American children, 26 percent of Latinx children, and 11 percent of White and Asian American children live in poverty (Annie E. Casey Foundation 2019).

Poverty, particularly when it is deep and persistent, can impede children's ability to learn. It can contribute to poor mental and physical health. Children may have low energy due to lack of proper nutrition or suffer from environmental poisoning (e.g., from lead paint in their homes, toxic waste in their neighborhoods, or lead in their drinking water). They may not be fully immunized or they may have untreated chronic illnesses. They may live in neighborhoods with few parks, libraries, or public spaces and with high levels of violence. And they may be living in cars, on the streets, or in shelters.

In addition to experiencing the effects of their family's income insecurity, young children also absorb value-laden attitudes and beliefs about themselves and others. These include economic class messages about where and how they live, what they do and don't own, how they travel, and what they wear. They receive these messages both directly, through comments from adults and other children, and indirectly, from what is misrepresented or invisible in media and from attitudes and behaviors they observe. Explicit and implicit biases toward people with lower income levels tend to be negative, while biases about people with wealth are more likely to be positive. Since classism most profoundly injures children in families with lower income levels and those living in poverty, it is important to critically analyze some of the biases their families face.

Myths About Families with Low Income

Several social myths reinforce the systemic inequities of economic class.

Myth: People Are Poor Through Their Own Fault

A pervasive social belief is that if people work hard, they will succeed and flourish. This myth ignores the realities of low-income work and of class privilege in education, resources, and contacts. Most people with lower income levels work very hard and yet remain poor (Wagmiller & Adelman 2009). It is not unusual for adults in the family to hold more than one job, and even if there are two wage earners, family income may still be below the poverty line. The reality is that in the United States today, the single biggest predictor of economic success is the economic success of the family in which you are raised (Wagmiller & Adelman 2009).

Myth: Families with Low Income Do Not Value Education

Families in low-income communities generally highly value and are supporters of education and teachers. However, they may not always show this support in ways that teachers recognize. The reality for most of the families is that they are less likely to have the means to purchase educational materials, to be able to take time off from work to volunteer in the classroom, or to have much time and energy to attend school functions. In addition, many family members may have had negative experiences with schools in the past and may not feel safe asking questions of teachers or even sharing their concerns. Their silence should not be interpreted as lack of interest in their child or a lack of support for your program.

Myth: Families with Low Income Are Not Good at Parenting

This classist idea comes from cultural deprivation explanations for why children from families with low income of all ethnic groups do not do as well in school as children from middle- or upper-income families. Such thinking implies that a good family is one that provides advantaged conditions (a private room, tutors, music lessons, etc.) for their children. This notion lessens the responsibility of educational institutions and educators to find ways to recognize and build on each child's strengths and to effectively promote children's growth regardless of their family's economic status.

Myth: Only Families with Low Income Contend with Substance Abuse and Incarceration

Substance abuse crosses all class, racial, and cultural lines. Although middle- and upper-income families also face the same issues, families with low income are more likely to experience jail time regardless of the charges, and their children are more likely to be placed in foster care as a result (Alexander 2012). See "Families with an Incarcerated Family Member" on page 172.

Myths such as these negatively affect how early childhood educators think about and work with children and families living in poverty. It is necessary to replace those biases with a positive, accurate understanding of how economic class inequities affect children and their families.

Stop & Think: What Messages Have You Absorbed About Economic Class?

- When you were a child, what did you think about your family's economic status? Was it a source of anxiety, embarrassment, comfort, or pride?

- When did you first realize that some people had more money and others had less? How did you feel about that? What did you think was the reason for the difference?

- What misinformation or myths about economic class did you absorb as you grew up? Where did you hear them? Which ones still show up in your thinking today?

Play as an Equity Issue

A fundamental tenet of early childhood education is that engaging in play is one of the most effective ways for young children to learn. Despite this, there has been a steady erosion of play time in many early childhood programs. The decision to focus on discrete, easily measured learning outcomes, taught through direct, one-size-fits-all teacher instruction, has resulted in minimizing or eliminating time for play for many children. So, too, has an over-focus on test scores. Loss of time to learn through play in early childhood programs most affects children from families with low income (NCTE 2016; Nicholson & Wisneski 2018).

The restriction, and sometimes loss, of this central tool of learning for young children is a major equity issue of classism. Its long-term negative impact is of increasing concern to families, educators, psychologists, doctors, and researchers. For example, here are excerpts from the American Academy of Pediatrics' important policy statement on play (Yogman et al. 2018):

> Play is not frivolous: it enhances brain structure and function and promotes executive function (i.e., the process of learning, rather than the content), which allow us to pursue goals and ignore distractions.

> When play and safe, stable, nurturing relationships are missing in a child's life, toxic stress can disrupt the development of executive function and the learning of prosocial behavior; in the presence of childhood adversity, play becomes even more important. The mutual joy and shared communication and attunement (harmonious serve and return interactions) that parents and children can experience during play regulate the body's stress response. . . . At a time when early childhood programs are pressured to add more didactic components and less playful learning, pediatricians can play an important role in emphasizing the role of a balanced curriculum that includes the importance of playful learning for the promotion of healthy child development.

> An increasing societal focus on academic readiness (promulgated by the No Child Left Behind Act of 2001) has led to a focus on structured activities that are designed to promote academic results as early as preschool, with a corresponding decrease in playful learning. Social skills, which are part of playful learning, enable children to listen to directions, pay attention, solve disputes with words, and focus on tasks without constant supervision. By contrast, a recent trial of an early mathematics intervention in preschool showed almost no gains in math achievement in later elementary school. (1–2)

Young Children Construct Ideas and Attitudes About Economic Class

While less has been written about how young children think about economic class than about other areas of social identity, teacher experiences along with a modest body of research offer useful insights.

The Value and Importance of Different Kinds of Work

Children learn about whose work matters from the curriculum in their schools; from their families; and from children's books, media and advertisements, and videos and toys. What they learn often emphasizes the work of people in professional and middle- to higher-income careers. For example, children's books and posters often depict families going to private doctors' offices (not clinics), shopping in malls (not at garage sales), traveling in cars (not crowded buses), living in detached houses with trimmed lawns (not in apartments or aging buildings), and living one family to a home (not in shared quarters with extended families).

Curriculum themes on community helpers tend to focus on only a few types of work—doctors, nurses, firefighters, police officers—and ignore the many other types of work that also support a community's quality of life (restaurant staff, farm workers, store clerks, office staff, bus drivers). Children tune in to these messages about who matters, who is important, who is "real" and visible. The result for children from families who have lower income levels is often a beginning sense of shame and discomfort about themselves and their families.

> "Princess, princess, I'm the princess," Selina sings as she puts on an elaborate costume in the dramatic play corner. "You can be the maid," she tells Shanice sternly. "You have to do everything I tell you." The teacher who hears her wonders what connections, if any, Selina is making between her play and the reality that her mother cleans houses for others.

Preschoolers may also assume that rich people are happier and more likeable than poor people (Ramsey 2015).

> A group of 4- and 5-year-olds is selecting magazine pictures of families for a collage. The teacher notices how frequently they select pictures of families in fancy clothes and with new-looking furniture or cars, and that they are passing over pictures of families in garden clothes (with dirt), in crowded rooms, and on buses. She asks why the children are choosing the ones they are and is surprised that the answer is "They look happy." Yet all the family pictures have smiling people.

At the same time, preschoolers often say that it is not fair that some people have more money than others, and they suggest that those who have lots should share with those who have less. However, as children get older, they become more likely to absorb and believe the stereotype that people who are poor get what they deserve (Ramsey 2015).

The Value and Importance of Material Possessions

> A 3-year-old says at circle time, "Look it! Look it! I got new shoes! I was good, so Momma bought me princess shoes! Aren't they pretty!"

Messages about the desirability of new possessions are pervasive in most children's lives: "Oh, what a pretty new dress you're wearing," "You can show everyone your new truck at circle time," "How exciting that your momma brought you to school in her new car!" Many children also receive material things as rewards for good behavior, as solace for injuries, or as substitutes for time with loved ones. An underlying message is that good children have many new things and that families show their love by purchasing new things for them.

Children growing up in economically advantaged families may come to believe that they are more deserving than children growing up in families who have lower income levels. They may become competitive about who has the newest toys or certain clothing, creating a hierarchal order of who is better and who is lesser. Some psychologists write about children learning to relate to physical objects, especially toys, in terms of *getting and giving* instead of *using and enjoying* and that children also learn to identify and judge themselves and others in terms of their possessions (Gable 2014).

Attitudes of Entitlement and Superiority or Inferiority

Families with middle or upper incomes or in professional or management work may implicitly or explicitly communicate to their children a sense of entitlement—that they have a greater right to the material resources of the world—as well as a sense of superiority over families with lower incomes (Coles 1977). Similarly, family members in low-paying jobs, wishing to help their children grow up to have a better life, may explicitly or implicitly communicate that the type of work they do is unimportant and menial. They may also express a sense of struggle and frustration about not having higher-paying employment or being able to give their children the things that families with higher incomes can provide. Early childhood teachers report hearing comments from children such as the following:

> "I got lots more toys than you did. I got a scooter and a soccer ball and two new dolls and lots more! What did you get for your birthday?"

> "You can't play with us because you do not have _____!" (Fill in the latest expensive, well-advertised toy).

> When asked to clean up and put away her art materials, Amelia says, "I don't have to. My nanny does that for me."

Media Messaging Tells Children What They "Need"

> "But, Mama, I want to be supercharged!" Willie complains, quoting the advertisement for a sugary cereal. "I have to be supercharged. You gotta buy it, please!"

Young children do not yet have the skills to sort out and resist advertising messages telling them that they want and *need* to have the latest film spin-off toy, clothing, sugary cereal, electronic toy or game, action figure, or doll. They often respond to advertising by pleading with their family to buy certain toys, seeking out children who have the coveted item, feeling deprived at not having a new possession, or feeling superior when they do.

Learning Class and Gender Shame

by Nancy K. Brown, early childhood teacher, director, and consultant

Jessica comes to school every day in sturdy jeans and T-shirts, but as soon as she arrives, she changes into the frilliest clothes she can find in the dramatic play corner, stuffing her home clothes into the back of her cubby. As the day progresses, she staunchly insists that the clothes she wears are her own clothes, worn from home. Jessica also begins taking clothing, usually pink, out of her classmates' cubbies, again tearfully insisting they are really hers.

Her teacher speaks with Jessica's teenage sister, who brings her to school each day. The sister reports that Jessica's clothes are hand-me-downs from her two older brothers. "We'd all like new stuff if we could get it," her sister says. "But Mom doesn't have money for that."

With that information in mind, Jessica's teachers begin paying closer attention to the situation in the classroom. A number of the 4-year-old girls from affluent families show up every day in new, trendy pink or lavender outfits and spend a lot of time swapping clothes, changing in and out of clothes, and playing in front of the mirrors. The teachers have jokingly labeled this group "The Pink Connection" and often compliment them on their new dresses, lovely outfits, and appearances.

With a sense of shock, the teachers realize that the problem isn't Jessica's—it's theirs. Jessica's sense of not being good enough, of class and gender shame, is coming from her experience at school—and, they realize, it isn't a good environment for *any* of the children. They intentionally change their interactions with all the children, deemphasizing "new things" and stopping their comments on the children's appearance.

Adults may succumb to the messages of consumerism as well, even when they cannot afford to make these purchases. Being unable to buy the latest thing their children want may result in a sense of shame and embarrassment that can be unconsciously transmitted to their children.

Messages About Class Differences from How Adults Interact

Although they do not yet have words for the social dynamics that occur between adults, children are excellent observers of their world. For example, they pay attention to which staff member is in charge in the classroom. Whatever you may say about showing respect to everyone, children notice when the cook isn't considered as important as the center director:

> While eating her snack, 4-year-old Mariko states, "I love Pooz [the center's cook]. She's kind of the pretend mommy." "Pretend mommy?" the teacher asks. Mariko looks puzzled for a second, then clarifies, "Miss Ann [the center's director] is the real mommy of the school. Pooz is just pretend." "Why is Miss Ann the real mommy?" asks the teacher, perplexed. Mariko replies, "She's the boss. She tells people what to do."

Children observe when staff and families make subtle but discernible distinctions in their interactions with each other. They notice, for example, when only some family members speak up with teachers. They pay attention to which families participate in the classroom most often. If the children in the program come from homes with different income levels, it may seem to children from higher-income families that their family fits or is an acceptable part of the classroom world. Children from families with lower income levels may come to feel like outsiders because their families don't seem to fit.

Children's Resiliency and Skills for Handling Challenging Economic Realities

While it is necessary to pay attention to the harm that economic insecurity causes families and children, it is also essential to recognize the coping strengths that families pass on to their children. For example, many families with low income levels teach their children to be thoughtful caregivers to younger siblings and to be highly competent at life management skills (dressing themselves, getting cereal ready, etc.). The following vignette (Chafel et al. 2007) illustrates a child's skills and resiliency:

> One winter morning, a new student, 5-year-old Cassie, arrives at the school with hiking boots. She can hardly contain her pleasure. "Look!" she exclaims. "These ties are made of stuff that will not break and the tops will keep the snow off my socks." "They are amazing boots," the teacher agrees. "Where did you get them?" "Backstreet Missions store," Cassie responds with pride. "My grandma said she hit it just right this time—my size and nearly new!" Other children immediately join the conversation to discuss the best places around town to shop for shoes "other people haven't used up yet." Several tell Cassie they will remember the store the next time they need new shoes.

A wonderful follow-up activity to a situation like this might be a curriculum on shoes. Children could bring in shoes that no longer fit, scrub shoelaces, clean shoes (they love polish!), and play shoe store or donate the cleaned-up shoes to a local thrift shop.

Strategies and Activities About Economic Class and Fairness

Economic issues affect *all* children. The following suggestions will support all the children in your program, regardless of their economic backgrounds.

Create a Welcoming and Equitable Learning Community

As you pay attention to economic class issues in your program, instead of looking for what children don't know or what they are not able to do (a deficit approach to teaching), adapt activities to support the *strengths* children bring into your program.

- Have the same high expectations for children from every family.

This is important both for families with food insecurity and for families who have plenty and do not recognize how waste hurts others.

Foster Nonclassist Assumptions and Interactions

Counter the pervasive messages that people need to have possessions to be valued or even to be noticed. You have a responsibility to children of all economic backgrounds to combat this harmful message.

- Pay attention to each child's unique approach to learning, knowledge, and skills, which is shaped by their specific life experiences. Does the child tend to use words to show what she knows, or does she demonstrate what she can do? Does the child expect adults to tell him what they want him to do, or to *ask* him ("It's time to set the table" versus "Would you like to set the table now?").

- Create beautiful environments for *all* children. Fresh paint, live plants, and clean, bright cushions do not have to be costly. Ask for contributions from neighborhood stores (which can be surprisingly accommodating when they know it is for a children's program).

- Be mindful of families' concerns about keeping clothing clean. Make or buy aprons for children to wear during messy play, and make sure the paints you use are truly washable. (Purple is often particularly difficult to remove.) Thrift stores are wonderful places to pick up large long-sleeved shirts that children can wear buttoned up as smocks. Have children wear plastic ponchos during water play. Remember that it may be difficult for some families to purchase new clothes, and washing clothes in laundromats can be expensive and time consuming. Children outgrow their clothes in all income groups. Arrange an ongoing clothing swap where families can donate clothing their children have outgrown and take home what they want.

- Use sensory materials that are not food. For example, use birdseed rather than rice or cornmeal at your sensory table. Make finger paint instead of using pudding or yogurt. String leaves and seedpods rather than pasta.

- Make a decision not to focus on children's new possessions during circle time and sharing times. Encourage children to share information about *experiences* they have had with their families. Invite children to bring in the toy they have had the longest and talk about how they still play with it.

- Encourage children to use toys and materials cooperatively. While many early childhood settings provide several of the same item so children do not have to share, this conveys the message that private ownership and exclusive use are more important than collaboration.

- Make whole-class murals out of handprints or drawings.

- Create a class quilt, with each child contributing a square.

- Ask pairs or teams of children to do specific tasks together (setting the snack tables, cleaning up the block area). Celebrate the important work they do in a class book called *We All Work Together*.

- Focus on justice rather than charity. Be cautious of introducing activities to "help poor people," which can unintentionally convey messages of the superiority of the helper and the helplessness of the receiver. For example, asking children to contribute toys "for the poor" for a holiday or event may teach pity and lead children to question whether families with low income levels really love their children, because they do not buy them toys. Instead, frame activities as making things fair. Children can contribute to a toy bank throughout the year where children are able to exchange and choose toys they want.

- If your program celebrates or studies holidays, use them to emphasize gifts of the heart rather than purchased gifts. Ask children about the enjoyable activities their family did together for the event rather than what gifts they received. Create an ongoing class book about people being kind to one another, titled *The Best Gift of All*. Help children dictate stories for it throughout the year, and read it frequently at circle times.

- Create persona doll stories that help children recognize and challenge hurtful words and behaviors that demean children from families who have lower incomes. Acknowledge family strengths and skills for handling difficult economic realities in these stories. If you do not know much about families who cope with great economic challenges, talk to people in the community who do!

Work at Home Is *Real* Work

Help children appreciate that work at home is essential because it takes care of the people in the family.

Charley, a teacher in a state-subsidized children's center, asks the children at circle time about the work their families do. He is surprised to hear 4-year-old Kathie reply, "Nothing. My mommy doesn't work." This comment worries Charley. He knows Kathie's mother is home during the day caring for a new baby and takes classes in the evening at the local community college. At circle time the next day, Charley asks the children a few more questions and is surprised to find out that all the caregiving, homemaking, and life management tasks their family members do are invisible to the children.

At a staff meeting, the teachers decide to create several activities to address the many ways people work to sustain family life. One activity is to gather photographs of family members doing their part to keep their family functioning. They ask the families to share pictures of family members cooking, cleaning, bathing children, and so on. The teachers are sensitive to families who may not wish to take photographs in their homes, so they clarify that pictures do not have to be inside but can show them buying groceries, taking the bus

to deliver the child to school, or any activity that helps the family. The teachers stress the special importance of the family taking a picture of their child doing something helpful, such as putting away toys, playing with a baby sibling, or dumping out the cat's litter box.

The families are asked to either email the pictures or come in and download them so the teachers can make a book called *Everyone Works in My Family!* Conscious that every family may not have a functioning phone for pictures, they also offer to send home small disposable cameras, which allows the teachers to have the film developed.

The children love the book, and the teachers use it to talk about the many different ways people contribute to family life. Each child receives a badge with the words "Family Hero" that also identifies the child's particular contribution, such as "Emmett. Family Hero. Picks up toys and puts them away." (Adapted from Derman-Sparks & Ramsey 2011, 92–93)

Address Misinformation and Discomforts About Particular Jobs

Do not remain silent when you hear hurtful or prejudiced remarks by children or their family members that reflect biases about what people do. These are moments for clarifying and brave conversations (see Chapter 4) and for an intentional curriculum. Here's an example:

Teacher Marina suggests to her coteachers that their class garden might be a tie to a nearby community of Central American farm workers. The teachers decide to take the children on field trips to see who plants and picks the strawberry fields. They also explore how the strawberries get from the fields to the store and who takes care of the food in the store. And of course, how strawberries taste.

Marina feels that things are going very well until she hears Bradley say to Michael, "We're going to visit those aliens again tomorrow!" Stunned, she asks Bradley what he thinks an alien is. "You know," he replies, "those brown people from Mars who pick the strawberries." Checking with other teachers, she discovers that some families have been uneasy about the field trips. There have been conversations about illegal aliens and some are angry, especially those whose family members lost their union jobs when the frozen food plant relocated to Mexico.

The teachers decide to address these issues directly and call a special family meeting. Liz leads a discussion about how people often scorn and mistreat farm workers, who are often very poor. She names these attitudes and behaviors as stereotypes, misinformation, and social oppression. Teachers help the families make a connection between the struggles that many of the center's families are having and the struggles of the farm workers' families.

Not all the families are convinced. However, when a third teacher, Charlie, begins to talk about the children's hurtful misinformation regarding "aliens" and the emotional pain terms like this inflict, most of the families express concern. Together, the families and teachers identify ways to challenge the negative images and messages and convey ones that are more accurate. Another new curriculum focus begins to emerge. (Adapted from Derman-Sparks & Ramsey 2011, 163)

Loving Families Live in Many Types of Housing

Create a theme on where people live. Include apartments, trailers, and single-family dwellings. Be sure to represent a range of races, cultures, and kinds of families in various types of housing; don't perpetuate a stereotype by depicting all White families in middle-class homes and all families of color in low-income homes. Include a discussion of homelessness. Here is one example, which took place in a parent co-op preschool program:

The topic of the economic downturn is an ongoing conversation among the children's families. Some family members have lost jobs; some families have taken on extra jobs at lower pay. Everyone feels concerned. The teachers assume that the children are not aware of the adults' worries until two things happen on the same day. While walking to the post office with their teacher, a small group of children see a man sleeping in a

doorway. Aaron says, "Look at the lazy guy," and Habiba adds, "He's a bad guy. Good guys sleep in their own rooms." Later that same day, three other children are building a car with the big hollow blocks. "A big car," says Chen, "so we can go all the way to Legoland!" Carl looks around, finds some cushions and a pillow, and puts them in the back of the "car," saying, "That's for when it's bedtime and we can go to sleep." "People don't sleep in cars," Chen says emphatically, "They sleep in beds." "Well, sometimes when we go camping, I sleep in the car," says Letitia. Carl just looks upset and quickly leaves the game.

Later, when the teachers talk with each other about the two incidents, one of them explains that Carl's family is, in fact, living in their car. His parents had emphatically told Carl not to talk about it to anyone. The teachers also remind each other that two other children's families are now living with various friends and relatives, sleeping on couches, in sleeping bags, or on cushions on floors. If the children think that only bad or lazy people don't have their own rooms or their own beds, how do they make sense of how their families—or classmates' families—now live?

After checking with Carl's family and assuring them that they will not single him out, the teachers make a plan for group time the next day. First they begin a chart called "Everybody Sleeps Somewhere," on which the children help make a list of all the ways and places that people sleep (in hammocks, on mats, with grandparents, in shared beds, in cribs, in tents). They change the dramatic play corner from a kitchen setup to a camping setup, with a small tent, day packs, sleeping bags, and mosquito netting. "What," asks one teacher, "do you think people need to sleep comfy and happy at night?" The children have lots of ideas: a stuffed bear, a special blanket, Mommy to tuck you in, your dog sleeping on the floor.

"Do you have to sleep in a bedroom to be comfy and happy?" the teacher asks. This is a new idea, but the children soon decide that the bedroom isn't what is important. Getting out a persona doll named Maggie, the teacher then tells a story about Maggie and her family sleeping in their car until her mom or dad could get a new job. "What," she asks them, "could Maggie's family do to be sure she is comfy and happy?" The children suggest things like giving her a special pillow, singing a sleepy song, and making sure she's warm. To the teacher's delight, even though Carl says nothing about his own family, he joins in with a few good suggestions.

Appreciate All Families' Contributions to the Community's Well-Being

People in every family and of every economic background make important contributions to their communities. Help children to recognize and celebrate these contributions.

- Make a class book with photographs of all the people whose work keeps your program going, such as kitchen and office staff and the custodian. Invite them to talk to the children about their work. Help the children dictate thank-you letters to each person, and brainstorm with children ways they can make these individuals' work easier (cleaning up after themselves, cutting down on waste). This activity enriches staff relations at your program and makes visible the important work in your school community.

- Find books that honor the often invisible work done by members of the families in your program and others in your community. Read books about hair stylists and barbers, bus drivers, cleaners, cooks, and cashiers. Talk about how their important work helps us all to live. Invite

family members to come tell the children about *their* work if they can arrange some time off. If they can't come in, ask if they could describe their work in a letter to the class, in an audio or video recording, or in a phone call with you so you can share the information with the children.

- Introduce children to artists, musicians, and writers, whose work may be mysterious or invisible to children. One strategy is to talk about the authors of the books you read to them. If possible, invite artists or musicians from the community to talk about and demonstrate their work. Find children's books that show people from diverse backgrounds in these roles.

- Read children's books that tell stories about people's efforts to improve their lives: for example, *Somewhere Today: A Book of Peace*, by Shelley Moore Thomas, and *Pearl Moskowitz's Last Stand*, by Arthur A. Levine. Learn about local people who have been or are activists for the rights of people with low income levels or living in poverty. Invite them to school or tell the children about them.

Support Recycling to Teach Respect for Conserving Resources

Offer learning experiences that use old boxes, juice cartons, paper towel rolls, and other reusable objects that families can collect and donate. Use rectangles cut from brown paper bags for children to use in art

activities (the color and texture are beautiful when the paper is painted with tempera paints!). Provide a recycle bin for used bottles, paper, and plastic.

In a private kindergarten program serving children of well-to-do professional and business families, teachers Madhu and Nathan become concerned about the children's wastefulness with materials. They decide to promote a closer connection with the natural environment and to foster appreciation of its value.

They extend the time children spend outdoors and use natural objects to teach concepts that they usually teach inside the classroom, such as identifying leaf patterns and counting trees and stones. They bring natural materials into the classroom, using acorns and pinecones for counting and twigs and small logs for building. They invite a local environmental activist to talk to the children about local problems with waste and conservation efforts. With his help, the children start to keep track of the amount of trash that accumulates in their classroom. Madhu and Nathan encourage the children to come up with ways to cut down on the waste, such as drawing and writing on both sides of the paper, using only one paper towel to dry their hands, making sure they carefully cover paint containers, and protecting all the outdoor toys from rain. The class recycles classroom materials and takes a field trip to a recycling center. The teachers help the children write or dictate statements and draw pictures of what they are doing to conserve the environment. Children make copies of those for their families, asking them also to do more conserving at home. (Adapted from Derman-Sparks & Ramsey 2011, 165–166)

Many other teachers have also created activities to engage children in protecting their environments. For example,

One class focuses on a local park to which they regularly go. The children bring bags, wear gloves, and pick up trash in "their" park. The children like the idea of doing a community service. Families and teachers fashion "trash collector" hats for the children. They photograph the park before, during, and after the cleanup. With permission from the parks department, the children make and put up signs: "Keep Our Park Clean" . . . "Don't Make a Mess" . . . "I Like to Play in a Clean Park."

Support Families Across Economic Class

See yourself as a partner with *all* families, supporting their children's inherent strengths and building skills where needed.

- Make clear in your program's mission statement that you do not allow any hurtful, classist comments and behavior.

- Be thoughtful and respectful about the limitations on time and resources with which all families struggle to some degree.

- If children from more affluent families have nannies, with written agreement from the family, consider them family liaisons and include them in the same way you would the children's relatives.

- Find out what each family needs in order to participate in classroom activities, conferences, and family meetings. Many workplaces do not allow employees to take time off during the day. Getting to meetings may involve taking a bus or two with small children—an enterprise that can add hours to the family member's already demanding schedule. Without provisions for additional child care, many families may not be able to attend because they cannot afford to pay a sitter. Provide flexible times for conferences.

- Set up opportunities for families to get to know each other, which may lead to efforts to support each other through clothing swaps, supplying meals to a family with a new baby, or sharing interests at a family meeting.

- Get to know the children's neighborhoods if you do not already. Shop at the stores, visit community centers, use the library, and attend events in the community. As you do, collect resources for your class, such as photographs to turn into posters, books, and puzzles; donated materials from stores; ideas for field trip sites; names of community members to invite to your class.

- Compile a listing of family support resources in the community and learn the names of specific people in these agencies. Ask families to let you know which agencies have been helpful and treated them with respect. Build alliances between families by sharing this information with *all* families, regardless of need, so everyone learns what is and isn't available in the community.

Classism in the Early Childhood Profession

Economic dynamics and class issues affect everyone. Early childhood educators and programs are not exempt from their influence. We have all absorbed attitudes and assumptions about our own and others' class statuses.

Stop & Think: What Did You Learn About Economic Class?

- What messages did you learn about the comparative value of working with your hands (farming, trucking, carpentry, house cleaning), service work (practicing cosmetology, cashiering, waiting tables), or business or professional work (working as a programmer, teacher, nurse, business owner)? What are your thoughts now about these various kinds of work?

- What did you learn as a child or teenager about what success meant and why some people are successful and some are not? Where did you learn those ideas?

- If you or your family ever received public assistance, what was that like for you? If not, what messages did you receive from your family and teachers about people who did receive public assistance?

- What did you learn in your childhood about people asking for help? Was this seen as a defeat or shameful act? Was this seen as an appropriate strategy to manage? Did it make any difference from whom one asked for help?

Class Differences May Affect Family–Teacher Relationships

Families with lower income levels often encounter demands in their lives that may inconvenience teachers. It may be hard on teachers, for example, when a child arrives late because her family has to take unreliable buses to school. Resenting a family member for these types of situations, without any indication of understanding or empathy, is not a solution and serves only to harm the teacher–family relationship. And even though teachers may try to hide their irritation, children can sense the teacher's disapproval. Respecting the family's perspective, on the other hand, motivates the teacher to seek positive, mutual, third space solutions (see page 71).

Some families with higher incomes may not view early childhood teachers as equal to them. They may make unrealistic demands for particular curriculum experiences or supports for their child. They may be openly critical of families with lower incomes and not want their own child to become friends with the children from those families. If a program is dependent on the financial contributions of the families with higher incomes, teachers may acquiesce to their demands—even when doing so reinforces family messages of entitlement and conflcts with teachers' professional expertise and anti-bias values. This dynamic can also lead to teachers feeling resentful and adds to the sense of burnout for many teachers.

Classism Affects Relationships Among Early Childhood Educators

Inadequate wages, lack of benefits such as health care, and the low societal respect accorded those in the field all have a negative impact on professional relationships despite the best intentions and dedication of early childhood teachers. Staff turnover is one of the serious consequences of inadequate salaries. When staff leave because they cannot afford to stay, deep bonds and consistent relationships with children; ongoing, integrated curriculum; and strong family–school and staff relationships are all at risk. In addition, insufficient program funding often leaves little or no time for staff to plan together and reflect, one of the essential components for quality early childhood programs (Gable 2014).

Over the years we have listened to many early childhood professionals talk about the effects of economic class distinctions within their programs. This is some of what we have learned: Class distinctions among the staff can interfere with open, honest dialogue and shared growth. Some staff members from lower-income backgrounds may self-limit their contributions at staff meetings, keeping quiet about their knowledge and ideas. A hierarchy of authority may result in giving more status and respect to some teachers than to others, a dynamic that children pick up on and absorb. Sometimes this hierarchy intersects with racial and ethnic differences.

Strategies to Counter Classism in Early Childhood Programs

Recognizing and addressing classism within your early childhood program can have far-reaching, positive impacts on the staff and the children. Here are some suggestions:

- Work to create an atmosphere where you and your colleagues can openly share and discuss issues of economic circumstances and class, with the goal of creating rich, full participation from, and respect for all the people who make the children's program possible. At staff meetings or during staff development activities, take some time as a group to explore the Stop & Think questions throughout this chapter.

- Celebrate and model respect for the work of each staff member. Be sure that all staff members, not just the lead teachers and the director, are included and have a voice in decision making.

- Share information with families about the real costs of quality early childhood programs. Let the community know how little early childhood staff people are paid considering their education and responsibilities. Keep speaking up about how the low wages of early childhood staff subsidize other industries by making it possible for family members to go to work.

- Work to create equal access to professional learning and development. Create a program policy that reimburses staff who choose to attend conferences, take courses, or engage in other professional learning activities. This may require fundraising efforts, which can also serve as opportunities to educate the families and the communities about economic class issues within the early childhood profession.

. . .

Discussion about economic class in early childhood professional education is often invisible or limited to exchanges about how to help children from families with lower income levels "catch up" to their peers. Yet many teachers are aware of the multifaceted impact economic class has on the children and families with whom they work. You are well placed to help children begin to sort out their ideas and feelings about themselves and others, gain accurate information, and learn to interact respectfully across economic class differences. You can also be a major resource for families to learn the skills of advocating for their children and to trust they have the right to do so.

CHAPTER 11

Learning About Different Abilities and Fairness

It means that they can't do stuff, but they can still do the stuff you can do, but they can't do all the stuff you can, but they can almost do the stuff you can.

—A 4-year-old explaining about children with disabilities

Doralynn Folse, principal of the early childhood program at the California School for the Deaf, shares the following:

> I don't think of my students as "deaf kids." I teach kids. They are deaf, but they are still just kids who will have to figure out how to live in our world. Sure, they need to develop Deaf pride and feel strong and safe in in their Deaf culture. But there are all kinds of people who are deaf—different religions, different races, those with a variety of families and lifestyles. There are all kinds of people who are *not* deaf who our students will be interacting with. And the world is not a safe, just place. They need to know about injustice and how to change it, maybe even more than hearing children need to know this, and they need the skills to address it.

Young children are curious about many kinds of ability differences. While they sometimes exhibit discomfort and rejection of someone because of a disability, they also have the capacity to understand that a child with a disability is able to do much of what most children can do, even if it's done differently. And as Doralynn notes above, children with disabilities benefit from having tools to navigate the world and to advocate for themselves. This chapter explores the anti-bias issues of working with children in inclusive classrooms, in which children with and without disabilities play, grow, and learn together. It also includes ideas and examples for using anti-bias goals and strategies in programs for children with specific disabilities.

Anti-Bias Education in Action: When the Teacher Behaves Differently with Different Children

Carole Cole, early childhood and adult special education educator and consultant, shares this story and insight:

> **I had given Jesse a special chair and had him sit by me every day at lunch. Some children**

wanted a turn in that chair. "He doesn't do what he's supposed to, so why does he get to sit by you every day?" Some teachers felt I was reinforcing negative behavior.

To the teachers, I explained that, given Jesse's background (he was born with fetal alcohol syndrome), it was important that he experience the predictable structure and the individual attention that the chair next to me provided. This support would not need to last forever. To the children, I matter-of-factly explained that Jesse needed help now, and that someday he would not need the special chair. I helped them to recall things they could not do before but now could do. The other children joined in my plan and began reminding each other not to sit in Jesse's chair. Within the month, Jesse adjusted to classroom expectations. He chose to sit by his new friend Isiah instead of in the special chair.

Children generally are very receptive to explanations about why a teacher might use a different strategy with one child. They are more accepting than some adults are. Talking openly about one child needing help enables the rest to understand a teacher's rationale, and it lets them feel like part of the solution. Most important, the talk reinforces the idea that everyone sometimes needs help, and because their classroom is a learning community, when they are the one who needs help, someone will help.

Applying Anti-Bias Education Goals to Issues of Different Abilities

- All children will develop autonomy and independence (as they are able) as well as confidence and pride in their competence. **(Goal 1)**

- All children will learn accurate information about disabilities appropriate to their developmental stage. They will gain understanding about how their own abilities are the same as and different from the abilities of others. **(Goal 2)**

- All children will learn to interact knowledgeably, comfortably, and fairly with each other, whatever their abilities. **(Goal 2)**

- All children will learn how to challenge name calling and stereotyping with respect to their own or others' abilities. They will share ideas about accessibility in order to promote interaction and independence. **(Goals 3 & 4)**

The Big Picture: Attitudes and Options for Children with Disabilities, Historically and Today

Up until the mid-20th century, children with disabilities in the United States did not have the fundamental right to attend public schools. In general, children with any kind of disability were thought to lack intelligence and considered unable to learn or become independently functioning adults. Most children with disabilities were kept at home, sometimes hidden from the rest of the world, and taken care of by their families throughout their lives, or they were put into institutions. If families had the economic means, they sent children to private schools created for specific disabilities. Many of these were boarding schools, so children were separated from their families (Dudley-Marling & Burns 2014).

Like most struggles for social justice, the struggle for rights of children with disabilities has been uneven. Due to the pioneering efforts of advocates, often with families of children with disabilities leading the struggle, attitudes and conditions have slowly improved for children with disabilities. In 1975, the United States Congress enacted the Education for All Handicapped Children Act (EHA), which guaranteed a free, appropriate, public education to individuals aged 3–21 who had physical and mental disabilities. Children were to receive this education in the least restrictive environment appropriate to their individual needs, with the supports and services to enable them to succeed. Although this was a big step forward, in practice it usually resulted in school districts setting up separate classrooms or even separate schools for children with disabilities (Congressional Research Service 1975).

Families, advocates, and practitioners, using lawsuits, public education, research, and political pressure brought about further legislation in 1986. These amendments to EHA expanded service to include infants and toddlers (Brillante 2017). Subsequent amendments to the law, now known as IDEA, continue to uphold the rights of all children and provide "procedural safeguards that give families a voice in the educational decisions made for their children and protect their rights with regard to their children's education" (Brillante 2017, 2).

Despite these significant and positive legal changes, providing high-quality services and inclusive programs for children with disabilities in all parts of the United States remains a work in progress (Voulgarides 2018). Research studies in the 1990s and early 2000s found that large numbers of children of color, especially African American boys, were placed in special education programs. This resulted in a higher percentage of children of color placed in special education services than would be expected compared with the general school population (Harry & Klingner 2006; Skiba et al. 2008). Such disproportionate misidentification and placement of children continues. In addition, as of 2019 more than 10,000 children were awaiting services (Camera 2017).

The challenge of helping children and adults achieve full acceptance and participation in all aspects of society continues. Legal centers such as the Special

Needs Alliance now exist in many part of the country to assist families and advocates to continue the progress toward full rights and services.

Early childhood programs play an important role in furthering the human rights of children with disabilities. Families of children with disabilities face the same childrearing issues as other families. In addition, they handle the many responsibilities that children with disabilities require. These responsibilities are made harder by community services that are inadequate or lacking, as well as by biases of others (Hanson & Lynch 2013).

What Is an Inclusive Classroom?

Inclusion in early childhood programs refers to including children with disabilities in early childhood programs together with their peers without disabilities: holding high expectations; intentionally promoting participation in all learning and social activities facilitated by individualized accommodations; and using evidence-based services and support to foster their development, friendships with peers, and a sense of belonging. (US HHS & ED 2015, 3)

Children with disabilities must have the opportunity to be included in classrooms with their peers to the greatest extent possible. Inclusive classrooms require teaching staff to have intentional strategies and the skills to create an equitable, inclusive curriculum for *every* child. While no teacher can know *everything* needed to support a child with a disability, all teachers can develop the skills of working in partnership with specialists to meet each child's unique needs.

In high-quality inclusive programs, children with identified disabilities make better progress with physical skills, in cognition, in communication, and in social and emotional development, as compared with children who are in segregated special education programs. "Children without disabilities in inclusive early childhood settings show positive attitudinal changes such as an increase in compassion, empathy, and understanding of diversity and disability" (Cook, Richardson-Gibbs, & Dotson 2018, 10).

High-quality inclusive early childhood programs reflect the understanding that contact among children with different abilities, important as it is, is not enough. Neither is simply teaching superficial acceptance and politeness—like "Be nice," "Play with everybody." ABE goals are an important part of a high-quality inclusive learning environment. Children with disabilities need teachers who value them for who they are, know how to adapt and shape individualized curriculum, and provide a learning environment that supports diversity, fairness, and taking action.

In addition, children need teachers who make sure that people with disabilities are visible in their learning environment—even if there are no children with disabilities in the classroom. This means using learning materials in the classroom that accurately and respectfully depict children and adults with disabilities. It also means that all children have many opportunities to ask questions, get accurate information, explore their feelings, and learn positive ways to interact with all their peers. Early childhood programs practicing anti-bias education can also work with families to gain the knowledge and tools needed to advocate for quality resources for their children in schools and in the community.

Stop & Think: What Did You Learn as a Child About People with Disabilities?

- Did you grow up with a disability? How did your family, friends, and teachers interact with you? Did you feel supported? How did these experiences shape your childhood?

- As a child did you know and have relationships with people with disabilities? What were your experiences with and feelings about these relationships? Did people help you understand your feelings or what having a disability means to people?

- What did you learn as a child about how visible a person with a disability should be? Was it okay to notice and interact with a person directly? Was it okay to ask people questions about their disability?

Young Children Construct Ideas and Attitudes About Different Abilities and Disabilities

As with other areas of social identity, young children are curious about the differences and similarities in abilities they see and that adults label as disabilities.

Young Children Want to Understand What They Observe

Children ask questions about people with disabilities, sometimes at inconvenient times and places for adults, and frequently with inaccurate words. Adults often quickly respond with a comment like "Don't look—it's not polite!" or "It isn't nice to ask that question." But these responses can communicate discomfort and tension and convey to children that there is something wrong with the difference itself. Such responses teach children to stop asking questions. Children are left without the information they need to learn how to act comfortably and to ask questions respectfully. It's important to answer children's questions truthfully and, when possible, invite the person with the disability to participate in the conversation.

When talking with children, listen for tone and other expression of feelings to determine whether their question reflects bias or fear and requires more than a matter-of-fact, clarifying response. Be alert for situations in which a child may be curious but does not ask a question:

> Lucy, a new teacher in a 3-year-old class, has one arm that is shorter than the other and two short fingers on that hand. She and her coteacher, Darsha, agree they will not make an issue of it and that she will talk to the children about her arm if and when appropriate. One day as Lucy is leading circle time, Darsha notices 3-year-old Mia looking intently at Lucy's hand.

> After the song is over, Darsha says matter-of-factly to Mia, "I saw you looking at Lucy's hand, Mia. It doesn't look like your hand. Do you wonder why her hand and arm are like that?" Mia nods. Lucy explains, "I was born with my arm and hand like this." Mia asks, "Does it hurt?" Lucy shakes her head. "Will my hand be like that?" says Mia with a worried expression. "No," answers Lucy, "because you were born with your hand just like it is now. Do you want to touch my hand?" Mia feels all around Lucy's arm and hand. "Now, Mia," says Darsha, "why don't you show Lucy where we keep the juice, and you can help each other get snack ready?" The two go off together.

Children Need to Know What People with Particular Disabilities Can and Cannot Do

Young children try to make sense of what they observe within their limited experience and understanding. Children may conclude that a child who uses a wheelchair is a baby and cannot participate in activities, that a child with a hearing impairment cannot know what a hearing child knows, and that a child who is blind cannot be active ("She wouldn't know where to go, and she might hurt herself"). They may also think that a child who is not yet speaking can't be a good play partner, or an adult who uses a wheelchair or who has a hearing or vision impairment cannot be a parent or a teacher. To counter such misconceptions, children with and without disabilities both need accurate information. They also need positive role models who show children how adults with disabilities function in their daily home and work lives.

> A child with a hearing impairment is coming into the preschool program, so Kay decides to do a series of persona doll stories about Samantha—a persona doll who wears a hearing aid and communicates mainly through American Sign Language (ASL). After some introductory stories about Samantha, Kay asks the children, "How could you let Samantha know you want to play with her if you don't know sign language?" One child suggests, "We could talk loud in her ear." Kay explains that Samantha cannot distinguish words, no matter how loud someone speaks to her. The children think of other ways: "We can gently touch her arm," "We can show her what we want," "We can wave to her if she is too far to touch."

> With pleasure in her voice, Kay tells the children, "A new child named Hanna will be joining our class next week. Hanna, like Samantha, cannot hear voices clearly. She also uses ASL. I'll be using a special system of pictures to help us talk to Hanna. I'll also teach you Hanna's name sign so you can begin talking with your new classmate when she gets here."

When Hanna comes to the program the following week, the children are careful to make eye contact with her and invite her to play with them by patting a seat or pointing to a center or toy.

Children Wonder Why Some Children Are Treated Differently Than Others

Children are curious when a child receives one-to-one attention from the teacher or the help of an assistant or specialist or when the child leaves for part of the day to work with a specialist. Often, a clarifying comment is all that is needed.

> "Why is Wendy always with Rosa?" Aaron asks his preschool teacher. Wendy accompanies Rosa, a child with cerebral palsy, throughout the day. The teacher explains, "Wendy helps Rosa play, learn, and move from place to place so she can be part of what we do."

• • •

> "Ishaan is going with Mack so Mack can help him work on saying his words clearly. Ishaan will be back in a little while."

Young Children Can Appreciate Their Shared Abilities and Similarities

As children with disabilities and their peers play and learn together in high-quality, inclusive learning environments, they come to understand and appreciate each other's strengths and challenges.

> Four-year-old Jasper, who has Down syndrome, is pulling the wagon around the playground, one of his favorite activities. Elena joins him and gets into the wagon. She announces to the teacher standing nearby, "He's a messy painter, but he's a good wagon puller."

• • •

> "Benjamin acts like a baby. He doesn't talk right, and he doesn't even know how to write his name," observes 5-year-old Rebekah. "Benjamin isn't a baby, Rebekah," his teacher

says. "He is 5 years old, just like you. Benjamin can do many things that you can do. He can ride a bike, run, play ball, and climb. He will be able to talk more clearly and learn to write his name, but it will take him longer." Later in the day, their teacher notices Rebekah and Benjamin playing ball together.

• • •

> The Head Start teacher notices Miko, who uses a wheelchair, carrying blocks on her lap from the block area to the dramatic play center for two of her classmates. Seeing their teacher watching her, Miko comments, "I can take more blocks than they can. They are the builders. I am the truck driver bringing the blocks."

A Child with a Disability Needs Support to Handle Questions from Other Children

Children with disabilities are likely to be asked questions about themselves in the classroom and beyond, and indeed throughout their lives. They need cognitive and emotional strategies to know what they want to say and be able to say it. And they need to know they have the right to *not* discuss their disability if they choose. This is something that you can support children in doing.

The first step is to find out how the family explains the disability to their child and to others, including what specific terms they use and how they would like you to talk about it with the child and to the group. Ideally this discussion with the family takes place even before the child joins the classroom. If the child has been attending the program and recently received a diagnosis, you might still want to have that conversation with the family to see if they want you to share any new information with the group.

Talk with a child about the fact that classmates will ask questions because they are interested and want to know more, but assure the child that she has the right to choose whether and how to answer. For example, the child can answer, decline to answer, or ask someone else to respond, depending on the question, the questioner, and the child's feelings. You might say, "I know it's hard sometimes when other children ask why you wear a brace and that sometimes you wish they wouldn't ask so many questions. When you feel tired or sad or angry about kids asking so many questions, let me know and I will help you."

> "Why doesn't Miguel have to stay in the circle the whole time?" complains Mariko. Abram chimes in, "Yeah, how come he gets to sit next to you all the time?" Their teacher checks with Miguel. "Do you want to explain, or do you want me to?" Miguel shrugs but says nothing, so the teacher replies. "Miguel is learning how to sit still for the whole circle time. It helps him if he sits next to me while he is learning how to do this. He also still needs to get up and do something else for some of the time." She then invites Mariko and Abram to recall things they could not do but now can.

Children May Worry that a Disability Is Contagious

Sometimes a child has a misplaced worry that he can catch a disability. And some children may be afraid of the specialized equipment used by some children with disabilities.

> The teacher has brought a child-size wheelchair to the class. Eduardo refuses to touch it. His teacher asks, "Eduardo, you decided not to try the wheelchair. How come?" Eduardo backs away. "'Cause it's scary." The teacher probes, "What do you think will happen to you if you sit in the wheelchair?" Eduardo replies, "I won't walk." "You think that if you use a wheelchair then you won't be able to walk?" she asks. Eduardo nods. The teacher says reassuringly, "When a person needs a wheelchair, it is because something happened to his legs *before* he needed the wheelchair. Sitting in the wheelchair will not hurt your legs."

> Eduardo and the teacher check with other children who have tried the wheelchair, each of whom show him that they can still walk. Eduardo gingerly sits down in the wheelchair for a few seconds, then gets up. Eduardo starts to walk away, then smiles a little at the teacher, and goes off to a new activity.

Young Children May Reject a Child with a Disability Because of Fear, Impatience, or Misconceptions

Children need adult help when another child rejects them. So, too, do the children who do the rejecting.

> Four-year-olds Selina and Habiba are playing with blocks. Katya (who has burn scars on her face and arms and has limited use of her hands) tries to join in their play. Selina declares loudly to Habiba, "I hate Katya; she's ugly." Their teacher intervenes, keeping in mind the four-step clarifying conversations (see page 55). She starts by repeating what she has heard and then seeking to understand what the child truly meant. Then she provides clear information, a conversation about feelings, and finally a process to act fairly and kindly.

> **Teacher:** Selina, I heard you say that Katya is ugly. That is a hurtful thing to say. What makes you say it?

> **Selina:** Because her hands go funny and she has those things on her face. I don't like them. They're scary.

> **Teacher:** I know it looks different and scary to you. Katya, do you want to tell Selina how you feel about what she said?

> Katya shakes her head. The teacher puts one arm around Katya and one around Selina.

> **Teacher:** Katya, do you want to tell Selina and Habiba about how you got your scars?

> **Katya:** You. (*Indicates the teacher.*)

> **Teacher:** Okay. Selina and Habiba, Katya has scars on her face and arms because she was in an accident when she was a baby. When Katya was 2 years old, some very hot oil in a frying pan spilled on her and burned her and it hurt the muscles in her hands. It hurt her very badly at first, and she had to be in a hospital for a long time.

> **Selina:** Do they hurt?

> **Katya:** No. They used to itch, but not now.

Teacher: It is okay to want to know about Katya's scars, but it is not okay to say she's ugly or not let her play with you. Katya, how did you feel when Selina said you were ugly?

Katya: Sad.

Teacher: What do you want to tell her about how you felt?

Katya: (*Speaks with vehemence.*) Don't say *ugly*.

Teacher: Remember that in our classroom I expect us all to work and play together. Let's all four of us play with the blocks together. I'll play too.

Sometimes children express anger, frustration, or fear toward a child whose disability is emotional or behavioral.

Rhea has great difficulty controlling her feelings of frustration and anger. She often expresses these feelings loudly or violently.

"I don't like Rhea," says Corrine emphatically as she watches Rhea with Jessica, a teacher who is stopping her from throwing a puzzle. "Why not?" asks Nathanial, another teacher in the room. "She's too noisy! And she throws stuff." "Yes," Nathanial agrees. "She makes a lot of noise sometimes, and it can be scary when she throws things. Jessica is keeping her safe, and in a little while she'll be able to play again." Corrine frowns and mutters, "I don't like her!"

Nathanial responds, "I think some things are hard for Rhea, like not being able to put the puzzle together. Then she gets so upset she throws things. Someday Rhea will learn that when she is having a hard time, she can use her words instead of throwing things. Corrine, I remember when you first came to school and had a hard time pouring your juice. There were lots of spills, remember? But look how you learned; you sure are a good pourer now! And Rhea will learn too. She will stop throwing things and use words to tell us when she needs help. I think she will learn how to be a good puzzle solver too."

Guidelines for an Inclusive Anti-Bias Program

An inclusive learning community communicates this message in many ways: "Everybody here belongs, plays, and helps each other learn in her or his own time and way." In such a community, all children feel nurtured, encouraged, and respected for their whole selves by the staff and by their peers. The anti-bias concept "We are all the same; we are all different" holds as true for differences in ability as it does for other kinds of diversity.

Stop & Think: Reflecting on Your Attitudes and Skills

- What happens when you meet someone with a disability? How easy is it for you to initiate an interaction? How comfortable do you feel during it? Do you feel it is okay to ask questions as you get to know a person?

- What attitudes do you have that enable you to work well with children with disabilities? What attitudes do you think might hinder you?

- Are there specific disabilities that are harder for you to deal with? What can you do to change these attitudes?

- Who are some people you could approach to help you think about your feelings about working with children with disabilities and acquire the skills you need?

Be Thoughtful About the Words You Use

As with many social identity terms, the names used to indicate that people have a disability are not static and have changed over time. It's important to use—and to help children use—language that focuses on a person's humanity first, as it signifies that the disability is just one aspect of who the person is. So instead of referring to "the blind person," it is more respectful to say "the person who is visually impaired." Saying "she uses a wheelchair" recognizes the power the child has, as compared with saying "a wheelchair-bound child." This is called *people-first language*. The Centers for Disease Control and Prevention (CDC) has a helpful chart titled "Communicating With and About People With Disabilities" that offers suggestions for people-first language and language to avoid (CDC, n.d.). An example is describing a person as "successful and productive" rather than having "overcome his or her disability" or being "so courageous."

If families have other terms they use, it's helpful to be curious and thoughtful while engaging in a dialogue about why people-first language is used at school. Be aware that people-first language is not preferred by all people with disabilities, as they see their disability as an integral part of their identity. For example, some members of the Deaf or autism communities prefer identity-first language (*autistic person, deaf child*). As we have stressed throughout this book, always ask an individual's preference, and if you are unsure, use people-first language.

Pay Attention to How Well You Meet All Children's Needs

As in all areas of ABE, ongoing assessment of your learning environment and practices in relation to children with disabilities is essential. Assessment enables you to identify where you can improve in meeting children's needs and where you are already succeeding. When assessing your practices with children with disabilities, ask yourself these questions:

- Do I regularly observe how children are interacting? Do I intervene in negative incidents, reinforce positive interactions, and use my observations for planning further activities to support social skills?

- Are children with disabilities able to participate in every activity in some way?

- Are there opportunities for all children to contribute to the group and to help each other learn and carry out activities?

- Does my teaching reflect respect for children's own developmental timelines and ways of developing?

- Do I treat children's varying abilities, strengths, and challenges as *differences* rather than reasons for competitiveness and rankings? Is my teaching appropriately individualized so that the entire curriculum is accessible to all children?

- Do I assist children with disabilities only enough to enable them to help themselves? Do I provide ways for them to stretch their skills and support for them to do so?

Be Responsive to Children's Questions and Thinking About Disabilities

Encourage children to be open about their ideas, feelings, and questions about themselves and others. This helps you learn how they think, strengthening your ability to provide accurate information and to model respectful ways of interacting. In turn, this creates a sense of community among the children.

If you do not know the answer to a specific question, admit it. Tell children you will have to learn more before answering their question. You can even research the question together by involving children in going to the library or looking for other sources of information.

Do Not Deny Differences in Physical, Cognitive, or Emotional Abilities

For example, do not say to a child that his classmate with autism is "just like you." This is confusing and does not give either child the information needed for interacting positively with each other. Help children recognize how they are different *and* how they are the same: "Demetrius, you like to play firefighter, and Mitch does too. Sometimes it's hard for him to follow along when you give long instructions. It might help if you just say, 'Mitch, let's pick up the hose!'"

Do Not Dismiss Children's Expressions of Anxiety, Fear, or Rejection of Disabilities

If a child says, "I don't like Mina; she makes weird noises," don't dismiss or disrespect the child's concerns by making statements such as "Yes, you do; we are all friends here." Stopping children from expressing their negative feelings doesn't eliminate them; it just teaches children to stop voicing them. It also may lead to avoidance of the child with the disability because her peer's fears or biases have not been addressed. Unresolved anxieties can fester, laying a foundation for prejudice and discrimination.

Also avoid handling children's anxiety by conveying that the child with the disability is to be pitied. For example, don't say, "We must be nice to Oliver because he cannot walk." The goal is for the children to see Oliver as one of the members of the classroom community, each of whom contributes in unique ways. "Yes, it's challenging for Oliver to keep up with you when you are chasing the bad guys outside. He would really like to play with you. I wonder how you could figure out together how he might do that."

Interrupt Hurtful Language

By kindergarten, some children may have learned disrespectful terms for a person with a disability (e.g., *retard, dumb, cripple, spaz*). They may use these and other terms to tease or put down a child *with* a disability or to insult a child *without* a disability. Regardless of whether the children know what the words mean, they know the words are hurtful and disrespectful. Preschoolers also hear these insulting words and may use them, although usually with no idea they are hurtful.

Calmly yet firmly interrupt any use of such language. (See page 54 about clarifying conversations and discussion of interrupting hurtful language). Make sure to follow up with activities that help children gain accurate information and names for various disabilities as well as activities that expand their empathy and skills for interrupting others' hurtful behavior.

Be Aware of Your Own Assumptions and Biases

Children with disabilities come from every cultural and racial identity and economic background. Sadly, both now and in the past, societal and individual biases about specific social identities affect both the identification of developmental challenges and the placement of children in special education programs.

To avoid allowing unexamined assumptions and biases to affect your thinking about a child's possible developmental and learning challenges, consider these guidelines:

- Observe a child about whom you have concerns in many different contexts throughout the day to identify when learning, behavioral, or interactional difficulties occur most. Check with other teachers to see if their perceptions and observations match yours. If not, consider why that might be so.

- Ask yourself these questions: What is influencing my thinking about this child? What in the school environment could be contributing to the child's challenges? What aspects of my teaching style and methods might I need to change to be a better match for this child? Are specific cultural differences between school and home contributing to my concerns?

- Get further help from people with expertise in assessing and diagnosing cognitive and emotional learning and behavioral challenges. Find and use one of the several assessment tools that are available for this purpose. Make sure that children are assessed in the language with which they are most familiar.

Talk with Families About Their Child's Possible Disability

Letting families know that their child may have a disability and may require further assessment is one of the more difficult, though essential, tasks for a teacher or program director. Initiating this communication can be hard. It is important to know and objectively manage your feelings. As Carol Cole, a long-time experienced teacher, explains:

It can be heartbreaking for a family to hear for the first time that their child may have a disability, or in a parent conference to hear a teacher verbalize what they may have privately feared. So, I get upset if I hear a teacher or administrator say that the parents are in denial or that the family should have known there was a problem or that they should just accept it and move forward.

Such statements deny a family's right to their particular process of acceptance and coping. They also risk undermining the relationship between the program and the family. Even if the pace of a family's process is frustrating at times, it is better to say to them: "I know a lot about young children in general, but you will always be the expert of your own child. So, if we put our heads together and share what we each know, we can come up with the best plan." It's even better to truly *believe* this.

Careful, thoughtful listening is essential when talking with families about children's possible disabilities (see Chapter 5). This is a journey for the family and the teacher together. It takes patience and empathy to be an advocate for both the child and the family. Provide families your ongoing support as you partner with them in creating the plan for their child, implementing it, and being part of the evaluation and services their child receives.

Work with Families Who Have Concerns About Their Child Being in a Class with Children with Disabilities

Discomfort and misinformation about children with disabilities in inclusive classrooms are not uncommon. Families may worry that a child with disabilities will take time and attention away from their own child or that their child will be frightened by a child who has a disability. They may object to the classroom expectation that all children will learn to respect, make room for, and adjust to other children's fundamental needs. As always, it is important to listen carefully to parents' concerns, ask questions to understand those concerns, and engage in thoughtful, clarifying conversations (see Chapter 5). Sometimes families just need more information. Sometimes they need help seeing how their child benefits from interacting with diverse peers, since the child will encounter human differences throughout life.

Ultimately, you need to reestablish the basic philosophy of you program—that every child is special, that good practice individualizes curriculum for every child, and that their child's experiences are important to you too.

Strategies and Activities About Disabilities and Fairness

The following classroom-tested ideas support children in developing an anti-bias understanding of their own and others' abilities.

Use Materials that Depict People with Disabilities as Full, Competent Human Beings

- Regularly read children's books that honestly depict children and adults with various disabilities. Invite children to express their feelings and ideas about the stories, then plan activities based on what they say to counter any misconceptions or feelings of discomfort or fear. Choose books and pictures that show people as whole, competent human beings and that address both their disabilities *and* their abilities.

- Display posters and photographs that show people whose lives contradict children's misconceptions about disabilities.

- Provide commercial and homemade dolls that have various disabilities. These help children develop familiarity and ease with disabilities and open up conversations so children can share their ideas and concerns.

- Use persona dolls with disabilities to tell stories that explore similarities as well as differences with the children in the class. Use the dolls to talk about common challenges (getting used to a new sibling, dealing with a grandparent's death, making a trip to the doctor) and the joys (getting a new pet, going on a special family outing) that all young children share. Create stories that help children understand what people with various disabilities might need (a wheelchair, extra time during an activity, an assistant, some space away from others).

Provide Supervised Times to Explore Adaptive Equipment

Adaptive devices and equipment that children use might include wheelchairs, walkers, hearing aids, braille print, and prostheses. Handling and trying out such equipment can help take the mystery out of such equipment and out of specific disabilities and provide information and experience that foster understanding and comfortable interactions with people wearing or using them.

- Contact organizations that provide equipment rentals for people with disabilities or a medical supply store to inquire about borrowing or renting equipment. Be sure to get child-size equipment! If you plan a curriculum unit that includes exploring children's crutches, carefully fit them to each child for safety.

- Caution! Never let children touch a classmate's adaptive equipment. This is a good opportunity to teach children to respect for other people and for the things they own and use. Boundaries help every child feel safe.

Help All Children Find Ways to Learn from Each Other

Through your actions as well as your words, always convey the message that although people are all different, everyone contributes. Intentionally set up small groups for using the various learning centers. For example, eight children want to play in the block area, but there is room for only five at a time. You talk with the children, and they agree to a schedule that allows one group of four to play for a while and then the next group plays. You create the two groups, making sure that each group includes at least one of the three children with disabilities in the class. Keeping an eye on their play, you can enter in as necessary to help the children interact with each other.

- Model specific ways to interact. For example, the children are getting ready to sing and dance "The Hokey-Pokey." You bring Aliya into the circle next to you and move her wheelchair through the steps. (Aliya is not yet able to move her wheelchair herself.) The next time the children do this dance, you ask Ling to dance with Aliya while you continue to move her wheelchair. Eventually the children initiate involving Aliya on their own.

- Arrange partners or small groups to work together on a specific activity that draws on each child's abilities so the children can help each other. For example, you pair Aliya, who knows many color and shape names, with Isabella, who is just beginning to learn them. Sitting at a table just the right height for Aliya's wheelchair, the two play a classification game together and Aliya names several colors and shapes for Isabella.

- Provide resources to help children with disabilities and their peers communicate with and understand each other. For example, place an age-appropriate sign language dictionary in the room that you and the children can use. Also put up an ASL alphabet chart. Tell a persona doll story in which one doll teaches another doll how to sign frequently used words in the classroom *(block, paint, crayon, book, ball)*. Have braille alphabet cards for all the children to explore.

Plan Learning Experiences to Counter Misconceptions

Find out the children's ideas about what people with different kinds of disabilities can and cannot do—for example, an adult with a prosthetic arm, a child with hearing aids, an adult using a walker. Use this information to plan experiences that expand their awareness and understanding. For example, if you learn that some children think that a person who uses a wheelchair or has a hearing or visual impairment cannot be a mother or father, invite a parent who uses a wheelchair to talk with the class, or read a book about a parent who uses a wheelchair (such as *Mama Zooms,* by Jane Cowen-Fletcher).

- Invite people with disabilities to visit your program regularly. Ask them to tell the children about their families, their work, and their hobbies. Plan for them to interact with the children throughout ongoing activities (reading aloud, working on a craft project). Before they commit to coming, make sure that the visitors will be comfortable with answering children's very direct questions and that they can do so in a developmentally appropriate way.

- Visit workplaces that employ people with disabilities. Disability rights organizations are especially good places to visit because children can see people—those with and without disabilities—working together to improve the quality of their own and others' lives.

Teach Children Empowering Ways to Help Each Other

Learning how to offer help is as important as actually aiding. Teach children to always ask, "Do you want help?" before acting and to respect the other child's answer. If the other child does want help, the helper should find out what kind ("Is this the way to help?"). If the child being helped is unsure of how to answer, you can help the child find the words.

Juanita (age 4) is working on a collage. Cerebral palsy sometimes causes her hand muscles to spasm, and she is having trouble with one of the pieces. She gets a lot of paste on herself. Jasmine (also 4) says to her, "I'll do that for you." Juanita keeps pasting and ignores Jasmine. The teacher intervenes, "Juanita, do you want help now?" Juanita responds, "No. I do it myself."

Their teacher explains, "Jasmine, I can see that you want to be a friend to Juanita by helping her. But it is important that you help her only when she wants it. Next time, first ask, 'Do you need help?'" To Juanita, the teacher says, "Good for you, Juanita, for speaking up for yourself and keeping on with your collage!"

Foster Children's Awareness and Skills as Allies and Activists

Foster children's skills for taking action to make unfair situations fair on behalf of classmates who experience any form of prejudice or discrimination. Of course, activities should take into account children's experiences and abilities.

- If you have a child in your program who uses a wheelchair, ask him to help you check the accessibility of your classroom or building and give you some ideas about how to make things better. When you thank him for his help, say, "You are the expert! You know a lot about how to make things right."

- If a new child is coming who uses a wheelchair, ask the other children to explore the space with a borrowed chair and problem solve ways to make it work better for their new classmate. Introduce the word *ally*—a friend who supports someone else.

- Bring photographs you have taken of various modifications around the community. Then take an accessibility walk around your school: Are there workable ramps and doorways sufficiently wide for wheelchairs? Are bathrooms and water fountains accessible? Are there curb cuts on the streets near your school? Is there an identified parking space for people who need accessible spaces? Are there accessible pedestrian signals at the crosswalk nearest your school? If accessibility is insufficient, this can lead to an action project you work on with the children and their families.

It's important to support children both as activists on their own behalf and as allies to each other. Here are two stories of teachers making that happen. Doralynn Folse relates the first:

> At the early childhood program at the California School for the Deaf, a bilingual (ASL and English) program, the children often make videos to communicate in ASL as well as written English to send a letter or write a story. In the kindergarten class, a teacher invites a friend who is a little person (with achondroplasia) and uses a wheelchair to visit the class. When he arrives, he finds a closed building door, which he is unable to open. He texts the teacher, and she brings the class to him, where he demonstrates how he couldn't get in. The children are incensed! Ian takes them to the school map on the campus and finds there is only one building with an electric door that he can open. The children make a video letter for the school's superintendent, saying it is "not fair that our friend Ian can't get into our classroom. We need doors in every building that will open for everybody!" A few days later, they are invited to speak at the monthly community Advisory Committee. They prepare speeches and passionately present to the superintendent and the audience of 20 adults, who listen carefully and applaud. The children feel very proud and empowered!

• • •

> Marcus is enrolled in the 3-year-old room of the children's center, and the staff are still waiting for him to be assessed and a probable IEP (Individualized Education Program) developed. When the room becomes very noisy, or there is a lot of action near him, Marcus will suddenly scream, push children down, or rock back and forth while humming loudly. Unsurprisingly, several of the children go to great lengths to avoid him.

> The teachers try to keep an eye on Marcus and intervene before he becomes upset, but they are not always successful. After a particularly difficult morning for everyone, one of the teachers decides to ask the 3-year-olds what they think might help Marcus. "He needs a quiet hidey place," says one. "I think he'd like a snuggly blankie to hold," says another.

> After talking with Marcus and his mom, the teachers take the children's suggestions and create a "time-to-be-quiet hidey corner" behind a couch, with pillow, blankets, and several stuffed animals. Marcus uses it frequently, and it is often helpful. Even though it does not solve all of Marcus's needs, it changes the atmosphere in the classroom and enables the children to support Marcus rather than be frightened by him. And to the teachers' surprise, several of the other children use the space as well for calming, quiet, and comfort.

• • •

Helping children understand that "different is just how people are!" as one 4-year-old put it, is an important lesson for all children, regardless of their abilities or disabilities. Children need skills to stand up to stereotypes and biases that convey inferiority of those with disabilities. For children with a disability, these skills are essential for healthy self-identity. For *all* children, knowledge about and connection to people with disabilities reduces the likelihood of fear and discomfort when they inevitably encounter a person with a disability or when they themselves become disabled. Every child benefits from knowing how to speak up for one's own needs and how to step up to support others. So, too, does the whole classroom community.

CHAPTER 12

Learning About Who Makes Up a Family and Fairness

So, no matter the age, no matter the stage, no matter how you came to be.

And no matter the skin, we are all of us kin, we are all of us one family.

—John McCutcheon, "Happy Adoption Day," *Family Garden* (CD)

There's Mama and me and Grandma and PopPop and Daddy and Kerri and Jesse and, and, oh yeah, there's Dusty and Princess. (Teacher: Who are Dusty and Princess?) That's my dog and cat. You *said* "Who's in your family?"!

—Gabe, age 4

To truly reach and nurture all children, early childhood educators create a program where families feel welcome and comfortable in the setting. Feeling a sense of belonging will support children in coming to trust the environment, form strong attachments, and explore and learn. This is a fundamental principle explored throughout this book. Chapter 6 focuses on the family as the child's first cultural unit; Chapter 7 explores cultural diversity among families. Chapter 10 looks at the family in relation to economic class. This chapter offers another important way to support all children and their families: understanding and accepting a diversity of family structures.

Anti-Bias Education in Action: Who Takes Care of You at Home?

Mother's Day is near, and the teachers in the 3-year-old room reflect on how to acknowledge the day. They know several of the children live with grandparents or foster parents, one child has two dads, and several live in blended families with parents and stepparents taking care of them on different days. In addition, Father's Day always occurs in the summer when the program is not in session, and it seems unfair to celebrate only Mother's Day.

The teachers decide to develop a curriculum for the next two weeks called "Who Takes Care of You at Home?" They start with asking the children how the big people in their families take care of the children in their homes. The teachers write the children's responses on a wall chart. They also bring in several children's books (some new, some which the children already know and love) in which children live in diverse families: *Mama, Do You Love Me?* by Barbara M. Joosse (featuring a single mom); *Dear Child*, by John Farrell (three different kinds of families who adopt children); *Fred Stays with Me!*, by Nancy Coffelt (co-custody family); *The Ring Bearer*, by Floyd Cooper (blended family); *A Tale of Two Daddies,* by Vanita Oelschlager (dads who are gay); and *Last Stop on Market Street*, by Matt de la Peña (grandma and grandson). The teachers read the books and ask the children about what they see the adults doing to take care of the children. The teachers add the children's insights to the list.

As the week of Mother's Day approaches, the teachers ask the children if they would like to make gifts for the people at home who take care of them. The response is enthusiastic. One of the teachers brings in tiny cuttings of succulents and the children decorate small yogurt and milk cartons to plant them. Most of them also want to dictate notes: "'cause I want Nana to see it's for her!"

The teachers make a display of all the plant gifts and notes before the children take them home, and they have a wrap-up conversation at group time about all the ways their family members take care of their children. No child is left out. No family is marginalized. The children love it. The families are delighted.

Applying Anti-Bias Education Goals to Diversity in Family Structure

- Children will talk comfortably about their own families from their personal experience. **(Goal 1)**

- Children will show awareness and acceptance of different kinds of families beyond their own and appreciate that different kinds of families love and care for their children. **(Goal 2)**

- Children will develop skills to recognize and question unfair depictions or invisibility of different kinds of families. **(Goal 3)**

- Children will learn and practice language and actions to resist teasing or rejection of themselves or classmates based on their own and others' family structures. **(Goal 4)**

The Big Picture: Family Inclusiveness

Family is central to the life of every child. It is through this earliest relationship that children first learn to view themselves and others and to find their place in the world. Families enter into a crucial relationship with teachers in their children's early childhood programs. They trust teachers to care for the most precious part of their lives—their children. Families also expect early childhood programs to serve as a bridge for their child between the family and the larger society. As the NAEYC (2016) Code of Ethical Conduct declares,

> Because the family and the early childhood practitioner have a common interest in the child's well-being, we acknowledge a primary responsibility to bring about communication, cooperation, and collaboration between the home and early childhood program in ways that enhance the child's development. (11)

Young children most commonly understand *family* as the people who live with them or the people who take special care of them. Their ideas reflect NAEYC's Code of Ethical Conduct, which states that "the term *family* may include those adults, besides parents, with the responsibility of being involved in educating, nurturing, and advocating for the child" (NAEYC 2016, 11). Validating each child's family requires creating and sustaining a learning environment that communicates this definition. To do this, early childhood educators need to have a broad concept of family that includes all variations and structures.

Who Makes Up a Family?

Family structures come in many forms. Variations exist across class, race, and culture. It is not uncommon for a child's family structure to change. For example, "approximately 50 percent of American children will witness the breakup of a parent's marriage. Of these, close to half will also see the breakup of a parent's second marriage" (Parker 2019). Children may start out in a two-parent family, which becomes a family of single parenting or grandparent parenting, and later transforms into a two-parent blended family. In 2014, fewer than half (46 percent) of children in the United States under 18 years of age were living in a home with two married heterosexual parents in their first marriage (Livingston 2014). In 2017, 32 percent of children were living with an unmarried parent (Livingston 2018).

Stop & Think: What Do You Know/ Not Know About Family Diversity?

- Which of the following kinds of families are familiar to you? Unfamiliar? Which ones do you know the most about? The least?

  Adoptive families

  LGBTQ families

  Biracial or multiracial families

  Immigrant families

  Blended families

  Migrant families

  Co-custody families

  Multigenerational families

  Conditionally separated families

  Nuclear families

  Extended families

  Single-parent families

  Foster families

  Transnational families

  Grandparent custody families

- Are there other family structures in your community?

- What types of family configurations feel most natural to you? What family structures feel unfamiliar or uncomfortable to you? How might that impact children you work with?

Knowing the structure of a family does not in itself reveal anything about how well that family functions. In every family structure, at any given time, people may be living joyfully or in pain. The family may operate harmoniously or in discord. Don't assume that just because a family has a specific structure, they will or will not need support and connection.

The degree to which families experience being included or excluded, approved of or negatively judged in the dominant society, also influences how a family functions. While raising children causes stress at different times in all families, some families face additional stressors from societal prejudice and discrimination. Family identities also include the dynamics of a family's ethnicity and culture, economic class, racialized and gendered identities, and emotional and physical characteristics specific to them.

Along with the general support you offer to *all* families and to *all* children in stressful family situations, an anti-bias approach means you are aware of the relationships between bias and the day-to-day struggles of each of these types of families. Understanding how the issues vary for various family types, as well as for the particular families you serve, makes it possible to be as thoughtful and supportive as possible. Always keep in mind that each family offers strengths to their children while also dealing with specific challenges.

The Many Kinds of Families in Early Childhood Programs

As you think about the families of the children you teach, you may find that more than one of the following definitions apply to a family. In addition, some families may use different terms than those listed here. Find out which word(s) each family uses to name itself, and then use that term.

Adoptive Families

A major task for young children who are adopted is understanding the distinction between their adoptive parents and their birth parents. This is partly a developmental issue complicated by children who are adopted having to struggle with their own and other children's questions about whether their adoptive parents are "real" parents. Adults add to this confusion and potential anxiety when referring to a child's family of birth as "your *real* mom" or "your *natural* dad" instead of the more accurate "birth mom" or "birth dad." A child's adoptive parents are the "real" parents because they are raising the child.

When adoption is transracial (a child and parent have different racialized identities), the core issue of adoptive versus birth parent can be more confusing to young children. Because some differences are visible (the parent and child have different skin colors), other children may ask, "Is that *really* your mother (or father)?" Even adult strangers in public

places may feel free to openly comment to parents "Is that child yours?" Families who adopt transracially often face racial biases directed at them and need to develop skills to help themselves and their child cope with these incidents of prejudice or discrimination (see Chapter 8).

White families become a multiracial family when they adopt a child of color. Having White adoptive parents, however, does not protect children of color from experiencing racial bias, and their families may find that they lose some of the advantages of being White, such as easily finding housing in some areas.

Adoptive families face issues specific to them. They may hear judgmental comments from others who believe the old bias that children who are adopted are flawed because of a birth parent's behavior. Social service and educational professionals sometimes believe, and act on, the misinformation that adoption is *the* source of any emotional or behavioral problems a child who is adopted may display. Adoptive families themselves may buy into this bias. While it is true that at different points in their development children rethink what adoption means to them, as with all children, the cause(s) of problematic behaviors may be developmental or circumstantial, or the behaviors may have deeper roots.

Families want to make sure their children who are adopted feel truly loved and secure. They may be unsure or uneasy about when and how to tell a young child about being adopted. As an early childhood teacher, you can support the adoptive family by reassuring them what matters is that they care for and love their child through good times and hard times. You validate children who are adopted by making their family visible and respected and by reinforcing the message that their family is a *real* family that chose them, loves them, and cares for them.

Biracial, Multiracial, and Multiethnic Families

The terms *biracial, multiracial,* and *multiethnic* cover a wide range of racial and ethnic combinations of family and individual identities. This range includes family members whose ethnic and cultural identities and/or racialized identities differ from each other, or family members who identify as racially or ethnically mixed. Families may also become multiracial if they adopt children whose ethnic or racialized identity differ from theirs.

It's important to know what names the family uses to describe their racialized identities and then to honor their choices. No matter what words the family uses, a child is never "half and half" but is always fully themselves, incorporating their entire family into their identity.

Blended and Extended Families

Some children live in a blended family, a family that has members from two or more previous families. Some live in an extended family where grandparents, aunts, uncles, and others have major roles in their care. In certain cultures of families, cousins may be as significant as siblings. In others, grandparents may be significant decision makers about the child's experiences. This may be in addition to the parents or instead of the parents. Families where grandparents have custody of the children are increasingly common in the United States (Henig 2018).

Families have a variety of names for various extended and blended family members, such as *my stepdad, Gary,* and *Pop-pop.* Many standard forms that families fill out, such as intake forms, have a section that asks families to write the parents' names and contact information. To reflect the variations in

family structures, it is more inclusive and respectful to use the term *Family* than *Parent* and let the family fill it in as they see fit.

Invite blended and extended family members who play major roles in children's lives to school events and conferences. Model to all the children in your program your conviction that all family members are "real" and are important to the child.

Co-Custody Family (Joint Custody Family)

When a child's parents live apart, they both may have legal responsibility for their children. Children may alternate living with each parent or live with one and have visitation with the other. For early childhood teachers and programs, it is important to know who is responsible for the child on which days and to be clear about legal issues, such as who is notified in case of illness or an accident. Equally important is to support both parents. This includes welcoming them to conferences, including them in communications, and acknowledging that both parents are trying to do the best they know how.

Children in co-custody families usually have two homes, where rules and parenting styles may differ. Teachers can clarify nonjudgmentally that "Your daddy wants you to wear your shoes when he picks you up. Your mom says you can be barefoot when you go home with her." Neither parent is wrong; they just have different ways of doing things.

Conditionally Separated Families

It is hard on a family when a member is far away for an extended period. This may be due to employment, military service, incarceration, hospitalization, or another reason. Even when family members are not physically present, they remain significant to the family.

The specific challenges of conditionally separated families vary depending on the reasons for the absence. When a family member goes to the hospital for a mental health condition or is incarcerated, families have to deal not only with the absence but also with negative social messages (see "Families with an Incarcerated Family Member" on page 172). When a family member serves in the military, there is fear for that person's safety as well as loneliness. When a family has immigrated and a family member has stayed behind, the child may feel divided about where "home" really is.

When family members are absent, children may feel uncertain or at a loss (Allen & Staley 2007). Making drawings for the separated family member, dictating letters or stories about recent experiences, and sending photos of favorite activities to the person can help the child and the separated family member stay connected. Regularly reassure the child that although absent family members are not around, they are still part of that child's family.

If a child shares a letter, email, or other communication from the separated family member, listen closely and help the child identify how he or she feels.

> Carlos's dad is deployed to a war zone overseas. He shows his teacher a crumpled letter from his dad and asks her to read it to him. As she reads it, Carlos leans close, resting his head on her shoulder. "You're looking sad, Carlos," she says. "It's hard to have someone you love be far away." Carlos grabs the letter back and pulls away, saying loudly, "I'm a big boy—I don't cry! And he's a stupid dad to go away!" The teacher replies, "I think your dad loves you a lot, that's why he's writing to you. And you know what? You get to be mad and sad both at the same time. You can be mad he's not here and sad because you miss him."

Children may be confused by what they have heard about why the person left and where the person is. Where you can, provide information. Where you can't, it is always better to say "I don't know" than it is to brush off the issue. Telling the truth includes avoiding saying "Everything will be all right"—as much as you might want to be reassuring.

Foster Families

Some children may be in foster care for brief periods, others for their entire childhoods. Children in foster care may not know how long their current living situation will last. They may also be in transition from one type of long-term family structure to another—for example, their foster parents could be in the process of adopting them, or their grandparent may soon be awarded custody. For all these reasons, children in

foster care need special support, as they may suffer some degree of trauma and struggle with a great deal of confusion.

Be particularly careful regarding family terminology. Children in foster care have two families. Use whatever terminology the child uses for the foster family: Dad, Michael and Emma, Mommy Val. Never ask a child to choose who and which family is most important to him. If the birth parents are allowed and able to visit, welcome them in your classroom or program.

Check with the foster parent(s) regarding what they have told the child about her family and the likelihood of reuniting. Also, once the child is comfortable with you, find out what the child understands—it may not be same as what the child has been told. Reassure the child that although parents sometimes need help taking care of their child, which might mean the child goes to live with someone else, the child's parent or parents still love her. The wonderful children's book *Kids Need to Be Safe*, by Julie Nelson, addresses these situations and children's emotions in an honest but very supportive way.

Foster parents need support too. They may or may not know much about child development and what to expect at various ages. They may not have a community of people who understand what they are doing or why they have chosen to be foster parents. They may not have been given much information on the child's experiences. Foster parents must cope with balancing their own feelings toward the child's family with the need to help the child feel lovable, secure, and safe. As a teacher, you are an ally to all three—the child, the birth parents, and the foster parents. You can be a significant source of strength and help to all.

Families with Members of the LGBTQ Community

adapted from Aimee Gelnaw & Margie Brinkley (Derman-Sparks & Edwards 2010, 122–124)

Many children in early childhood programs grow up with family members who are gay, lesbian, bisexual, or transgender. LGBTQ is an umbrella term that includes these families (see the glossary). These family members come from all racial and ethnic groups, and they create all kinds of family structures, including single-parent families, two-parent families, and families with parents living in two different

households. People who are gay or lesbian become parents in many ways, including partnering with a person who already has a child. Sometimes children are the result of a heterosexual relationship or marriage; some are adopted or in foster care. Some children are conceived through insemination with a known or unknown donor, some through surrogacy.

Despite some changes in the legal status of LGBTQ families (notably, Obergefell v. Hodges in 2015, the Supreme Court decision that marriage between same-sex people was legal), these families often still face discrimination and bias. It may or may not be safe for them to be open with their children's schools about who they are. Several incorrect, stereotypical, hurtful ideas about people in the LGBTQ community continue to circulate in US society. It is important to be aware of these biases so that they do not influence your work as an early childhood educator or undermine children's thinking about diverse kinds of families, including families of classmates. Here are some examples:

- Some people incorrectly worry that including LGBTQ families as part of teaching about different kinds of families is the same as teaching about sexuality. But learning about families who are members of the LGBTQ community is no more about sexuality than is learning about a family with parents whose identity is in the heterosexual community.

- Children learning about different kinds of families does not influence their eventual sexual development. Children's interest in family has to do with who lives in their home, who takes care of them, and who loves them. And the reality is that all kinds of parents can love and raise their children well.

- Some people argue that they do not need to introduce family structures that include members of the LGBTQ community unless they have families who are LGBTQ. They may not realize that unless programs make visible their commitment *all* families, some families may not be safe enough to share their identities. In addition, knowingly or not, children in families with parents who are heterosexual are likely to have people who are LGBTQ among their siblings or other family members, neighbors, and friends. Additionally, some of the children in your program, regardless of the kind of family they grow up in, may grow up to be LGBTQ, and the attitudes they learn in childhood can hurt or support who they become.

Given the prevailing stereotypical attitudes about LGBTQ families in many communities, it is important for both the families and the children that program staff reach out and make these families welcome. You can include specific mention of families with parents who are LGBTQ in your mission statement or family handbook.

Never "out" someone's social identity. All people have the right to determine how they identify and with whom they share information about themselves. Find out from each family what terminology they use and what names they have taught their child. Also find out what terms the child uses for each parent. Support their choices. Do *not* ask, "Which one is the natural mom or dad?" This is offensive and hurtful yet continues to be asked in some programs.

Migrant Families

Similar to any other family, migrant families have diverse family structures. What distinguishes them is that they move from place to place for work, often agricultural work. Families stay in one place as long as needed to harvest a particular crop and then move on to another area. Migrant farm worker families too often live in substandard housing. They often have little access to health care or even safe water. The children of migrant agricultural families move from school to school and attend as they can. Many communities have migrant education early childhood programs that take children's living realities into account. Some use a total family support approach, providing literacy education to adults as well as helping with other needed resources. Sometimes children of migrant families attend local early childhood programs, although rarely for an entire school year.

Migrant agricultural workers still face bias from people living in local communities, and their children may be teased or rejected by classmates. Pay attention to these community attitudes and adapt your curriculum to counter the biases migrant children experience (see Chapters 6, 7, and 10).

Military Families

Children growing up in military families may also experience the dynamics of frequent moves, often with a year or less in one place before being reassigned. Most military bases provide early childhood programs, which are set up to accommodate the realities of frequent moving. If children from military families attend your local program, pay attention to the impact frequent moves may have had on the children. Children who are part of a military family also live with the reality that their parent may be called into active duty and be required to serve in dangerous, faraway places. (See "Conditionally Separated Families" on pages 168–169).

Single-Parent Families

More than 35 percent of children in the United States lived in a single-parent household in 2015, and the numbers are increasing (Annie E. Casey Foundation 2018). Children's experiences in single-parent families vary widely. Single parenting can be by choice or by life circumstances such as divorce or death. The other parent may have been part of the family at one time or not at all, or may still play a role but in a separate household. There may be extended family who share childrearing responsibilities, or the single parent may be going it alone.

Ask the parent about who else plays a significant role in the child's life and what supports, if any, the parent has. If the parent wishes, find ways to connect the parent with other families who can be friends, share ideas, and provide community. Be on your guard against both your own and others' assumptions or value judgments about single parents. Never use derogatory terms such as *broken home,* and intervene

if you hear others do so. Be clear that there is no such thing as a "broken" family. Each family form is what it is—and *is* a family!

Transnational Families

Transnational families, those that move back and forth between two countries on a regular basis, are another type of conditionally separated family. The child may spend time being cared for by different family members in each country. The child may be left in the care of one parent or grandparents while the other parent travels to another country to work.

Culture clash is often an issue for transnational families as they work to have their children feel at home in both places (see Chapter 6). Learn the words the children use for their various family members in each country and what, if any, kinds of group care the child has experienced. Ask the family to share photos, artifacts, and stories from the child's other country. Ask children to tell you about what they find the same and different between the two countries.

Stop & Think: What Did You Learn in Childhood About Different Family Structures?

- When you were growing up, who did you consider the members of your family? What was your family structure? Did your family structure stay the same throughout your childhood? How was it the same or different from the other families in your community?

- What did others in your school and community communicate to you about your family? Was your family accepted and/or admired? Did you experience invisibility, teasing, or rejection?

- What did you learn from your family about family structures that were different from yours? Did your family indicate what kind of family they hoped you would have when you were an adult?

- How have your current values about family structure changed or stayed the same as your family of origin (the family you in which you grew up)? Do you have some new ideas or attitudes as a result of reading the information in this section?

Young Children Construct Ideas and Attitudes About Family Structures

Young children take the family in which they live for granted. They also initially think that all families are like their own—an idea that often gets challenged when young children enter an early childhood program.

Young Children Have Their Own Definitions of Family

Definitions of family are unique to each child and may include every living creature in the child's household. For example,

> To draw her family, Carolina makes four small stick figures, three large ones, and one very large one. Pointing to the largest

---

Families with an Incarcerated Family Member

by Louise Rosenkrantz, teacher leader

The United States has the highest percentage of its citizens incarcerated of any country in the world (Wagner & Sawyer 2018). Increasingly, early childhood programs are working with children where someone in their family has been incarcerated. Louise Rosenkrantz, who was the director of a children's center in a federal prison, also experienced the incarceration of her own father when she was a child. The insights she presents here focus on incarcerated parents. They also apply for a child who has a brother, sister, or other loved one who is incarcerated.

For 10 years, I worked with a nonprofit project called Prison MATCH (Mothers and Their Children). For 6 of those years, I was the director of a play-based, community-administered visiting program in a federal prison. It was there that I gained an enormous amount of experience.

It's not surprising that children of incarcerated parents experience many strong feelings, including shame, embarrassment, loneliness, uncertainty, anger, and confusion. However, in my experience, the most devastating issue for children is the unpredictability of the prison system. You think you're going to visit your mother, but you arrive at the prison and, for a reason that has nothing to do with your parent, visiting has been canceled for the day. Never mind that you're 5 and have been counting on this visit all week, and you've told other people you're going to see your mom. You're expected to just get back on that bus and travel another four hours home without complaining because, after all, everyone's upset.

The bond between children and their parents is extremely strong even in the most difficult of times. Children with parents in prison must deal with difficult questions, which we can start to answer:

- Why is this happening to me? ("It's not your fault. Nothing you did made this happen.")

- Does it happen to anyone else? ("Many children have someone in their family in prison.")

- Is my parent safe? ("Yes. And you are safe, too.")

- Do I still have a family? ("Of course you do! And they love you very much.")

As you listen to a child's feelings and ideas, also recognize and affirm both the child's and parent's love. For example, my youngest sister doesn't remember knowing much about my father's imprisonment until it was imminent. Then she remembers being told he was going to prison, and the picture that formed in her mind was of the gun towers and cement cell blocks she had seen on television shows. Since our dad was going to a less restrictive federal prison, it would have been comforting if someone had asked my sister to describe what she *thought* was going to happen, and then given her accurate details about the *actual* situation.

Children want and need basic, practical information. They want to know if people sleep, eat, or work in prison; whether their mom can call them on the phone; and when they will get to see their brother. Until you know the specifics of the child's situation, it's best to keep the conversation supportive but general. Through ongoing conversations with the child, family, and community one, she says with a big smile, "That's me!" Pointing to the three large figures, she says, "Mama, Papi, Tia Yolanda." Then she points to the smaller ones and names her sister and her three cousins. "Oh," says the teacher, "do your cousins and auntie live with you?" "No," says Carolina shaking her head. "They're my cousins. You know, mi familia!"

Young Children Perceive Their Family as an Extension of Themselves

Young children's sense of self first develops within their family, whatever its composition or structure. Allow each child to define his family, and actively support that definition.

agencies, you will find concrete, specific answers for the actual experience of that child and her loved ones. For example, some jails allow physical contact, some don't. Some prisons let you bring in presents or money for the incarcerated person, some don't.

Here is another example from my own family's experiences. My middle sister was in second grade when our father was sentenced to a year in federal prison. A well-intentioned adult did the math, subtracted the time for good behavior, and was pleased to tell my sister the good news that her dad would be home for her next birthday. Unfortunately, this well-meaning adult did not know that at that time people didn't get time off for good behavior on a 1-year sentence and that our dad would serve his full term. On her birthday my sister waited all day, thinking he would appear. This experience still affects my sister's feelings about her birthday, and it happened more than 40 years ago. It's another example of why I place unpredictability at the top of the list for issues children of incarcerated parents grapple with.

Sometimes you learn about the incarceration of a child's family member from a child blurting out the information at circle time or from hearing it in the community. The first step is letting both the child and the family know that you treasure the child and want to support the family, recognizing that it a very difficult time.

It's also important to talk with a family member about how they want the child to answer the inevitable question about why the child's family member is in prison. With that information, you can help the child give a simple, truthful answer: "He took some drugs that were bad for him" or "He got mad and hit my mommy." Or they can choose not to answer at all: "I don't want to talk about that." You can help a child practice the chosen answer until it becomes comfortable.

The subject of why a person is incarcerated is always a difficult one. Other children may pronounce, "Only bad guys go to prison." Imagine what it is like for a child to hear that someone they love is bad. Your first response is clear: don't go silent. Always step in. Ask the child how she feels about what she just heard. Listen carefully and remind her that whatever happened, she can go right on loving that person. Ask open-ended questions about what the child knows or has seen. (See page 55 about clarifying conversations). Assure the child that even if the parent has been hurtful to the family, the parent *wants* to be a good parent and wants the child to be safe and loved.

Over the years working with families through Prison MATCH, inmates consistently talked about their concerns for their children. After checking if the family wants contact between the child and the inmate, a child's teacher is in a unique position to help the parent and child keep in touch. Here are some ideas:

- The wonderful drawings that children make in class can be hung on the parent's cell wall.

- Photos of the child on a field trip give the inmate something to talk or write about.

- Dictations, with child-drawn pictures, give a parent a sense of how the child is growing.

- A recording of the parent reading a storybook is a great way to help a young child remember the parent's voice.

- Being remembered with a child-drawn birthday or holiday card is a great present.

Akemi's mother and stepfather have just had a new baby. She breaks down in tears when her friend Tressa says that the new baby brother is not Akemi's real brother. Tiffany, whose family includes half-sisters, says the baby is Akemi's half-brother. When Akemi calls the teacher over, the teacher agrees with Tressa because she is technically correct. This leaves Akemi unhappy and confused. However, another teacher comes by and adds, "Akemi, your 'real' brother is the brother you love. Tressa meant that your baby brother has a different birth daddy than you do. But he's still your real brother."

Children Are Curious About Other Families

As children come in contact with other children whose family structures differ from their own, they are curious and observant. Their matter-of-fact statements about each other's families may require little, if any, comment from adults.

On the playground, a child who has played at Zachary's home comments to Zachary, "Your mom is a lesbian." Zachary responds, "Yeah, she is." Both children resume their play.

Because children take their own family structures for granted, their curiosity often takes the form of wanting to know why another child's family is not like their own.

Savannah's two sets of cousins and two neighborhood friends all live in households with single mothers. She asks her mother one day, "How come their daddies don't live with them?"

• • •

Malcolm shares a bedroom with his two brothers. When he hears that Radley is an only child, he says in disbelief and worry, "But who sleeps with him at night?"

How families and teachers respond to these questions and comments creates the foundation for children's feelings about the many ways of being a family. In the example of Savannah, above, there are several possible reasons why those daddies don't live with their children: the mothers may be single by choice,

divorced, or widowed. The father may work far away, be in the military, be hospitalized, or in prison. If you do not have accurate information about the separated person, explain that you don't know but that you will help the child find out. In all cases, what matters most is affirming that there are many ways to be a family. The key message is, "We all have families. Our families love and take care of us. Our families have different people in them."

Some Family Configurations Are Less Visible Than Others

To a great extent, the dominant culture image of families with a mother and father and one or two children living in a well-furnished, never messy, modern home is portrayed in the media (ads, films, videos). Children risk concluding that this image represents the normal family and that there is something wrong with any other configuration. As a result, teachers report hearing children question the validity of a family in which the child is being raised by a grandparent, a single parent, or parents who are gay or lesbian.

Strategies and Activities About Family Structure and Fairness

Some adults mistakenly assume that teaching children about the diversity in family structures devalues "traditional" families. ABE does not disparage or advocate any family structure—but it does adhere to early childhood education's fundamental ethic of positively representing and supporting each child's family regardless of its structure.

High-quality early childhood programs already include the topic of families in the curriculum. Addressing the theme of family diversity is about ensuring that existing activities are inclusive. It is about addressing and correcting misinformation and pre-prejudice about particular family structures. Even if the families you serve appear to be homogeneous, it is important that children learn that many different kinds of families exist and that they can like their own family and at the same time be open to and supportive of other children's families.

Every Family Matters and There Is Room for All of Us

- From your first contact with families, stress how important it is for their child that program staff and families build strong relationships. It may take a while to gain the trust and open relationship with all of the children's families, but when families feel welcome, children will greatly benefit.

- In your initial contact with families—when they visit to see whether they will enroll their child or during their intake interview—clearly state your program's commitment to supporting diversity of all family structures. Specifically list various kinds of families throughout your handbook so people will not have to ask, "Do you mean *our* kind of family?"

- Create an inclusive language environment about family for the children. Avoid language that excludes some children's family members, such as "Everyone take this home to your mom," "Let's make an invitation for your mom and dad for the family picnic," or "Where are your parents taking you for vacation?" Instead, use inclusionary statements: "Everyone take this home to your family," "Let's make invitations for the family picnic. Who would you like to invite?," or "What kinds of things will you do this summer?" Always talking about *mommies and daddies* as if they are one long word leaves out many children's experiences.

- Make sure the learning materials you use in your classroom represent a wide notion of family. Purchase several sets of small people figurines representing various ethnicities, ages, and genders. Put all these family sets together in one container so that children have enough figures to select those that best represent their own family. Provide or make lotto, matching, and number games that show all kinds of families. Use photos of the children in your class and their families to supplement commercial games.

- In the dramatic play area, support children's play about their own experiences with family roles. Intervene if children make fun of other children's families. (See Chapter 4 for strategies.)

- During group times, be sure that all children have the opportunity to discuss the people in their lives who take care of them. Use children's questions and conversations as teachable moments, clarifying and expanding on their concepts about family. Incorporate literacy development by creating a chart about who is in each child's family.

- Make your own books about the children in your program. Children love these classroom books where they get to hear about their classmates and themselves. Your books might include *All the Different People You Call Your Family, Who Puts You to Bed at Night?*, or *Who Fixes Things That Break?*

- If your class includes only one or two children whose family structures are different from those of the rest of the children, do not shine a spotlight on those one or two during these suggested activities. Rather, intentionally read children's books and tell persona doll stories that reflect the children's families.

  Pay attention: children who remain silent during discussions about families may be signaling that they do not feel safe talking about their family. Explore this individually with the child and with the child's family.

- Adapt familiar songs and make up new ones that allow children to sing about their own family. For example, change the lyrics to "The More We Get Together" to "Oh, we belong together, together, together; Oh, we belong together; we're one family." Each child who wants to can name family members ("With Pedro and Papa and Abuelito and Chico / Oh, we belong together / We're one family" or "With Mama and Daddy and me and my kitty / Oh we belong together / We're one family").

- Read books to children about common family issues facing children with diverse family structures. For example, *Something Special for Me*, by Vera B. Williams, is about a young girl in a single-parent, working-class family who wants a special birthday gift. *Donovan's Big Day*, by Lesléa Newman, is about a young boy who is a ring bearer in a wedding. Not until the last page do you find out the wedding is between his two moms. Even when the specific story line in some books may not be the same as the lives of the children in your class, they can relate to the feelings of the children in the story.

- If a family in your program expresses discomfort, fear, or bias about another family, first listen thoughtfully. Try to learn why they believe as they do. Thank them for letting you know their feelings and respond with clear statements about the staff's commitment to welcoming and respecting *all* families. Address discomfort, fears, and inaccurate beliefs with factual, clear information. Explain how making hurtful comment about someone's identity harms the person, the person's child, and their own child.

. . .

Early childhood education programs are where many children first experience how the world feels about their family—and that not all families are like theirs. Cherishing every family is foundational to high-quality early childhood programs. When you assure families that you support and treasure their strengths and gifts—and recognize the biases and challenges they may face—then you create a classroom community where children belong and thrive.

Anti-Bias Education for Young Children and Ourselves

Carry It On: A Letter to Our Readers

As you come to the end of this book, ABE work may seem challenging. And it is. It is also empowering. Early childhood educators have a unique role to play in building a society in which all children and families can—and do—thrive. Across the United States and around the world, people like you are making changes in their classrooms, their programs, and their research; in policies, regulations, and laws; and at local, regional, and national levels.

Working for social justice change can be hard. Yet, it is also exciting and satisfying and brings healing and greater equity. When new understandings and new tools enable everyone to work and live in healthier, caring ways, change feels like a triumph. Over time, many small changes add up to bigger changes that can positively shift early childhood programs, communities, and the world. The challenge is to keep on keeping on. Here are some guideposts for embarking and carrying on the ABE journey.

Begin Where You Are

Identify the early childhood spheres where you have influence. It may be as a teacher of young children, program director, teacher educator, researcher, writer, and/or leader of an agency or organization. *Begin there.* One step leads to another as your experience, knowledge, and skills increase.

Understand Why You Do Anti-Bias Work

Your vision of the kind of world you want for children and families is the fuel that energizes your commitment to anti-bias work. It gives you courage to keep on keeping on. Use your vision to explain *why* you do anti-bias work, what it means to you, and what it means to the children and their families. Work with colleagues to help them articulate *their* vision and to then create a mission statement for your early childhood program: "In our program we have an anti-bias education approach because . . ." Remind everyone that a quality program means equity for all children.

Work with Others

Engaging in anti-bias education and working for change is both an individual and collaborative process. Connect with at least a few people who share your passion and your vision. Create or join a support group at work or in your community. They can celebrate with you when your work goes well and support you when things don't work the way you hoped. Attend and participate in workshops at local, state, and national conferences where you will find other people who share your interests.

Remember that Dissonance and Disagreement Are Part of Learning

When you do anti-bias work with children, their families, your colleagues, and others in the field of early childhood, conflicts may arise from diversity of experiences and differences in ideas about child development, childrearing, educational practice, and political or religious beliefs. View these dissonances as raw material for learning and personal growth. Combined with mutual respect, they open opportunities to explore different perspectives and try out new ideas and behaviors.

Be Strategic

Focus on the journey as well as the destination. Decide where your energy will be most effective at any given moment as you work toward your objectives and mission. To help you decide that, use what Paolo Freire (2000) calls the *cycle of praxis*. This is the interaction between three essential actions: *naming* (the specific situation), *reflecting and analyzing* (the situation in its immediate and broader contexts), and *acting* (dealing with the situation).

Stay Informed

Collect data about the demographics of your community, the children's families, and the program's staff. Find out about local, state, and federal governmental policies and oversight bodies such as boards of directors and licensors. Don't simply accept someone telling you "you can't do that" or "it has to be done this way." Find out *why* the limitation exists and look for where it is possible to make needed changes.

Advocate at All Levels of Early Childhood Education

Making equity and diversity fundamental elements of early childhood education includes joining with colleagues to improve the working conditions, benefits, and salaries of early childhood practitioners, including regular time for staff reflection and planning. The principles of honoring diversity and creating equity for all children need to permeate every part of the early childhood education field: classrooms; program-wide policies and leadership; teacher preparation and staff development; state and federal policies, regulations, standards, and assessment criteria and tools; research topics and methodologies and publications; and professional associations and leadership. The NAEYC's advancing equity position statement (2019) provides a powerful foundation you can use as a tool at all levels of advocacy.

Join Social Justice Movements

Be a voice for children and families in the larger world. This can be in places of worship, unions, and community organizations. Keep in mind that all structural isms and individual biases—which treat children and families as anything less than deserving of their full rights as human beings and deny anyone opportunities to develop intelligence and competence—violate the basic ethics of the early childhood profession. That is the reason the NAEYC Code of Ethical Conduct calls on us to

- Work through education, research, and advocacy toward an environmentally safe world in which all children receive health care, food, and shelter; are nurtured; and live free from violence in their home and their communities. . . . and in which all young children have access to high-quality early care and education programs (I-4.3 & 4).

- Promote knowledge and understanding of young children and their needs. To work toward greater societal acknowledgment of children's rights and greater social acceptance of responsibility for the well-being of all children (I-4.6).

- Support policies and laws that promote the well-being of children and families, and to work to change those that impair their well-being. To participate in developing policies and laws that are needed, and to cooperate with families and other individuals and groups in these efforts (I-4.7). (NAEYC 2016, 19)

Gather an Anti-Bias Education Village

Look for like-minded, committed colleagues across the country and beyond to form your ABE village. Having these relationships will stretch you, teach you, and support you in many ways. Together, you can look critically at what you are doing and problem solve difficult situations, share information and ideas, balance what is urgent with what is important in the long run, reassure and energize each other when you feel stuck or depleted, and celebrate small steps and accomplishments (Derman-Sparks 2017).

Continuing the Journey—a message from Catherine Goins

Anti-bias education is the North Star that guides all of my work with young children and their families. It was a central part of my work as a preschool teacher, Head Start teacher and supervisor, and college educator and remains so now as an assistant superintendent of early education. I started my anti-bias journey when, as a preschool teacher, I read *Anti-Bias Curriculum: Tools for Empowering Young Children* (Derman-Sparks & the A.B.C. Task Force 1989). I saw the possibilities of an early child community where everyone belongs, is respected and accepted, and has the tools to speak up for themselves and others. I felt hope, and I felt at home in the world of ABE.

While the basic principles of ABE have stayed the same, the social, political, and cultural contexts in which they work has undergone changes. This third edition of this book takes the best ideas from the 1989 and 2010 editions, adds tools and resources, and builds the anti-bias concepts so that they resonate with a new generation.

One central reality ABE must now address is that most states have moved toward a Quality Rating Improvement System (QRIS); early learning standards; standardized curricula; and formalized approaches to measuring and assessing environments and teacher–child interactions.

Developing tools that help teachers and administrators use these mandated tools to embed anti-bias concepts into everyday routines and activities is essential and calls on us to advocate for change in these public policies at the local, state, and national levels.

I have learned that ABE is not a final destination as much as it is a lifelong journey, guided by a vision, core values, and goals. Those who are on this journey remain explorers and travelers. My own stories about the transformative power of ABE, along with the stories of the many, many folks who engage in this work, energize and keep me going. I get inspiration from people I have never met, and from those with whom I work every day.

As I pick up the baton to continue the next leg of the anti-bias journey, I invite each of you to join me in taking collective responsibility for ABE, to engage deeply with it and with others who are also doing ABE.

Most of all, I remain hopeful. My anger and frustration that not all children are free from discrimination or have positive outcomes in life keeps me up at night. But the promise of anti-bias education gets me up every morning.

Keeping On

The reasons that drew us to ABE and social justice work are also the reasons that motivated and sustained us for all our professional lives.

We yearn for a time when every child will grow up fully nurtured and able to be fully who they are, with no barriers of prejudice, discrimination, poverty, or war. We dream of the time when quality and equity in all early childhood programs—and in our society—are the norm and at the core of what we do. [We long for the possibility of living in a society where] learning about and valuing one another's differences will be a natural part of growing up. Until that day comes, we must keep on keeping on with faith in our dreams and the possibility of positive change—in ourselves, in others, in our programs, and in our larger society. (Derman-Sparks 2017, 23)

As Dr. Martin Luther King Jr. declared in a speech on March 31, 1968, "We shall overcome because the arc of the moral universe is long, but it bends toward justice" (Washington 1991, 277).

Checklist for Assessing the Visual Material Environment

The toys, materials, and equipment you put out for children; the posters, pictures, and art objects you hang on the wall; and the types of furniture and how you arrange them all influence what children learn. What children do not see in the classroom teaches children as much as what they do see.

Rate each item:
N—not yet; **S**—still working on it; or **Y**—yes, we do this well

Dramatic play materials that support . . .

____ The home lives of children, families, and staff in the program

____ Diversity of gender roles

____ Diversity of cultures in your community, city, and state (supplementing the diversity of children, staff, and families in the program)

____ Economic class diversity

____ Accessibility and diverse abilities

____ A variety of ways to care for a family, cook and eat, keep house, play, and so on

Manipulatives that reflect . . .

____ Diversity in racial identity, ethnicity, gender, physical ability, and occupation (for all manipulatives, including puzzles, memory games, reading and number literacy games, and other small toys)

____ Diversity of skin tones, body shapes and sizes, physical abilities, clothing, and ages for play figures of people

____ Accurate depictions of people in terms of current life in the United States, avoiding stereotypes of all kinds

Language: Every day the staff support . . .

____ The languages that children, families, and staff speak through songs, labels and signs, stories, and interactions among children and with adults

____ The ongoing development of children's home languages and the development of English language skills

____ Regular opportunities to engage with American Sign Language and braille

____ Children's different communication styles, giving everyone equal opportunity to voice their ideas and feelings

Art materials are regularly available, including . . .

____ A range of skin tone paper, paint, crayons, markers, and playdough

____ Mirrors for children to reflect on their own physical features

____ Collage materials with images of diverse people and cultures

____ Items meant for individual and for group art activities

Dolls (purchased and homemade) that represent . . .

____ A fair balance of the physical characteristics of children, staff, and families in the program and in the community

____ Diversity in the United States beyond what is represented in the classroom

____ A fair balance of males and females, and also some anatomically correct dolls

____ People with different kinds of disabilities (along with a range of doll-size equipment that supports people with disabilities)

____ A variety of types of clothing (e.g., not gender stereotyped; not just dominant culture styles)

Children's books that contain accurate, nonstereotypical depictions of . . .

____ Physical characteristics and lives of the children, families, and staff in the program

____ Different languages, especially those spoken by children, families, and staff in the program and in the community

____ Diversity of gender roles, racial and cultural backgrounds, and abilities

____ A range of occupations and income levels (that support and supplement the diversity present in the program)

____ Many different family structures, so there are no token books of any particular type of family

Books that . . .

____ Present accurate images and information, with no overt or covert stereotypes

____ Challenge unfairness and prejudice

____ Encourage children to take action when faced with unfairness toward themselves or others

Posters, signs, photographs, puzzles, and games that authentically reflect . . .

____ All aspects of identity of the children, families, and staff in the program (e.g., economic class; aspects of physical appearance such as skin color, hair texture, eye color, and body size; physical abilities; language)

____ Children and families from the racial and ethnic groups in your community, city, and state

____ Diversity in families: single parents, extended families, LGBTQ families, interracial and multiethnic families, adoptive families, etc.

____ Elderly people of various backgrounds doing different types of activities

____ A balanced ratio of images depicting women and men doing jobs in the home and outside the home, and all different kinds of work (e.g., doctor, teacher, factory worker, truck driver, chef, firefighter, artist)

____ People of various backgrounds with different abilities and disabilities with their families and working. People with disabilities as active and independent

____ Creativity of artists of diverse backgrounds and cultures (e.g., paintings, drawings, sculptures, weavings)

____ Images of influential people, both past and present, including people who participate(d) in important struggles for social justice

____ Balance and variety, so that there are no token images of any particular group

Glossary

ableism: Beliefs or practices that discriminate against people with disabilities.

allies: People who stand up against unjust treatment of members of an identity group other than their own. An **alliance** is when people from two or more identity groups act together to stop inequitable treatment of either one or all groups.

anti-bias: An approach to education that explicitly works to end all forms of bias and discrimination.*

bias: Any attitude, belief, or feeling that justifies or results in unfair treatment of a person or a group of people because of their identity.

biracial, multiracial: Describes a child whose parents are from two or more different racialized identity groups. These terms cover a wide range of racial identity combinations.

body shaming: The action or practice of humiliating someone (regardless of intent) by making critical or mocking comments about their body shape or size.

classism (or classist): Any attitude, action, institutional policy, or practice that give societal advantages, such as greater opportunities, resources, and/or preferential treatment, to those with greater economic means and that denies access to and/or treats as inferior those with fewer economic means.

cultural continuity/discontinuity: The degree to which children or adults do or do not experience a match between their family culture ways of thinking, speaking, and behaving and those of the dominant culture. Cultural continuity and discontinuity between children's home culture and their early childhood program's culture are important variables in how much children feel they belong and how well they thrive.

culture: A set of shared beliefs, values, expectations, rules or patterns of behavior, goals, and practices that characterizes a group such as a family, community, institution, or organization. The characteristic features of everyday existence (how people live their lives) shared by people in a place or time.

developmentally appropriate practice (DAP): Adult–child interactions, materials, teaching methods, and learning experiences that promote young children's optimal learning and development. DAP takes into account what is individually appropriate for each child. This includes children's development and learning at different ages and each child's social and cultural context. *Note:* At the time of this writing, NAEYC is revising its position statement on developmentally appropriate practice, which will reflect the evolving understanding of this term.

disability: A physical, cognitive, emotional, or neuro-divergent challenge that impacts a person's abilities in some area(s) of daily living and learning, such as a vision or hearing impairment, intellectual impairment, autism spectrum disorder, dyslexia, or cerebral palsy.

discrimination: Action by institutions or an individual that denies access, opportunity, and resources to a person or group of people based on one or more of their social identities. *Outcomes* of such actions, rather than their intent, are the basis for determining discriminatory actions.

dominant culture: The way of life defined by the dominant group(s), as the normal and right way to live. Other cultural groups are judged based on how they differ from the dominant culture standards, which then become the justification for disrespect, prejudice, and discrimination.

dominant group: The social identity group(s) within a society that have greatest structural power, privileges, and social status. The dominant group may or may not be the majority of the population. In the United States, the dominant social identity groups have historically been White, Christian, affluent, heterosexual, and male. A dominant group achieves and maintains its position by controlling economic, political, and social institutions such as communications/ media, education and health institutions, the legal system, the arts, and business.

dual language learners: Children who are developing knowledge and fluency in their home language while also developing skills in a second (or third) language.

economic class: The financial conditions in which a person or family lives, which determine their access to the institutions and resources of their society and their degree of financial security. Unlike more rigid societies, in the United States the lines between classes are regarded as potentially permeable, though the extent to which movement from one economic class to another actually takes place varies by social identities and by historical periods.

equity (equitable)/equality: Equity is providing the conditions and supports that children and adults need to be successful. These take into consideration individual capacities, needs created by a person's current social conditions, and historic and current inequities connected to the individual's social identities. Equity is judged on the actual *outcomes* of the provided conditions and supports, not on their intent. The concept of *equity* goes beyond *equality*, which implies treating everyone the same—providing the same conditions and resources to all individuals— despite their differing needs and capacities.

ethnic group (and **ethnicity):** A group of people whose members identify with each other through a common heritage derived from where their ancestors lived (e.g., Mexico, Ireland, India). *Ethnicity* refers to the group members based on this shared heritage that make the group into a people. Individuals are born into an ethnic group but choose the elements of this culture to claim for themselves or leave behind.

explicit/implicit (overt/covert): Explicit and overt statements are social messages that directly spell out their meaning, in contrast to implicit and covert statements that are indirect, subtle, or hidden. Implicit

and covert messages have a strong impact on both children and adults, in part because they are not identified, analyzed, or critiqued.

family of origin: The family in which you grew up.

family structure: The specific people who make up a family, which includes adults or adults and children. Families provide each other shelter, food, childrearing, and love. Families exist in many different combinations of people, of which the heterosexual model of a father and mother and their biological children is only one such structure.

gender: A social identity resting on the assigned sex given to people at birth or earlier based on their visible anatomy. This assigned, legal identity carries with it a set of beliefs and social structures about **gender role**: the behaviors, appearances, capacities, and expectations that societies define in specific ways.

gender binary: Classification of gender roles into two opposite forms, male and female.

gender expression: The way people present themselves to the world; the observable behaviors, appearances, clothing, play choices, interests, and so on, that are interpreted as demonstrating a person's gender identity. At any given time, a person may appear to be **gender conforming**—appearing and behaving in ways that mostly match binary expectations—or **gender expansive or gender creative**— dressing and expressing themselves in ways that push the boundaries of binary expectations.

gender identity: One's deeply held sense of self as it relates to the world of gender. It is both imposed by the society from the outside and internally constructed by the child from the inside, starting in infancy. This internally constructed awareness and sense of gendered self may shift throughout one's lifetime. There are many terms people use to describe their gender identity. **Cisgender** describes a person whose gender identity matches the one assigned at birth. Additional identity terms currently in use include **gender fluid** (gender identity varies over time), **agender**

(identifying as neither male nor female), and **nonbinary** (gender identities that do not fit within the binary model). **Intersex** refers to people who are born with anatomy and/or body chemistry that is neither clearly male nor female. **Transgender** refers to a person whose assigned sex at birth does not match their gender identity.

heterosexism: An attitude, action, or practice of an individual or institution, backed by societal power, which assigns legal, social, and cultural advantages to people who are heterosexual while denying legal, social, and cultural rights to people whose sexual identity contradicts a heterosexism norm. **Homophobia** refers to individual or institutional attitudes and behaviors that reflect misconceptions, fear, or prejudice toward people who are part of the LGBTQ community.

inclusion: The practice of including children with disabilities in all learning, social, and educational programs alongside their peers without disabilities while providing specialized supports and accommodations for each child's success. More broadly, inclusion seeks to ensure equitable participation of all historically marginalized children.

income insecurity: Not having the amount of income necessary to cover basic expenses over time; living very close to the official definition of poverty.

internalized inferiority (internalized oppression): The internalization and acceptance of externally imposed hurtful, inaccurate beliefs, information, and judgments about one's social identity group(s)—and by extension, about oneself. These beliefs may result in self-restriction, self-limitation, and self-hate.

internalized superiority (internalized privilege): The internalization and acceptance of externally imposed misinformation and messages of superiority about one's social identity group(s)—and, by extension, oneself. These messages create a sense of entitlement and the belief that one's group is the norm by which all others should be judged. Internalized superiority functions as a social lens that justifies mistreatment of all others who are not part of the entitled social identity groups.

intersectionality: The overlapping and interdependent systems of oppression across, for example, race, gender, ability, and social status.* It highlights the complex and cumulative effects of different forms of structural inequity that can arise for members of multiple marginalized groups.

isms: The many forms of institutionalized prejudice and discrimination based on social identities such as ability, culture and ethnicity, economic class, sexual orientation, and racialized or gendered identity. Resultant isms would be, for example, *ableism, ethnocentrism, classism, heterosexism, racism, sexism.*

LGBTQ: An acronym for lesbian, gay, bisexual, transgender, queer or questioning, and more, reflecting the expansive, fluid concepts of sexual orientation, gender identity, and gender expression.* Other initials are sometimes added, such as I for intersex and A for asexual. Sometimes + is used with the acronym to indicate that other identities fit under it.

microaggressions: Indirect, subtle, and sometimes unintentional, statements, actions, or incidents that express prejudice and/or bias that support any of the isms.

misinformation: False or inaccurate information, whether intended or unintended and whether a reflection of ignorance or of prejudice.

misrepresentation: Inaccurately teaching about an individual's or group's culture due to lack of information (e.g., using historical examples rather than current examples, mixing up distinct cultures by generalizing them into one category) or due to bias.

multiracial family: May be either a family in which the parents are racially different from each other or one in which the children have differing racial identities. See **transracial adoptive family**.

nationality: The status of belonging to a particular nation by origin, birth, or naturalization. **Citizenship** is the legal status of being a citizen of a country either by birth or by naturalization. You are a citizen of the country or countries from which you may receive a passport.

nativism: Favoring people born in your own country and having prejudice toward immigrants. Xenophobia is another term with the same meaning.

norm, normative: The definition of certain actions, identities, and outcomes as the standard ("the norm" or "normal"), with everything else as outside the norm. While some research-based norms provide guidance regarding healthy child development and appropriate educational activities and expectations, these norms have too often been derived through research that has only or primarily included nonrepresentative samples of children.*

oppression: The systematic and prolonged mistreatment of a group of people.*

people-first language: A way of identifying an individual's humanity before describing the person's disability (e.g., *child with a disability, child who uses a wheelchair*). Some individuals prefer **identity-first language,** such as *autistic person* or *Deaf person,* as a way of taking pride in their full identity, including the way their differences structure their experience of the world and themselves.

people of color: A socially and politically created category referring collectively to the various groups—and the members of those groups—who have historically been made targets of racism in the United States. This label has changed throughout US history and has been applied to African Americans, Asian Americans, Latino Americans, and Native Americans. Arab Americans may also be included in this category. (Use of the inclusive term *people of color* in this book is not intended to deny the significant cultural, historical, and class differences among these groups.)

personal identity: Attributes that give each person a sense of individuality. Includes factors such as a person's first name, personality, talents, interests, age, and the specifics of and relationships with family members. Primarily fostered by a child's temperament, home, and extended family, and then by community and school experiences.

power of silence: The negative impact on children when adults do not talk openly about issues that are controversial and/or have strong emotional meaning for adults.

prejudice: An attitude, opinion, or feeling formed without adequate prior knowledge, thought, or reason. Prejudice can be prejudgment for or against any person, group, or gender.

pre-prejudice: Beginning, inaccurate ideas and feelings in very young children that may develop into real prejudice if reinforced by prevailing societal biases. Pre-prejudice may be a misconception based on children's limited experience and developmental level or may reflect imitations of adult behavior. More serious forms are behaviors that reflect discomfort, fear, or rejection of differences.

privilege: Unearned advantages that result from being a member of a socially preferred or dominant social identity group. Privilege is often invisible to those who experience it without ongoing self-reflection. Privilege is the opposite of marginalization or oppression that results from racism and other isms.

public assistance: Government assistance to people with low income (e.g., vouchers for child care, food-purchasing assistance, temporary cash assistance).

race: A social and political construct that creates and assigns people to different hierarchal racial groups and assigns racialized social identities. The scientific consensus is that the concept of race has no biological basis; all people are members of one biological race—that of human beings. Historically, the socially and politically created idea of race became the center of systemic racism, which justified European countries', and then the United States', acts of enslavement, economic exploitation, and colonization of other peoples' lands. The false concept of race continues to justify economic exploitation and discrimination.

racialized identity: One of the fundamental social identities in societies built on the false social and political concept of race and the practices of systemic racism. Racialized identity is imposed on every individual and becomes the basis for societal advantages and disadvantages. Individuals vary in the degree to which they accept or reject the societal messages about their own and others' racialized identity and the degree to which they work to end the practices of racism and racialized identity. In this book, the term *racialized identity* is used to indicate that racial identity is imposed upon us from outside, while individuals construct it internally, beginning with very young children.

racism: An institutionalized system of economic, political, social, and cultural conditions that assigns power, advantage, and privilege to one racial group over another group(s). Institutionalized policies, structures, ideologies, and behaviors, as well as individual acts of bigotry, prejudice, and discrimination, create and maintain racism throughout society. This includes the imposition of one racial group's culture in such a way as to withhold respect for, demean, or attempt to destroy the cultures of other races **(cultural racism)**.

refugee: A person who has been forced to leave his country in order to escape war, political persecution, violence, or natural disasters. While all refugees are immigrants, not all immigrants are refugees.

religious literacy: An educational approach to supporting children's individual families' specific beliefs while also promoting children's awareness of and respectful language and behavior toward differences in other people's beliefs and practices.

sexism: Any attitude, action, institutional policy, or practice that gives societal advantages, such as greater opportunities, resources, and/or preferential treatment, based on a person's assigned sex. Sexism operates at a systemic level through deeply embedded structural and institutional policies that have assigned power and prestige to those society calls men, and caring and nurturing roles with little economic reward to those defined as women.*

sexual orientation: Describes to whom a person is sexually attracted. A person can be heterosexual (attracted to those of the opposite sex), homosexual (attracted to those of the same sex), bisexual (attracted to both sexes), asexual (not attracted), polysexual (attracted to many sexes). All these terms reflect binary terminology about sex.

sexuality: The state of being sexual; how individuals live out their sexual lives.

social identity: Assigned memberships in groups defined by the society and shared with many other people. Identities include economic class, gendered identity, heritage, racialized identity, and religion. Each of these social identities is connected to societal advantages and disadvantages. Individual identity, in contrast to social identity, is about an individual's specific personality, interests, abilities, and beliefs about themselves (self-concept).

stereotype: Any depiction of a person or group of people that makes them appear less than fully human, unique, or individual or that reinforces misinformation about that person or group. An oversimplified generalization about a group, race, or gender, which presumes all members of the group share the same characteristic.

transracial family: A family in which an adopted child has a different racialized identity than member(s) of the child's adoptive family. **Transethnic family** refers to a family in which an adopted child has a different ethnic identity than member(s) of the child's adoptive family.

White: A socially and politically constructed racial group that historically and currently receives the benefits of racism in the United States. The category now includes all ethnic groups of European origin regardless of differences in histories, languages, or cultures. The designation of White, as well as the degree and amount to which different White groups have received economic social, political, and cultural benefits, has varied historically.

White normalcy: The notion that Whiteness is the normal way of being. This gives White people the assumed benefit of being thought of as simply human without having a racialized identity. The assumed cultural rules of White people become the standard against which all other cultures are judged.

*Indicates definitions adapted from NAEYC, "Advancing Equity in Early Childhood Education" (position statement), 2019.

References

Adair, J.K., & A. Barraza. 2014. "Voices of Immigrant Parents in Preschool Settings." *Young Children* 69 (4): 32–39.

Alexander, M. 2012. *The New Jim Crow: Mass Incarceration in the Age of Colorblindness*. New York: The New Press.

Allen, M., & L. Staley. 2007. "Helping Children Cope When a Loved One Is on Military Deployment." *Young Children* 62 (1): 82–87.

Annie E. Casey Foundation. 2016. *A Shared Sentence: The Devastating Toll of Parental Incarceration on Kids, Families and Communities*. Policy report. www .aecf.org/resources/a-shared-sentence.

Annie E. Casey Foundation. 2018. *2018 KIDS COUNT Data Book*. Baltimore, MD: Annie E. Casey Foundation. www.aecf.org /resources/2018-kids-count-data-book.

Annie E. Casey Foundation. 2019. 2019 KIDS COUNT Data Book. Baltimore, MD: Annie E. Casey Foundation. www.aecf.org/m/resourcedoc /aecf-2019kidscountdatabook-2019.pdf.

Baker, V.C. 2010. "A Window into Four Children's White Identity: Exploring Racial Identity Development Among White Children in a Diverse Preschool Classroom Located Within a Predominantly White Community" [a project submitted in partial fulfillment of the requirements for the degree of Master of Arts in human development]. Pacific Oaks College, Pasadena, CA.

Barbarin, O., & G. Crawford. 2006. "Acknowledging and Reducing Stigmatization of African American Boys." *Young Children* 61 (6): 79–86.

Barndt, J. 1991. *Dismantling Racism: The Continuing Challenge to White America*. Minneapolis, MN: Augsburg Fortress.

Beirich, H. 2019a. "New FBI Report Shows Increase in Violent Hate Crime in 2018." www.splcenter .org/news/2019/11/12/new-fbi-report -shows-increase-violent-hate-crime-2018.

Beirich, H. 2019b. "The Year in Hate: Rage Against Change." *Intelligence Report* (Spring) 166: 35–61. www.splcenter.org/fighting-hate /intelligence-report/2019/year-hate-rage -against-change.

Belenky, M.F., B.M. Clinchy, N.R. Goldberger, & J.M. Tarule. 1997. *Women's Ways of Knowing: The Development of Self, Voice, and Mind*. New York: Basic Books.

Bian L., S.J. Leslie, & A. Cimpian. 2017. "Gender Stereotypes About Intellectual Ability Emerge Early and Influence Children's Interests." *Science* 355 (6323): 389–91. https:// doi.org/10.1126/science.aah6524.

Bisson, J., & L. Derman-Sparks. 2016. "Holidays and Anti-Bias Education: Being Thoughtful and Creative." *Exchange* 231 (September/October): 75–78.

Blumenbach, J.F. [1795] 1865. "On the Natural Variety of Mankind." In *The Anthropological Treatises of Johann Friedrich Blumenbach*, ed. and trans. T. Bendyshe. London: Longman, Green, Longman, Roberts, & Green.

Bredekamp, S., ed. 1986. *Developmentally Appropriate Practice*. Washington, DC: NAEYC.

Bredekamp, S., ed. 1987. *Developmentally Appropriate Practice*. Expanded ed. Washington, DC: NAEYC.

Bredekamp, S., & C. Copple, eds. 1997. *Developmentally Appropriate Practice in Early Childhood Programs*. Rev. ed. Washington, DC: NAEYC.

Brillante, P. 2017. *The Essentials: Supporting Young Children with Disabilities in the Classroom*. Washington, DC: NAEYC.

Bronson, P., & A. Merryman. 2009. "See Baby Discriminate." *Newsweek,* September 14, 53–59.

Brown, C.S., H. Ali, E.A. Stone, & J.A. Jewell. 2017. "U.S. Children's Stereotypes and Prejudices Toward Arab Muslims." *Analyses of Social Issues and Public Policy* 17 (1): 60–83. https://doi.org/10.1111/asap.12129.

Brown, C.S., & E.A. Stone. 2016. "Gender Stereotypes and Discrimination: How Sexism Impacts Development." In *Advances in Child Development and Behavior*, Vol. 50, eds. S.S. Horn, M.D. Ruck, & L.S. Liben, 105–133. Philadelphia: Elsevier.

Burchinal, M., S. Field, M.L. Lopez, C. Howes, & R. Pianta. 2012. "Instruction in Spanish in Pre-Kindergarten Classrooms and Child Outcomes for English Language Learners." *Early Childhood Research Quarterly* 27 (2): 188–97.

Butler-Wall, A., K. Cosier, R.L.S. Harper, J. Sapp, J. Sokolowe, & M.B. Tempel. 2016. *Rethinking Sexism, Gender, and Sexuality.* Milwaukee, WI: Rethinking Schools.

Byrd, D. 2018. "FBI Report: Religion-Based Hate Crimes in 2017 Increased for the Third Consecutive Year." BJC (blog), November 13. https://bjconline.org/fbi-report-religion -based-hate-crimes-up-22-in-2017-111318.

Camera, L. 2017. "New Study Questions Links Between Race, Disability in Students." *U.S. News & World Report.* Aug 31. www.usnews .com/news/education-news/articles/2017-08-31.

Cárdenas-Hagan, E., C.D. Carlson, & S.D. Pollard-Durodola. 2007. "The Cross-Linguistic Transfer of Early Literacy Skills: The Role of Initial L1 and L2 Skills and Language of Instruction." *Language, Speech, and Hearing Services in Schools* 38 (3): 249–59. https:// doi.org/10.1044/0161-1461(2007/026).

Castro, D.C. 2014. "The Development and Early Care and Education of Dual Language Learners: Examining the State of Knowledge." *Early Childhood Research Quarterly* 29 (4): 693–8. https://doi.org/10.1016/j.ecresq.2014.08.003.

CDC (Centers for Disease Control and Prevention). n.d. "Communicating With and About People with Disabilities." www.cdc.gov/ncbddd /disabilityandhealth/pdf/disabilityposter _photos.pdf.

Chafel, J.A., A.S. Flint, J. Hammel, & K.H. Pomeroy. 2007. "Young Children, Social Issues, and Critical Literacy: Stories of Teachers and Researchers." *Young Children* 62 (1): 73–81.

Christensen, O., & K. Gast. 2015. "Addressing Classism in Early Childhood Education: How Social-Class Sensitive Pedagogy and the Montessori Method Can Work Together." In *Discussions on Sensitive Issues*, ed. J.A. Sutterby, 113–35. Vol. 19 of *Advances in Early Education and Day Care.* Bingley, UK: Emerald Group Publishing Limited.

Chu, J.Y. 2014. *When Boys Become Boys: Development, Relationships, and Masculinity.* New York: New York University.

Churchill, W. 2004. *Kill the Indian, Save the Man: The Genocidal Impact of American Indian Residential Schools.* San Francisco, CA: City Lights Publishers.

Clark, K.B. 1963. *Prejudice and Your Child.* Boston, MA: Beacon Press.

CNN. 2010. "Study: White and Black Children Biased Toward Lighter Skin." May 14. www.cnn .com/2010/US/05/13/doll.study/index.html.

Cole, K., J-Y. Plaisir, M. Reich-Shapiro, & A. Freitas. 2019. "Building a Gender-Balanced Workforce: Supporting Male Teachers." *Young Children* 74 (4): 39-45.

Coles, R. 1977. *Privileged Ones: The Well-Off and the Rich in America.* Boston, MA: Little Brown.

Collins, P.H., & S. Bilge. 2016. *Intersectionality.* Cambridge, UK: Polity Books.

Congressional Research Service. 1975. "Education for All Handicapped Children Act." Washington, DC: Library of Congress. www.govtrack.us /congress/bills/94/s6/ summary#libraryofcongress.

Cook, R., A. Richardson-Gibbs, & L.N. Dotson. 2018. *Strategies for Including Children with Special Needs in Early Childhood Settings.* Boston: Cengage Learning.

Cooper, E.J. 2016. "Guarding Against Damaging Implicit Racial Bias—Even in Our Preschools." HuffPost, September 27. www.huffpost.com/entry/guarding-against-damaging_b_12220386.

Copple, C., & S. Bredekamp, eds. 2009. *Developmentally Appropriate Practice in Early Childhood Programs Serving Children from Birth through Age 8*. 3rd ed. Washington, DC: NAEYC.

Crenshaw, K. Forthcoming. *On Intersectionality: Essential Writings*. New York: The New Press.

Cummins, J. 2001. *Negotiating Identities: Education for Empowerment in a Diverse Society*. 2nd ed. Walnut, CA: California Association for Bilingual Education.

Cummins, J., & M. Early, eds. 2011. *Identity Texts: The Collaborative Creation of Power in Multilingual Schools*. Stoke-on-Trent, UK: Trentham Books.

Day, C.B. 2013. "Culture and Identity Development: Getting Infants and Toddlers Off to a Great Start." In *A Guide to Culturally Sensitive Care*, 2nd ed., eds. E.A. Virman & P.L. Mangione, 2–10. Sacramento: California Department of Education.

DeAngelis, T. 2009. "Unmasking 'Racial Micro Aggressions.'" *Monitor on Psychology* 40 (2): 42. www.apa.org/monitor/2009/02/microaggression.

Derman-Sparks, L. 2013. "Developing Culturally Responsive Caregiving Practices: Acknowledge, Ask, and Adapt." In *A Guide to Culturally Sensitive Care*, 2nd ed., eds. E.A. Virman & P.L. Mangione, 68–94. Sacramento: California Department of Education.

Derman-Sparks, L. 2017. "Keeping On: Reflections from a Long-Time Anti-Bias Education Activist." *Exchange* 237 (September/October): 20–24.

Derman-Sparks, L., & the A.B.C Task Force. 1989. *Anti-Bias Curriculum: Tools for Empowering Young Children*. Washington, DC: NAEYC.

Derman-Sparks, L., & J.O. Edwards. 2010. *Anti-Bias Education for Young Children and Ourselves*. Washington, DC: NAEYC.

Derman-Sparks, L., D. LeeKeenan, & J. Nimmo. 2015. *Leading Anti-Bias Early Childhood Programs: A Guide for Change*. New York: Teachers College Press; Washington, DC: NAEYC.

Derman-Sparks, L., & C.B. Phillips. 1997. *Teaching/Learning Anti-Racism: A Developmental Approach*. New York: Teachers College Press.

Derman-Sparks, L., & P. Ramsey. With J.O. Edwards. 2011. *What If All the Kids Are White? Anti-Bias Multicultural Education with Young Children and Families*. 2nd ed. New York: Teachers College Press.

DiAngelo, R. 2018. *White Fragility: Why It's So Hard for White People to Talk About Racism*. Boston, MA: Beacon Press.

Dudley-Marling, C., & M.B. Burns. 2014. "Two Perspectives on Inclusion in the United States." *Global Education Review* 1 (1): 14–31.

Dunbar-Ortiz, R. 2014. *An Indigenous Peoples' History of the United States*. Boston, MA: Beacon Press.

Edwards, J.O. 2017. "How to Get Started with Anti-Bias Education in Your Classroom and Program." *Exchange* 233 (January/February): 78–79.

Ehrensaft, D. 2016. *The Gender Creative Child: Pathways for Nurturing and Supporting Children Who Live Outside Gender Boxes*. New York: The Experiment.

Feagin, J.R. 2000. *Racist America: Roots, Current Realities, and Future Reparations*. New York: Routledge.

Freire, P. 2000. *Pedagogy of the Oppressed*. 30th anniversary edition. New York: Bloomsbury.

Gable, S. 2014. *The States of Child Care: Building a Better System*. New York: Teachers College Press.

Gates, H.L. Jr. 2019. *Stony the Road: Reconstruction, White Supremacy, and the Rise of Jim Crow*. London: Penguin Press.

Gilliam, W.S., A.N. Maupin, C.R. Reyes, M. Accavitti, & F. Shic. 2016. "Do Early Educators' Implicit Biases Relate to Behavior Expectations and Recommendations of Preschool Expulsions and Suspensions?" New Haven, CT: Yale University Child Study Center.

Gilligan, C. 1993. *In a Different Voice: Psychological Theory and Women's Development.* Cambridge, MA: Harvard University Press.

Goodman, M.E. 1952. *Race Awareness in Young Children.* Cambridge, MA: Addison-Wesley.

Hannaford, I. 1996. *Race: The History of an Idea in the West.* Washington, DC: The Woodrow Wilson Center.

Hanson, M.J., & E.W. Lynch. 2013. *Understanding Families: Supportive Approaches to Diversity, Disability, and Risk.* 2nd ed. Baltimore, MD: Brookes.

Harry , B., & J.K. Klingner. 2006. *Why Are So Many Minority Students in Special Education? Understanding Race and Disability in Schools.* New York: Teachers College Press.

Heckman, J., & G. Karapakula. 2019. "The Perry Preschoolers at Late Midlife: A Study in Design-Specific Inference." Cambridge, MA: National Bureau of Economic Research. https://doi.org/10.3386/w25888.

Henig, R.M. 2018. "The Age of Grandparents Is Made of Many Tragedies." *The Atlantic,* June 1. www.theatlantic.com/family/archive/2018/06/this-is-the-age-of-grandparents/561527.

Jaboneta, N., with D. Curtis. 2019. "Challenging Gender Stereotypes: A Teacher's Reflections on Counteracting Gender Bias." In *Spotlight on Young Children: Equity & Diversity,* eds. C. Gillanders & R. Procopio, 71–74. Washington, DC: NAEYC.

Jordan, M. 2019. "More Than 2,000 Migrants Were Targeted in Raids. 35 Were Arrested." *New York Times*, July 23. www.nytimes.com/2019/07/23/us/ice-raids-apprehensions.html.

Katz, P.A., & J.A. Kofkin. 1997. "Race, Gender, and Young Children." In *Developmental Psychopathology: Perspectives on Adjustment, Risk, and Disorder*, eds. S.S. Luthar, J.A. Burack, D. Cicchetti, & J.R. Weisz, 51–74. New York: Cambridge University Press.

Kaye, J. 2010. *Moving Millions: How Coyote Capitalism Fuels Global Immigration.* Hoboken, NJ: John Wiley & Sons.

Kendi, I.X. 2016. *Stamped from the Beginning: The Definitive History of Racist Ideas in America.* New York: Nation Books.

Kirwan Institute for the Study of Race and Ethnicity. 2015. *Understanding Implicit Bias.* The Ohio State University. http://kirwaninstitute.osu.edu/research/understanding-implicit-bias/.

Kissinger, K. 2017. *Anti-Bias Education in the Early Childhood Classroom: Hand in Hand, Step by Step.* New York: Routledge.

Koball, H., & Y. Jiang. 2018. "Basic Facts About Low-Income Children: Children Under 18 Years, 2016." Fact sheet. National Center for Children in Poverty. http://nccp.org/publications/pdf/text_1194.pdf.

Lane, J. 2008. *Young Children and Racial Justice.* London, UK: National Children's Bureau.

LeeKeenan, D., & J. Nimmo. 2016. "Anti-Bias Education in Challenging Times." *Exchange* 232 (November/December): 66–69.

Letzter, R. 2018. "How Parents and Doctors Support Transgender Children." Live Science, June 22. www.livescience.com/62893-transgender-kids-puberty-blockers-hrt-hormones.html.

Levin, B., & L. Nakashima. 2019. "Report to the Nation: Illustrated Almanac—Decade Summary: Hate and Extremism." Center for the Study of Hate and Extremism, California State University, San Bernardino. https://csbs.csusb.edu/sites/csusb_csbs/files/Report%20to%20the%20Nation%20Illustrated%20Almanac%20%28November%202019%29.pdf.

Livingston, G. 2014. "Fewer than Half of U.S. Kids Today Live in a 'Traditional' Family." Fact Tank: News in the Numbers, Pew Research Center, December 22. www.pewresearch.org /fact-tank/2014/12/22/less-than-half-of-u -s-kids-today-live-in-a-traditional-family.

Livingston, G. 2017. "The Rise of Multiracial and Multiethnic Babies in the US." Fact Tank: News in the Numbers, Pew Research Center, June 6. www .pewresearch.org/fact-tank/2017/06/06/the-rise -of-multiracial-and-multiethnic-babies-in -the-u-s/.

Livingston, G. 2018. "About One-Third of U.S. Children Are Living With an Unmarried Parent." Fact Tank: News in the Numbers, Pew Research Center, April 27. www.pewresearch.org/fact -total/2018/04/22/about-one-third-of.

Madison, M. 2015. "Building a Diverse, Anti-Bias Library for Young Children: A Masterpost." Equity in Early Childhood (blog), August 12. https ://earlychildhoodequity.tumblr.com/post /126556770455/building-a-diverse -anti-bias-library-for-young.

Marable, M. 2016. *Beyond Black and White: From Civil Rights to Barack Obama.* Reprint ed. Brooklyn, NY: Verso.

Mardell, B., & M.M. Abo-Zena. 2010. "'The Fun Thing About Studying Different Beliefs Is That . . . They Are Different': Kindergartners Explore Spirituality." *Young Children* 65 (4): 12–17.

McIntosh, P. 1989. "White Privilege: Unpacking the Invisible Knapsack." *Peace and Freedom* (July/August): 10–12.

Moore, D.L. 2007. *Overcoming Religious Illiteracy: A Cultural Studies Approach to the Study of Religion in Secondary Education.* New York: Palgrave Macmillan.

Murray, C., & M. Urban. 2017. *Diversity & Equality in Early Childhood: An Irish Perspective.* Dublin, Ireland: Gill & Macmillan Ltd.

NAEYC. 1995. "Responding to Linguistic and Cultural Diversity Recommendations for Effective Early Childhood Education." Position statement. www.naeyc.org/sites/default/files/globally -shared/downloads/PDFs/resources /position-statements/PSDIV98.PDF.

NAEYC. 2005. "Screening and Assessment of Young English-Language Learners: Supplement to the NAEYC and NAECS/SDE Joint Position Statement on Early Childhood Curriculum, Assessment, and Program Evaluation." www.naeyc.org/sites /default/files/globally-shared/downloads/PDFs /resources/position-statements /ELL_Supplement_Shorter_Version .pdf. Washington, DC: NAEYC.

NAEYC. 2016. *Code of Ethical Conduct and Statement of Commitment.* Brochure. Washington, DC: NAEYC.

NAEYC. 2019. "Advancing Equity in Early Childhood Education." Position statement. Washington, DC: NAEYC. www.naeyc.org/resources/position -statements/equity.

NAEYC & CLASP (Center for Law and Social Policy). 2018. "Sensitive Locations and Beyond: Roles and Responsibilities for Early Childhood Educators Working with Children in Undocumented Families" (webinar). www.youtube .com/watch?v=eTnW8zLv7wc.

National Academics of Sciences, Engineering, and Medicine. 2017. *Promoting the Educational Success of Children and Youth Learning English: Promising Futures.* Washington, DC: The National Academies Press. https://doi.org/10.17226/24677.

National Indian Child Welfare Association. 2015. "Setting the Record Straight: The Indian Child Welfare Act Fact Sheet." Portland, OR: National Indian Child Welfare Association. www.nicwa .org/wp-content/uploads/2017/04/Setting -the-Record-Straight-ICWA-Fact-Sheet.pdf.

Nayani, F. 2017. *Being All of Me: A Handbook for Teachers and Parents of Multiracial, Multiethnic, and Transracially Adopted Children.* Los Angeles: Multiracial Americans of Southern California.

NCCP (National Center for Children in Poverty). 2019. "Child Poverty." http://www.nccp.org/topics/childpoverty.html.

NCTE (National Council of Teachers of English). 2016. "Equity and Early Childhood Education: Reclaiming the Child." Brief. Washington, DC: NCTE.

Nicholson, J.M., & D.B. Wisneski, eds. 2018. *Reconsidering the Role of Play in Early Childhood: Towards Social Justice and Equity.* New York: Routledge.

NIEER (National Institute for Early Education Research). 2007. "Rx for Behavior Problems in Pre-K." Preschool Matters 5 (5): 4–5. http://nieer.org/wp-content/uploads/2016/08/55.pdf.

Nimmo, J., M.M. Abo-Zena, & D. LeeKeenan. 2019. "Finding a Place for the Religious and Spiritual Lives of Young Children and Their Families: Taking an Anti-Bias Approach." *Young Children* 74 (5): 37–45.

NMAI (National Museum of the American Indian). 2018. *Do All Indians Live in Tipis? Questions & Answers from the National Museum of the American Indian.* 2nd ed. Washington, DC: National Museum of the American Indian and Smithsonian Institution.

Nutt, A.E. 2015. *Becoming Nicole: The Transformation of an American Family.* New York: Random House.

Oh, J.S., & A.J. Fuligni. 2010. "The Role of Heritage Language Development in the Ethnic Identity and Family Relationships of Adolescents from Immigrant Backgrounds." *Social Development* 19 (1): 202–20. https://doi.org/10.1111/j.1467-9507.2008.00530.x.

Ovando, C.J. 2003. "Bilingual Education in the United States: Historical Development and Current Issues." *Bilingual Research Journal* 27 (1): 1–24. https://doi.org/10.1080/15235882.2003.10162589.

OWH (US Department of Health and Human Services Office on Women's Health). 2019. "Body Image." Last modified March 27. www.womenshealth.gov/mental-health/body-image-and-mental-health/body-image.

Oyate. n.d. "Resources: Living Stories." www.oyate.org/index.php/resources/45-resources/living-stories#parent-story.

Paradis, J., F. Genesee, & M.B. Crago. 2011. *Dual Language Development and Disorders: A Handbook on Bilingualism & Second Language Learning.* Baltimore, MD: Brookes.

Parker, W. 2019. "Statistics About Children of Divorce." Verywell Family, August 8. www.verywellfamily.com/children-of-divorce-in-america-statistics-1270390.

Pastel, E., K. Steele, J. Nicholson, C. Maurer, J. Hennock, J. Julian, T. Unger, & N. Flynn. 2019. *Supporting Gender Diversity in Early Childhood Classrooms.* London: Jessica Kingsley.

Pew Research Center. 2015. "What Census Calls Us: A Historical Timeline." https://www.pewsocialtrends.org/wp-content/uploads/sites/3/2015/06/ST_15.06.11_MultiRacial-Timeline.pdf.

Piaget, J. 1953. *The Origin of Intelligence in the Child.* New York: Routledge & Kegan Paul.

Pierce, C.M. 1980. "Social Trace Contaminants: Subtle Indicators of Racism in TV." In *Television and Social Behavior*, eds. S.B. Withey & R. Abeles, 249–57. Hillsdale, NJ: Lawrence Erlbaum Associates.

Rajunov, M., & S. Duane, eds. 2019. *Nonbinary: Memoirs of Gender and Identity.* New York: Columbia University Press.

Ramsey, P. 2015. *Teaching and Learning in a Diverse World: Multicultural Education for Young Children.* 4th ed. New York: Teachers College Press.

Religious Literacy Project. 2019. "What is Religious Literacy?" Harvard Divinity School. www.rlp.hds.harvard.edu/our-approach/what-is-religious-literacy.

Roediger, D.R. 2005. *Working Toward Whiteness: How America's Immigrants Became White—The Strange Journey from Ellis Island to the Suburbs*. New York: Basic Books.

Rojas-Flores, L. 2017. "Latino US-Citizen Children of Immigrants: A Generation at High Risk." Summary of Selected Young Scholars Program Research. Working paper. New York: Foundation for Child Development.

Rojas-Flores, L., M.L. Clements, J. Hwang Koo, & J. London. 2017. "Trauma and Phycological Distress in Latino Citizen Children Following Parental Detention and Deportation." *Psychological Trauma: Theory, Research, Practice, and Policy* 9 (3): 352–61.

Rothenberg, P.S. 2016. *White Privilege: Essential Readings on the Other side of Racism*. 5th edition. New York: Macmillan Learning.

Rothstein, R. 2017. *The Color of Law: A Forgotten History of How Our Government Segregated America*. New York: Liveright Publishing.

Schweinhart, L.J., H.V. Barnes, & D.P. Weikart. 1993. *Significant Benefits: The High/Scope Perry Preschool Study Through Age 27*. Ypsilanti, MI: High/Scope Press.

Schweinhart, L.J., J. Montie, Z. Xiang, W.S. Barnett, C.R. Belfield, & M. Nores. 2004. *Lifetime Effects: The High/Scope Perry Preschool Study Through Age 40*. Ypsilanti, MI: High/Scope Press.

Skiba, R.J., A.B. Simmons, S. Ritter, A.C. Gibb, M. Karega Rausch, J. Cuadrado, & C-G. Chung. 2008. "Achieving Equity in Special Education: History, Status, and Current Challenges." *Exceptional Children* 74 (3): 264–288.

Smith, S., M.R. Granja, & U.S. Nguyen. 2017. "New York State Profile of Young Children in Deep Poverty." New York: National Center for Children in Poverty, Mailman School of Public Health, Columbia University. http://www.nccp.org/publications/pdf/text_1190.pdf.

Sue, D.W. 2010. *Microaggressions in Everyday Life: Race, Gender, and Sexual Orientation*. Hoboken, NJ: John Wiley & Sons.

Sue, D.W., C.M. Capodilupo, G.C. Torino, J.M. Bucceri, A.M.B. Holder, K.L. Nadal, & M Esquilin. 2007. "Racial Microaggression in Everyday Life." *American Psychologist* 62 (4): 271–86.

Tatum, B.D. 2017. *Why Are All the Black Kids Sitting Together in the Cafeteria? And Other Conversations About Race*. 20th anniversary edition. New York: Basic Books.

Trager, H., & M.R. Yarrow. 1952. *They Learn What They Live: Prejudice in Young Children*. Problems in Race and Culture in American Education series, 8. New York: Harper & Brothers.

Turkewitz, J. 2017. "Thanksgiving for Native Americans: Four Voices on a Complicated Holiday." *New York Times*, November 23. www.nytimes.com/2017/11/23/us/thanksgiving-for-native-americans-four-voices-on-a-complicated-holiday.html.

UN OHCHR (United Nations Office of the High Commissioner for Human Rights). 1989. "Convention on the Rights of the Child." www.ohchr.org/en/professionalinterest/pages/crc.aspx.

US Department of Education Office for Civil Rights. 2014. "Data Snapshot: School Discipline." Brief. Civil Rights Data Collection. https://ocrdata.ed.gov/Downloads/CRDC-School-Discipline-Snapshot.pdf.

US HHS & ED (US Department of Health and Human Services & US Department of Education). 2015. "Policy Statement on Inclusion of Children with Disabilities in Early Childhood Programs." www2.ed.gov/policy/speced/guid/earlylearning/joint-statement-full-text.pdf.

Van Ausdale, D., & J.R. Feagin. 2001. *The First R: How Children Learn Race and Racism*. Lanham, MD: Rowman & Littlefield Publishers.

Voulgarides, C.K. 2018. *Does Compliance Matter in Special Education? IDEA and the Hidden Inequities of Practice*. New York: Teachers College Press.

Wagmiller, R.L., & R.M. Adelman. 2009. "Childhood and Intergenerational Poverty: The Long-Term Consequences of Growing Up Poor." National Center for Children in Poverty. www.nccp.org/publications/pub_909.html.

Wagner, P., & W. Sawyer. 2018. "States of Incarcerations: The Global Context 2018." Prison Policy Initiative, June. www.prisonpolicy.org/global/2018.html.

Wallis, J. 2017. *America's Original Sin: Racism, White Privilege, and the Bridge to a New America.* Ada, MI: Brazos/Baker Publishing.

Washington, J.M., ed. 1991. *A Testament of Hope: The Essential Writings and Speeches of Martin Luther King, Jr.* New York: HarperCollins.

Weikart, D.P. 1993. *Longitudinal Results of the Ypsilanti Perry Preschool Project.* Ypsilanti, MI: High/Scope Educational Research Foundation.

William, T.K. 2012. "Understanding Internalized Oppression: A Theoretical Conceptualization of Internalized Subordination." Dissertation. Amherst, MA: University of Massachusetts Amherst. https://scholarworks.umass.edu/cgi/viewcontent.cgi?article=1628&context=open_access_dissertations.

Yang, J.E. 2013. "Gender Balance in Early Childhood Education: Reasons for the Lack of Male Involvement, Encouraging Men into Early Childhood Teaching, and the Impact on Children, Families, Colleagues and the Early Childhood Sector." *He Kupu* (3) 3. www.hekupu.ac.nz/article/gender-balance-early-childhood-education-reasons-lack-male-involvement-encouraging-men.

Yates, T.M., & A.K. Marcelo. 2014. "Through Race-Colored Glasses: Preschoolers' Pretend Play and Teachers' Ratings of Preschool Adjustment." *Early Childhood Research Quarterly* 29 (1): 1–11. https://doi.org/10.1016/j.ecresq.2013.09.003.

Yogman, M., A. Garner, J. Hutchinson, K. Hirsh-Pasek, R. Michnick Golinkoff, Committee on Psychosocial Aspects of Child and Family Health, & Council on Communications and Media. 2018. "The Power of Play: A Pediatric Role in Enhancing Development in Young Children." *Pediatrics* 142 (3): e20182058. https://doi.org/10.1542/peds.2018-2058.

About the Authors

Louise Derman-Sparks, MA, worked for more than 50 years as a preschool teacher, child care center director, college teacher, author, consultant, and social justice activist. She began as an early childhood educator in the Ypsilanti Perry Preschool Project, directed a cooperative child care center, and was a professor at Pacific Oaks College for 32 years. Louise gave conference keynotes, conducted workshops, and consulted widely on anti-bias education with children and adults throughout the United States and internationally. Her published work includes several books and numerous articles. A member of the NAEYC Governing Board (1997–2001), Louise received the McCormick Center for Early Childhood Leadership's Visionary Leader award in 2012. Now retired from teaching, she is active with the Social Justice Committee of the Pasadena Jewish Temple and Center. Louise is also the mother of two professionals in the human service field, Douglass and Sean.

Julie Olsen Edwards began her early childhood education career as a family child care home provider and fell in love with young children and their amazing capacity to learn and create. Over the years she taught in public and private programs with infants through 8-year-olds, always working closely with families. She was the founding director of the Cabrillo College Children's Center and served as faculty and department chair during her 40 years at the college. She was a key organizer of the faculty union, insisting on the inclusion of the Children's Center teachers. A lifetime activist for children and families, Julie is currently a consultant to the Early Childhood Education Department at the Smithsonian National Museum of African American History and Culture. She continues to write, teach, and consult on issues of equity, diversity, and anti-bias; emerging literacy; and family life and empowerment. She served on the NAEYC Governing Board from 2003 to 2007.

Catherine M. Goins is assistant superintendent of Early Childhood Education for the Placer County Office of Education and adjunct faculty member at Sierra Joint Community College. She has more than 30 years of experience administering private, nonprofit, and publicly funded early education programs and speaking, coaching, and training on diversity, anti-bias education, and equity issues. An outspoken advocate for children, Catherine served as president of the Child Development Policy Institute; is a member of numerous national and statewide organizations; and has served on many early childhood boards and committees. She was honored as Educator of the Year from the California State University Sacramento (CSUS) College of Education. Catherine holds a BA in Child Development from CSUS, an MA in Human Development/Leadership in Education from Pacific Oaks College, and an MPA from the University of San Francisco. Catherine currently consults as a senior policy advisor for the First 5 California Children and Families Commission.

Photo courtesy of Rob Edwards.
Clockwise from top left: Catherine M. Goins, Julie Olsen Edwards, Louise Derman-Sparks

Index

A

ABE. See Anti-bias education

Ability differences, ABE core goals and, 151

Ableism, 9

Academic readiness, 139

Acknowledge, Ask, Adapt, 70–71

Acting, 177

Action projects, 102

Activism
as ABE goal, 5, 17, 49
adults and, 19
group, 69
talking about, 18

Activists
children as, 162–163
visits from, 102

Adaptive devices and equipment, 161

Adoptive families, 167–168

Adults
ABE goals and, 19, 65
class difference messages and interactions between, 142
relationships between, 65

"Advancing Equity in Early Childhood Education." *See* Advancing equity position statement

African Americans, 35, 108, 117
special education programs and, 152
suspension rates, 11

AFT. *See* American Federation of Teachers

Aggressive behavior, 17

AI/AN. *See* American Indian and Alaska Native

Allies, children as, 162–163

***All the Colors We Are/Todos los colores de nuestra piel* (Kissinger),** 118

American Academy of Pediatrics, 139

American Arab Anti-Discrimination Committee, 78

American Federation of Teachers (AFT), 22

American Indian and Alaska Native (AI/AN), 14

American Indians, 101

American Sign Language (ASL), 154

Anatomy, curiosity about, 126

Anti-bias activities, disagreements with, 69–72

Anti-bias commitments, 72

Anti-bias conversations, 54–57

Anti-bias core goals, 4, 5, 15–18
ability differences and, 151
adults and, 19, 65
children's lives and, 41
conversations with children and, 52
curriculum planning and, 43
economic class and, 137
families and, 68
family structure and, 165
gender identity and, 122
holidays and, 49
persona dolls and, 47
racialized identity and, 107
religious diversity and, 104

Anti-bias education (ABE), 1
activity planning, 43
avoiding missteps in, 41–43
children's lives and, 41
content and activity idea sources, 40
curriculum guidelines, 39–43
defining, 4–5
dual language learning and, 79
families included in, 68
implementing goals of, 17–18
inclusive, 157–160
materials guidelines, 43–44
need for, 6–8

personal experience and, 53
reasons for doing, 177
world view of, 5

Anti-bias libraries, financing, 45

Anti-bias relationships, 64–69, 72–74

Anti-bias values and goals, 71–72, 89

Anti-Semitism, 10

Anxiety, about disabilities, 159

***Apple Picking Time* (Slawson),** 120

ASL. *See* American Sign Language

Assessment, immigrant families and, 83

Assigned sex, 123, 124, 127

B

Behavior
aggressive, 17
documenting, 59
implicit bias and, 11
sexual, 124
stereotypes transcended through, 132–133

Bias
acting on child's, 59–60
children learning, 16
development undermined by, 57–60
explicit, 10–11
family views and, 72
implicit, 10–12
interrupting development of, 90
isms and, 10
race and, 107

Bill of Rights, 20, 103

Binary gender expectations, 123, 124

Binary gender roles, 127–129

Biracial children, racialized identity and, 113

Biracial families, 168

Try More NAEYC Resources
Great Books for Early Childhood Educators

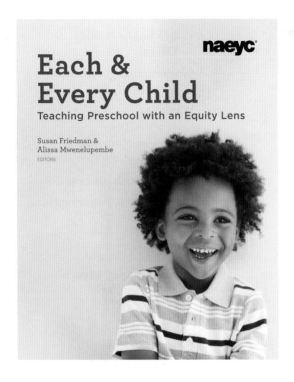

Each and Every Child: Teaching Preschool with an Equity Lens

All educators have a part to play in advancing equity in early childhood. But what does equity look like day to day in the classroom? This thoughtfully curated collection provides concrete strategies and tips for implementing recommendations from NAEYC's position statement "Advancing Equity in Early Childhood Education" in your work with children ages 3 through 5.

Featuring diverse voices from the field, this book explores practical topics ranging from examining your own biases to supporting children's conversations about identity to preventing preschool expulsion. With these and more engaging insights, you'll create and foster learning environments that promote equity for all.

Item 1144 • 2020 • 160 pages

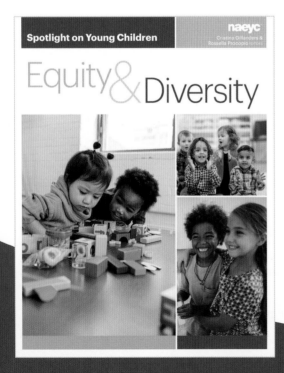

Spotlight on Young Children: Equity and Diversity

Informed and influenced by NAEYC's forthcoming position statement on equity and diversity, this collection of articles contextualizes how educators of children from birth through third grade can advance equity and embrace diversity. It features a broad spectrum of topics, including how to

› Examine your own implicit biases and reflect on their influence on your beliefs and actions
› Address and navigate conversations about race and racism with children and their families
› Welcome and support families of all structures in your program
› Incorporate policies and practices that recognize and value immigrant and refugee children and their families

Item 2843 • 2019 • 136 pages

The Essentials: Supporting Young Children with Disabilities in the Classroom

This guide is filled with practical information that will help educators who work with children ages birth through 8 teach children with disabilities alongside their peers. Learn the essentials of what you need to know:

› What developmental delays and disabilities are
› How special education laws apply to you and your program or school
› The process of referral, assessment, IFSP/IEP development, and service delivery
› Which supports and interventions can help children be successful socially and academically
› How to work with families, special education professionals, and the medical community

Item 1131 • 2017 • 160 pages

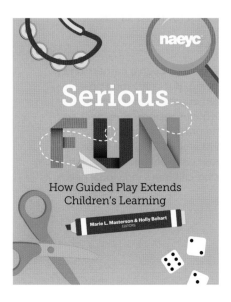

Serious Fun: How Guided Play Extends Children's Learning

Guided play is a powerful tool educators can use to help preschoolers and kindergartners learn essential knowledge and skills in the context of playful situations. Young children's natural curiosity and dynamic imaginations can lead to exciting and meaningful learning opportunities. Discover how to provide guided play experiences along with opportunities for unstructured play to support children's knowledge in key areas and their lifelong enjoyment and pursuit of learning.

Item 1137 • 2019 • 144 pages

Big Questions for Young Minds: Extending Children's Thinking

Questions are powerful tools, especially in the classroom. Asking rich, thoughtful questions can spark young children's natural curiosity and illuminate a whole new world of possibility and insight. But what are "big" questions, and how do they encourage children to think deeply? With this intentional approach—rooted in Bloom's Taxonomy—teachers working with children ages 3 through 6 will discover how to meet children at their individual developmental levels and stretch their thinking. With the guidance in this book as a cornerstone in your day-to-day teaching practices, learn how to be more intentional in your teaching, scaffold children's learning, and promote deeper understanding.

Item 1132 • 2017 • 160 pages

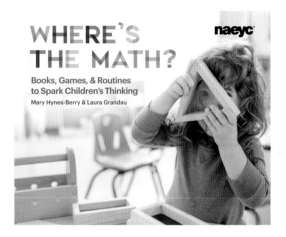

Where's the Math? Books, Games, and Routines to Spark Children's Thinking

Make math learning both meaningful and fun by building on children's natural curiosity to help them grow into confident problem solvers and investigators of math concepts. Using five math-related questions children wonder about as a framework, this book helps you go deeper into everyday math with children.

Item 1140 • 2019 • 128 pages

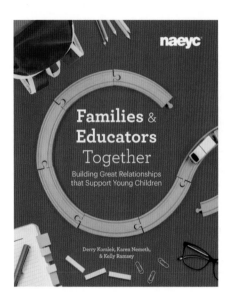

Families and Educators Together: Building Great Relationships that Support Young Children

Home–school relationships have always been a cornerstone of children's success and well-being. But cultivating positive, supportive partnerships between educators and families is an ongoing process, one that requires reciprocal respect and communication to grow. Use the practical information and ideas in this book to develop and embed a culture of family engagement in all aspects of your early childhood program, from curriculum planning to addressing children's individual needs.

Item 1139 • 2019 • 140 pages

This Is Play: Environments and Interactions that Engage Infants and Toddlers

This book is a delightful, easy read, full of insights like how to provide play choices for even very young children and why sportscasting is not just for TV but for infant and toddler classrooms, too. With its spot-on ideas and delightful anecdotes, you'll gain a new appreciation for infants' and toddlers' competence and curiosity and how important your role is in the birth-to-3 adventure.

Item 1141 • 2019 • 136 pages

Making and Tinkering With STEM:
Solving Design Challenges With Young Children

This practical, hands-on resource includes
› 25 engineering design challenges (ages 3–8)
› Suggestions for creating a makerspace environment
› A list of 100 picture books that encourage STEM-rich exploration and learning
› A planning template so you can create your own design challenges

Item 1130 • 2016 • 144 pages

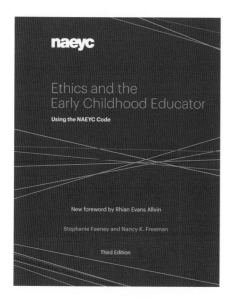

Ethics and the Early Childhood Educator:
Using the NAEYC Code, Third Edition

Do you need support and guidance to help you navigate tough ethical issues in your work? The NAEYC Code of Ethical Conduct is every early childhood educator's foundation for moral practice, and this book shows you how to use the Code to guide your actions and responses to challenging situations in the workplace.

Here, you'll find real cases from early childhood programs that illustrate the process of identifying and addressing ethical issues by applying the NAEYC Code. Reflection questions encourage you to think deeply about how your own experiences relate to the examples. Ethical conduct is critical, and the Code and this book are resources you can turn to again and again as you seek to make the right decisions for young children and their families.

Item 1134 • 2018 • 160 pages

From Survive to Thrive: A Director's Guide for Leading an Early Childhood Program

With so many demands and limited time, being an early childhood program leader is more challenging than it's ever been. This guide, grounded in current research and based on the experiences of the authors as well as directors from across the country, blends theory with practical tips you can implement immediately. Plus, each chapter recommends additional resources you can explore to take your knowledge and professional development to the next level. Use the guidance and strategies contained in this book to go from surviving in your role as director to thriving in it.

Item 1136 • 2018 • 176 pages